SOCIAL STRATIFICATION AND CHANGE IN INDIA

Social Stratification and Change in India

YOGENDRA SINGH

MANOHAR

1997

First published 1977
Reprinted 1989
Revised edition 1997

© Yogendra Singh, 1977, 1997

ISBN 81-7304-188-1

Published by
Ajay Kumar Jain for
Manohar Publishers & Distributors
2/6 Ansari Road Daryaganj
New Delhi 110002

Typeset by
Kumud Print Service
Near Railway Station, Tutu
Shimla

Printed at
Rajkamal Electric Press
B-35/9, G.T. Karnal Road Indl. Area
Delhi 110033

Contents

Contents

Preface to the Second Edition

Social Stratification and Change in India, first published in 1977 has since been widely read through successive reprints. It contained two long essays on concepts and theories of social change and social stratification, each prepared for the Indian Council of Social Science Research. These essays placed in perspective the development of sociology in our country with special reference to the studies of social change and social stratification, and offered a critical review of these in terms of concepts, theories and substantive concerns.

It has since been felt that the book should be revised and enlarged to bring the debate on concepts, theories and substantive issues on social change and social stratification in India to address and take account of the contemporary processes and orientations on these problems. Both conceptually and substantively many new developments have taken place during the decades of the 1980s and 1990s in the studies of social change and stratification in India. In the present edition we have attempted a comprehensive analysis of these developments. Five new chapters have been added. Each of these attempts to analyse not only the changing ground realities and processes but also the emerging conceptual and theoretical concerns.

NEW ORIENTATIONS IN
SOCIAL STRATIFICATION STUDIES

Compared to the studies of social stratification from the 1950s to the mid-1970s, the decades of 1980s and 1990s have reflected some basic changes in the comprehension of issues and their theorizing. This we have discussed in the new essay on 'Sociology of Social Stratification'. An identifiable new orientation that seems to have emerged during this period is that of concerns with the origins and evolutionary processes of the institutions of caste and class. This has further resulted in two contingent developments: one, there is new sensitivity to take into account history in the studies of sociology, and secondly, the emphasis is upon in-depth exploration of the ideologies of caste and class from an evolutionary perspective. The two orientations have reinforced each other. One major result of these changes is the emergence of a non-Brahmanical paradigm for the study of caste, class and processes of social stratification in India. The question of origin and formation of these institutions has assumed new significance in the literature.

The ascendance of Dalit and Backward Class movements has brought out the ideological debate on caste and class to the foreground of its cultural and sociological matrix. An alternate cultural construction of India through the historical stages of the evolution of protest and revolt against Brahmanical orthodoxy has gained momentum which traverses Indian history from the Vedic (particularly Upanishadic) to the Buddhist-Jain, to the *Bhakti* protest traditions onward to the non-Brahmanical rationalist movements of modern India. Counter-cultural models of stratification are revived through focus on local *Jati-puranas* in many regions of India. Here the ideology of caste is presented in an ambiguous yet critical language of protest.

An important implication of these developments is a shift in focus on the studies of caste, class and ethnic groups. It moves away from the established ideology of change and mobility to concerns with questions of *identity, domination* and *exploitation*, hidden in this ideology. The last decade has witnessed an explosion in the consciousness of identities and concern with autonomy and cultural pluralism all over the world. This development in India, however, is further bounded by its own historical processes where it has resulted in, first, a much critical appraisal of the notions of 'integration' and 'mobility' within the system, and secondly, there is new emphasis on the recognition of the autonomy of cultural and social identities of the 'marginalized groups' and its preservation in the process of economic development and modernization of the nation. We have analysed this problem in the essay on 'Sociology of the Integration of the Marginalized Groups (Scheduled castes, Tribes and Backward Classes) into Indian Society'. The paradigm of 'integration', which essentially implies not total assimilation but inter-cultural linkages without jeopardizing identities of cultural pluralism, evolved during the phase of the national movement. This movement itself generated counter-paradigms of which the model suggested by Dr. Ambedkar is the one which is most exhaustive and analytically vigorous. This contributed to the emergence of what we have termed as the 'Constitutional paradigm' of integration of the various marginalized groups of the Indian society into a nation-state. As indeed, the working of the Constitution has so far revealed, there are many more adjustments and accommodations to be made in the future years. The policy of protective discrimination has a central place in this regard.

Ironically, as the agenda of integration takes a new turn in the context of social stratification and nation-building process the traditional categories of stratification such as caste and class are exposed to new theoretic tensions. As we shift our focus in such studies from issues of 'ranking' and 'hierarchy' to elements of 'domination' and 'exploitation', the need for empowerment and not mere intra-systemic mobility assumes significance. Also the scope of the conceptual categories of social stratification is widened to include gender, which cuts across the boundaries of caste or class. The need for their protective discrimination also assumes significance. In addition, the groups uprooted from their economic and cultural moorings either due to political strife or due to ecological displacement (developmentally generated or due to natural catastrophes), the groups suffering from marginalization and exploitation due to political oppression or human rights violation or groups having practices, customs and beliefs dissenting from those in the mainstream or dominant cultural majority, etc., come increasingly within the conceptual and methodological ambit of social stratification studies. Sensitivity to such issues is gaining momentum in India, and the studies of social stratification in the future years would increasingly reflect this reality.

These developments have deeply influenced the theoretical orientations in contemporary social stratification studies. The early emphasis on systemic conceptualizations anchored either in the functionalist or historical materialist (Marxist) theoretical frames is undergoing serious rethinking. A clear enunciation of the alternate theoretical paradigms has not yet fully emerged, and in most studies of social stratification one may find a good mix of both the functionalist and historical-materialist theoretical orientations. Yet, it is realized that in order to have a fuller theoretical grasp over the problems of social stratification where the categories through which its processes are comprehended go beyond the issues of 'hierarchy' to that of 'domination' and 'exploitation', there is need for new theoretical sensitivities. This sensibility should be able to fully comprehend the richness of identities, subjectivities and pluralities of the relevant processes of stratification as also their deeper and individualized symbolic contents. The theoretical choices, therefore, tend to be moving towards a range of orientations from hermeneutics, to cultural analysis to phenomenology. Some studies of social stratification have been attempted employing these perspectives. But the overall theoretical preferences continue to be synthetic and pluralistic in orientation.

PERSPECTIVES ON SOCIAL CHANGE

The treatment of social stratification encompasses the perspectives on social change. The two processes are deeply interrelated. In this edition we have attempted to offer our assessment of the contemporary processes of social change with the inclusion of two new essays: 'Country-Town Nexus: Social Transformation in Contemporary Indian Society' and 'Present Social Situation in India: A Sociological Analysis'. These essays read along with others should provide a comprehensive picture of social change in India today. No doubt, the processes of change are imbued with elements of crisis and contradictions arising out of both successes achieved through our developmental policies as also failures in some sensitive areas.

Some of the changes which could be termed as indicators of 'success' are: emergence of a strong rural middle class as carriers of the 'green revolution'; widening of the social base of the industrial entrepreneurial classes and increase in their numbers; the emergence of strong social movements of Dalits, women, tribals and other marginalized groups and the sharpening of their political and cultural awareness; the emergence of a substantial middle class of professionals in the fields of management, science, technology, medicine, law and engineering, etc., due to the successful policy of higher education and finally the widening and strengthening of the base of democracy in India. Each of these developments, which are mainly the result of five decades of planning for the modernization of our society, has contributed towards stability and resilience of the national economy and our social system. Yet each specific case of success has led to related social consequences which generate contradictions and tensions in our society.

For instance, the emergent powerful rural middle classes drawn largely from among the rich peasantry and the middle level castes have taken the country out of the era of humiliating food scarcities. The class is imbued with a new sense of work culture and entrepreneurial ethos. As the motor force of the Backward Class movements in India it has enlarged and intensified the agenda of social justice and equality. This class traditionally had an ambivalent relationship with Brahmanical orthodoxy, and its ascendance today on the national political scene may harbinger a movement towards cultural liberalism and strengthening of the processes of secularization of society. Yet, ironically, the cultural and social practices of this class show increased levels of ideological conservatism and conflictual relationship with the marginal-ized and under-class groups such as the tribals, Dalits and women. The strong tradition of work culture of this class seems to be neutral to or even violative of the ethical social contents of liberalism. In the past, the peasant tradition was symbolized by its commitment to *Bhakti* movements in most parts of the country. The present de-ethicization of the rural middle class peasantry which is increasingly gaining access to political power in the country does engender cultural and social contradictions. It is reflected in the changing inter-caste and inter-class relationships and also in the crisis of legitimacy of institutions of State and polity.

The same tendency is recurrent among all other new middle classes in India such as the industrial entrepreneurial, professional-technological and educational classes. On the one hand, there is an increase in their aspiration to achieve, to succeed, to move upward in social stratification for which all possible facets of instrumental rationalities are mobilized and acquired. On the other hand, these instrumental rationalities are defined in ethically neutral terms or tend to be violative of the ethical norms. This leads to two immediate cultural and social consequences: first, it leads to the awakening of the commitment to ideology of sharing and social justice towards the poor and the marginalized. Secondly, the under-class and the Dalit perceive this attitude of the middle classes towards them as justification for aggressive responses on their side. This leads to new social contradictions. This is increasingly observed in the emergent relationships between the slum dwellers and the urban middle classes in cities and the rich peasantry and the Dalits and the landless laboureres in the villages. The same pattern is repeated in the attitude of the professional, technical and intellectual middle classes towards the underprivileged and the deprived sections of the society.

The substantial rise in the number of the middle classes makes a critical contribution to the overall processes of social change and development in our society. The positive contribution of this class is indeed obvious as it contributes to the growth of economy and mirrors societal resilience. Its problematic side is rather complex, and cannot be analysed on a purely negative-positive dimension. It is imbedded in the dynamic cultural matrix of the middle classes in India which lends itself to more fruitful analysis from a phenomenological or psycho-cultural mode of theoretical treatment. The notion of ethical commitment is itself a complex and a multilayered phenomenon. It has dissimilarities of expression and judgement at the subjective-objective levels and at the levels of the real versus the normative praxis. The middle class social psychology about ethical commitments in ideal terms is certainly that of approval and affirmation. It is apparent from their support to the causes that seek establishment of morality and cleanliness in public and private life. At the same time, at the behavioural level or at the level of day-to-day social practice middle class commitment to ethical values tends to be ambiguous and dithering. It suggests that a great churning process is on in the cultural realm of India today and a level of equilibrium is yet to emerge. In the future studies of social change and its diagnosis this dimension of cultural change should form a vital component.

Despite successes in several fields, the process of social change in India also reveals failures and handicaps in many areas. Some of these could be identified as: the failure in the removal of illiteracy; the failure in the abolition of destitution of a large section of our society and the failure in the successful implementation of the family welfare policies. As we review the successes and failures of our policy of social change and development today we increasingly realize the crucial role that literacy plays not only in the access to employment but also as a prime-mover in reduction of poverty, in the enhancement of productive potential of the individual, in the acceptance of family welfare norms, and in the overall empowerment of the deprived and the marginalized groups in society. Comparative studies in most East Asian societies have shown a close relationship between the levels of literacy and the extent of the removal of poverty and the empowerment of women and other deprived groups.

The rate and the scale of population growth in India is bound to have a detrimental influence on the growth and distribution of the resources of the nation. It has also cultural and ecological consequences and gets invariably enmeshed with all other processes of development and change in society. It is revealed by our own internal experiences of development in the country that in order to overcome those problems empowerment of women and mass literacy (particularly the education of the girl child and the women in the reproductive age group) are essential. The growth in this domain is bound to have positive consequences in overcoming the emerging social and cultural contradictions in our society. It may also add a moral or an ethical corrective to our emerging value-neutral achievement-oriented democratic society.

In a larger sense, social change in present-day India reflects a revolutionary process of social and cultural re-structuration. The rise of the backward classes and castes to power, the assertiveness of the Dalits and the marginalized groups, particularly women in our polity, the increasing recognition of the role of the voluntary people's movements to supplement and forewarn in the context of the State apparatus of social engineering, etc., reflect how the strategies of reconciliation and consensus are being reinforced. It is a dynamic and complex process. However, it is clear that both resilience and contradiction are at play in this process of social transformation of our society.

Jawaharlal Nehru University   YOGENDRA SINGH
New Delhi
14 September 1996

Preface to the First Edition

Social stratification and change, the themes of the two essays in this volume, constitute the fundamental processes of society. Despite the apparent contradistinction between social stratification—which refers to the principal mechanism of social order in society—and change—which reflects its inner contradictions and motions, the two processes converge theoretically as well as substantively. An objective analysis of social stratification is not possible without reference to the processes of social mobility, the cleavages and contradictions that the system brings about as the scheme of social differentiation or hierarchy leads to the tensions of status crystallization on the one hand and status dissonance on the other. The cleavage between the 'have' and the 'have-not' in the process of status crystallization within the class or caste principles of social stratification reflects this reality, whether the bases of deprivation are wealth, privilege or power. One would notice this continuity of concepts and substantive social process in the treatment of both social stratification and social change in India, which have been reviewed in the two essays in the context of the growth of Indian sociology.

The sociology of social stratification in India has been reviewed with special reference to the contribution that studies in this field have made in theory, method and substantive domains. In terms of theory, a distinction may be drawn between 'master theories' of social stratification and 'conceptual schemes'. The same holds true for studies in social change. It would appear that in the analysis of both 'social stratification' and 'social change', Indian sociology, as also sociology in general, has been more oriented to the uses of conceptual schemes rather than master theories. Master theories comprise nomological and systematic variety. The nomological or law-like theories using a set of sociological propositions in logical interrelationships and calculi of abstraction or inference are limited in scope, far less relevant in studies of social change or social stratification. The use of nomological theory in the analysis of social stratification or social change in India has been rare. The application of systematic theory in the analysis both of social stratification and change has been more pronounced, particularly among sociologists who use a dialectical model of analysis. In theory, these too resemble 'conceptual schemes' rather than theory proper. Most studies, of course, use neither nomological nor a systematic theoretical model.

Systematic theory in sociology holds great promise. It is latent in most analyses of change and social stratification even when the sociologist only uses conceptual schema for a descriptive or analytical treatment of the phenomena. Its proper application, however, imposes certain conditions on the sociological operations. These are: historical contextuality combined with empirical observations of its contemporary social formations; rigorous uses of the principles of confirmation or disconfirmation of propositions; and imposition of logical norms in the operationalization of concepts and methodological strategies. A systematic theory, whether it is dialectical or functional in nature would fall short in its explanatory power if it deviates from these standards. The inadequacy of the conceptual schemes in the study of social stratification or change is derived mainly from these shortcomings. Consequently, in Indian sociology one comes across many conceptual schemes which appear to be a systematic theory, either dialectical or functional, but are devoid of its power. The roots of this contradiction can be traced through the studies that form the bases of the two essays on social stratification and concept of change respectively.

The theoretical and methodological issues in the studies of social stratification in India relate mainly to the formulation of conceptual schemes and their operationalization through indicators of status, levels of equality and inequality, occupational differentiation or degree of homogeneity and heterogeneity of groups in status hierarchy and of interaction variables such as pollution-purity (through exchange of food articles, co-dining, etc.), dominance, fusion, fission, etc. The predominant method of analysis is through conceptual schemes, in which either attributional or interactional criteria are used to define the dimensions of cultural and structural differentiation in caste, class, elite or other status groups and categories. Both attributional and interactional criteria are used for ranking groups or strata in a system of hierarchy. Attributional criteria are mainly nominalistic and refer to the ranking of individuals, through a set of characteristics, such as income, occupation, housing, education, etc. A good example is the operationalization of Victor S. D'Souza's definition of caste and class or the role of income, education and occupation in the status mobility of individuals or families in urban centres analysed by McKim Marriott (cf. Chapter 1). This method of ranking also assumes the weakening of the corporate structure of the groups or communities concerned. In a village it is assumed that the significance of individual ranking through attributes such as those of income or education would be highly circumscribed by the fact that caste and subcaste groups, and not individuals, would operate as units of social stratification. Here, not 'individual ranking' but the principle of 'corporate ranking' prevails and status is collectively defined. Hence the significance of interactional criteria such as pollution and purity, social distance in day-to-day interaction, etc., for understanding the structure and change in the rural social stratification system. Such criteria also assume a certain degree of close-ended social structure.

The utility of attributional criteria of ranking in the urban centres and of interactional criteria in the villages as formulated by Marriott may not be as valid as his statement that wherever the social system is closed rather than open, interactional criteria of ranking or the principle of corporate ranking would operate. This is particularly relevant considering that the distinction between rural and urban is not territorial but structural, and in the structural sense, the neat dichotomy between the two continues to be problematic. Despite the dissimilarity between the social structures of the city and the village, many village-like structures persist in urban centres.

Yet another context in which the theory and method of social stratification studies need to be evaluated is their power of generalization. In this respect, assuredly systematic theory has greater power than mere conceptual schema. The conceptual schemes used in the treatment of caste social stratification emphasize this very clearly. These help in the systematic description or even analysis of the structure of caste and its role in social hierarchy. We have been able to classify the various shades of approaches to the definition of caste as a reality using a two-dimensional property space. This is: Universalism-Particularism and Cultural-Structural. The universalism-particularism dimension refers to caste either as a universal or cross-societal reality or a typically Indian social reality. The cultural-structural dimension refers to whether caste, as a social phenomenon, could be understood primarily as an ideological or cultural system enshrined in a system of normative principles or whether it could be treated as a system of social relationships *par excellence*. Obviously, this scheme of classification helps more in the ordering of the varied interpretations of the nature of caste and its socio-logical constructions than in any forecasting about its future course of change. The same could be said about other dichotomous conceptual schemes, such as the distinction between the 'closed' and 'open' and 'segmentary' and 'organic' properties of the caste stratification system.

Moving from caste to class as a principle of social strati-fication, we find that the theoretic and methodological bottlenecks of dependence on conceptual schemes rather than systematic theory continue to persist. Indeed, in the studies of class, there is an increased tendency towards using inter-actional categories through which dialectics of the processes of social stratification rather than its mere formal properties could be analysed. This is particularly true of studies using Marxist theoretical models with their pre-supposition of evolutionary system constructs. But such studies are few, and of more recent origin. Otherwise, schematization of class based on attributional criteria also abounds in the analysis of class stratification. Most formulations of agrarian strata use such criteria. There are many who depend on income, size of land holding, occupational differentiation, etc., to arrive at class categorization. Quite often, students of class stratification start with attributional properties, such as occupational categories, and then transform them for analytical interpre-tative purposes into interactional categories (cf. Ramakrishna Mukherjee on class in Chapter 1). Nevertheless, most studies on agrarian class structure use only attributional criteria for the classification of classes.

In recent years, however, there has been a more intensive and systematic effort by economic historians, economists, sociologists and social anthropologists to formulate interactional classificatory categories of classes from Marxist methodological frames of reference. Daniel Thorner, who in his early works on agrarian classes used interactional categories like 'malik', 'mazdur' and 'money-lender', has in the 1970s been trying to work out a more critical and systematic classification of historical bases of socio-economic formations. His critique on various modes of production such as 'primitive communism', 'Asiatic mode of production', 'ancient or slave mode of production', 'feudal mode of production', 'capitalist mode of production' and the 'socialist mode of production' takes into account several historical-existential variations within each mode of production, with some of them having a very precarious historical basis (cf. 'The Principal Modes of Production of Karl Marx: Some Preliminary Notes', October 1973, a paper presented at the seminar on the Emergence of Agrarian Capitalism in Africa, South of the Sahara, Dakar, 3-13 December 1973). Thorner has been particularly concerned with the 'multiple and contradictory disadvantages' of clinging to an analysis of changes in structure of societies on the basis of the above classification of modes of production. 'If we remind ourselves' he says, 'of another current question—"God, is he dead?"—may we not ask whether the series of modes of production of Marx still retains its *raison d'etre*.'

The interactional categories of class formation in the study of social stratification inhere systematic theoretical concern, and the neo-Marxist sociologists have contributed particularly richly towards this objective. The approach of these sociologists and social anthropologists differs from orthodox Marxists in several ways: their systemic theoretic interests do not cease merely with deductive constructions of system states based on classical Marxism; instead, they tend to be more theoretically conscious of the rules of confirmation and disconfirmation of propositions and of the limits of operativity of concepts and categories. They also place greater emphasis on the historical contextuality of events and use the observations derived in this frame for systematic verification. Daniel Thorner represents this new wave pre-eminently. In the mode of production thesis, he does not reject its philosophical and methodological relevance, but its doctrinaire usage as tool of analysis. In a note on 'The Peasantry Confronted with Industrial Capitalism, 1770-1970', he particularly highlights this point in connection with 'peasant economy' and 'feudalism'. He writes:

the term 'feudalism' or 'feudal mode of production' broke down because too much was asked of it. We should strive to avoid the same fate for 'peasant economy at the national level'. Around our core of structures at the level of Nation or States, we should expect to find several other sets of families of States or Nations which differ in one or more basic characteristics from our central core group. We probably have to deal here with what may amount to four or even eight or more different 'modes of production'. To lump them all together on the basis of a few purely qualitative criteria will doom us, in all probability, to an empty handed return to base zero! If, on the other hand, we start with a limited number of sufficiently similar peasant socio-economic formations at the national level, say twelve or at the most twenty, we may be able to progress toward the elaboration of *theory* of peasant economy at the State level. (Italics added.)

Commenting directly on the 'mode of production' approach to social analysis, Thorner writes:

From a methodological point of view, after having benefited from more than a full century from Marx's concept, 'mode of production'—brilliant, indeed a stroke of genius in its time, and incredibly fruitful for two or three successive generations of thinkers and scholars—is it not our duty today to try, standing on the shoulders of Marx, to work out further concepts useful and fruitful for our generation and, if the God so wishes, for that which will succeed us. (cf. Thorner 1973, op. cit.)

The innovative concern in Thorner's Marxist sociology is indeed representative of the orientation of several contemporary thinkers. Social and economic historians, E.J. Hobsbawm, Pierre Vilar, Witold Kula and social anthropologists, M. Godelier, M. Sahlins, G. Dalton and K. Polanyi among others have contributed substantively to the analysis of concrete structures and processes of societies in primitive, peasant and feudal-capitalistic stages of social formation within the Marxist methodological framework, but with deep innovative insights.

There is indeed a corresponding new awareness among some sociologists, economists and social historians in India. They use Marxist methods and categories in social analysis, be it the study of agrarian structure and class formation, or study of feudalism and capitalism as socio-economic systems, with emphasis on social and historical contextuality in operationalization and objective historical-empirical standards of confirmation and disconfirmation of propositions. The doctrinaire manner in which Indian societal processes and their structure were interpreted in the 1940s and the 1950s by several Marxist thinkers has now been replaced with an emphasis on the historical individuality of social formations and the consequent adaptive changes and innovations in categorical and methodological strategies. In their studies of class formation and its social processes in India, several Marxist sociologists and economists have not recognized the role of non-economic social factors such as caste, region and cultural prejudices which refract the nature of social contradictions in Indian society (cf. Y. Singh in M.N. Srinivas *et al.*, *Dimensions of Social Change in India*, New Delhi: Allied Publishers, 1977). In a Marxist analysis of class formation and its process in India Meghnad Desai writes:

The bourgeoisie cannot, because of its weakness, pursue unbridled capital accumulation. The petty bourgeois view of socialism and public sector expansion means a creation of unproductive government jobs and the policing of the Big Bourgeoisie with the paraphernalia of state agencies. In this curious alliance lies the contradiction of the Indian ruling class. Its mass support is in conflict with its class interest. The deadlock results in slow and uneven growth insufficient to alleviate unemployment and poverty. This slow and uneven growth also strengthens the other main contradictions: uneven regional development and inter-regional antagonism. Slow growth postpones the emergence of a national economy with division of labour on a national scale. In doing this, it also, however, frustrates the possibility of an alliance of the poor across regions. It keeps the class struggle fragmented regionally and diverts the energies of a regional struggle into chauvinistic channels. (Meghnad Desai, 'India: Emerging Contradictions of Slow Capitalist Development', in Robin Blackburn ed., *Explosions in a Subcontinent*, London: Penguin Books, 1975.)

More than in the analysis of class structure, it would be noticed that historical insights have been increasingly utilized by social historians and sociologists in the study of the elite structure in India. The dialectic of social change in our society is revealed most clearly when one looks at the processes of formation, uprooting and re-formation of status groups and categories including the class and elite in the course of history. Colonialism and its socio-economic aftermaths have contributed directly both to the uprooting of the traditional elite and middle classes in India as well as to the rise of new elite categories, be they of the bureaucracy, the business and economic enterprise or the political and intellectual categories. The process of elite formation in India also coincides with the growth of new institutional foci, economic, educational and industrial, which colonialism found necessary to introduce in India, and the response to which shaped the character and ethos of the middle classes and elite in our country. The literature generated by Indian sociologists and economic historians does not always sharply place the process of elite and class formation in India in the context of colonial and neocolonial historical forces. With a few exceptions, most studies on this problem tend to take a historical-descriptive rather than a dialectical account of these processes. The processes outlined, however, underline adequately the contradictions between the elite formations and the other classes of Indian society owing to specific social and economic bases from which the elite have emerged in India.

II

As one moves from studies in social stratification to those on concepts and theories of social change in India, one would notice a great deal of convergence of categories, methods and themes. Once again, the predominance of 'conceptual schemes' over 'theories' of social change is amply in evidence. The theoretical and methodological problems that studies on social change in India have encountered are of the same dimension as those encountered by the social stratification studies. It would, nevertheless be of interest to review the nature of conceptual schemes that have been used from time to time to explain social change in India. It would also be useful to locate the tensions in Indian sociology for going beyond mere conceptual schema and to highlight the successes and failures in this direction. The essay on 'Concepts and Theories of Social Change' is an attempt to study some of these problems through a review of the literature of Indian sociology on this theme.

Evolutionary constructions of stages of origin and growth of social institutions and forms of structures in India, the family, kinship, village, community, land tenures, political institutions, etc., mark the beginning of social change thinking in sociology. Much of this thinking was speculative and based on models of Western society, as it was also launched by Western sociologists. In this scheme of analysis, Indian society was seen as a representation of the underdeveloped form of the evolutionary stages, in comparison to which Western society stood at a higher level of advancement. With the exception of the Orientalists, who had a positive yet romantic appreciation of Indian culture and civilization, the above interpretation of Indian society was held to be valid by all other shades of the Western colonizers of India, be they the liberal-utilitarian administrators, the missionary zealots or the sociologists and social anthropologists. Though unscientific and soon to be discredited, this approach of conceptualizing social change in India did perform one unintended service to the Indian sociology of change. It engendered a reaction among Indian social scientists forcing them to reflect on the culture and structure of their society in a cross-cultural and comparative perspective. In fact, this process triggered the process of societal self-awareness which as a system of thinking crystallized in the discipline of sociology. This also logically paved the way towards looking at Indian society more intimately, to analyse its concrete social structures and their social processes.

The conceptual schemes for the analysis of social change resulted from two types of forces: the disenchantment from the evolutionary speculative interpretation of social change both in India and the West, and the deepening of interest in the structure and culture of one's own society. Sanskrit-ization and Westernization as a conceptual dichotomy reflects most sharply this change in the orientation of Indian sociology. It has many limitations as an explanatory model of social change. It is primarily oriented towards explaining the pressures of cultural mobility and change among the caste groups in India. It deals with the structural problems of social change only by implication through the processes of ideological changes in the outlook and customs of the caste groups. It is, nevertheless, oriented primarily to the structure and process of Indian society and captures significantly the central ethos of change in a society which harbours a deep ambivalence between tradition and modernity. The dichotomy of the 'Little' and 'Great' tradition which follows this conceptual scheme is based on the theory of tradition, its social organization and its inner structural differentiation. Its conceptual scheme tends to be more general and formal in shape, but its limitations as a theory of change are identical with those of the 'Sanskritization-Westernization' scheme.

The attempts to explain the structural forces bringing about change in Indian society constitute a second set of conceptual schemes used by sociologists in India. The focus here is on the processes of role differentiation, mobility of status groups and categories in terms of scales of access to the resources of wealth, privilege and power. Most studies in this category have focused on the analysis of fictional differentiation in village communities, fission and fusion processes in the family and caste structures and the social mobility of groups and categories. The implicit theoretical frame in most of them remains that of the structural-functional variety. Their contribution to the understanding of the processes of social change in India as compared to the 'dialectical approaches' needs to be evaluated. The contributions of Louis Dumont and Gunnar Myrdal, which we have categorized as 'cognitive historical' and 'institutional' approaches respectively, fit into the intermediate ranges of these two main theoretical models.

A perusal of the 'dialectical' approaches would reveal tensions that persist in meta-theoretic assumptions, value-loads and parameters of observation and analysis. The Marxist frame of analysis is predominant in most of these theoretical attempts, but curiously one notices tension between 'tradition' and 'modernity' on the one hand, and equivocation between 'dialectical' and 'diagnostic' on the other, in the writings of some of the prominent proponents of these approaches. The first type of tension one may find in the writings of D.P. Mukerji and the second in the dialectical reasoning of Ramakrishna Mukherjee. This is symptomatic of the ambivalence that most Indian sociologists have experienced in adapting a 'Western model' for interpreting Indian society. It also confirms that Marxism as a theoretic and methodological system does undergo adaptive changes when applied to historically distinct societies. This tendency in Indian sociology is significant as it is increasingly realized that there is no succession of paradigms in sociology, not even in Marxist sociology. As Worsley has rightly stated, the creative tensions in sociological theory are not so much paradigmatic as Thomas Kuhn had assumed for the natural sciences; they are, on the other hand, recurrent and inter-systemic. That is, from within the same paradigm or theoretical system, differentiation of theory might begin.

Taking note of the nature of the paradigm of Marxist sociology, Worsley writes:

The major ideology of our time, Marxism is a plural phenomenon... Nor is the problem resolved by taking non-Marxism as the reference-point for drawing boundaries of inclusion and exclusion, for Marxist sociology has never been as separate as Gouldner suggests and has exercised an increasingly powerful influence on its competitors and enemies even when quite excluded from the academy. We even use the label *marxisant* to express our uncertainty as to just when Marxism begins and ends. Even Engels himself identified only the theory of surplus value and the materialist theory of history as the crucial novel elements added by Marx and himself to the existing corpus of ideas inherited from the Enlightenment, from British political economy, French social (including socialist) thought, and German idealist philosophy. He might, with justice, have credited Marx and himself with the synthesis of these elements too. (P.M. Worsley, 'The State of Theory and Status of Theory', *Sociology*, January 1974, p. 3.)

Indeed the renaissance in Marxist sociological thinking today owes much to the basic creativity of this thought as a philosophical and scientific system. The dialectical approach, compared with all other approaches for the interpretation and analysis of social change or stratification in India, tends to be most viable. Its more creative contributions, however, have yet to come. As we stated previously, the process has now started. Against this background, when one looks at the elements of tensions or ambivalence in respect of concepts, categories or even value premises in the writings of Indian sociologists who professedly take a Marxist epistemological standpoint in interpreting the social reality of India, it becomes meaningful.

As we review broadly the processes of social stratification and change in Indian society, the contours of emerging social contradictions become visible. The class structure is slowly but steadily moving towards polarization. The upper and the middle classes both in the rural and industrial sectors have gained the maximum benefits and have expanded their base of social, economic and political power. The poor and the have-nots, the Harijans and the backward tribes remain at the bottom of the social hierarchy. Despite recent events leading to the breakdown and restoration of democracy in India, this stark structural reality of the Indian social system has not changed. With the increasing power of the middle classes the plight of these marginalized sections has also become more poignant. This process breeds tension, organized resistance and motivates people towards a search for ideologies which may not always be consonant with the ideology of the dominant sections. It would increasingly generate conflicts and contradictions. To grasp this reality of the Indian social system, a dialectical model of reasoning is assuredly more effective and offers greater promise. But it has to be a dialectic informed with the historicity of societies to render it more creative and innovative.

1

Sociology of Social Stratification: I

INTRODUCTION

The sociology of social stratification inheres many basic and complex theoretical issues. These relate to the nature of social order, social equality and inequality, social justice, power and the nature of man. These issues are strategic to sociology and also influence the postulates and presuppositions of other social sciences such as economics, political science, and psychology. The conceptual and theoretical frames of sociology of stratification have, therefore, naturally struck points of convergence with other social sciences. The issues themselves, however, have yet to be resolved.

In sociology these issues relate to questions of theory, structure and process of social stratification. The three are organically interrelated, though heuristically distinct. The theory of social stratification implies a set of concepts, propositions and assumptions that are verified and validated and constitute an explanatory system. Analysed by this criterion, most theoretic approaches in the sociology of stratification rarely reach the formal level of theory. Consequently, there is theoretic divergence in the explanations of social stratification: it is explained either in terms of (a) the *need* in society for ranking the roles and statuses of its members commensurate with their relative normative-utilitarian significance for society and the consequent rewards, or (b) the ranking and differential rewarding of roles and statuses commensurate with their access to the extent of institutionalized *power*. The first explanation corresponds roughly with what is known as the functionalist theory and the second with the conflict theory of social stratification. Both have many theoretical variations. A common presupposition in all functional theories is that social stratification results from a value consensus in society about the ranking of roles and statuses for rewards. Similarly, all conflict theories assume that 'consensus of values' manifests only the sanctions that the power elite in a society impose upon men entering into various roles and status situations. The stratification system is, therefore, inherently unstable, involving perpetual conflicts for mobility of status and challenge to the established structure of power.

Recent literature on social stratification in American and Continental sociology indicates trends towards narrowing down of the two theoretical positions. This has followed from the increased theoretical sophistication of the stratification studies and new substantive discoveries about social stratification in industrially advanced societies. These developments suggest two things: (1) neither the conflict nor the consensus model is by itself sufficient to explain fully all the sociological processes of social stratification (see Jackson 1968; Allardt 1968; Leach 1967; etc.); and (2) the ideological bases used to distinguish between the two approaches, e.g. that the functional theory is rationalisation of the established order and that the conflict (dialectical) theory has a revolutionary élan as it not only postulates a conflict between the privileged and the non-privileged but also predicts a classless society at a certain evolutionary stage, have proved to be less certain. In the industrially advanced capitalist countries, for instance, where labour radicalism should be high, we find labour conservatism (see Lipset 1960; Lockwood 1958 and 1960; Zweig 1961; etc.). This finding, though contradicted by some empirical studies (see Harrington 1963; Titmus 1962; Townsend 1965; etc.) continues to be significant in the context of other findings, viz., the capitalistic system need not lead to the growth of immiserized proletariats, and the socialistic societies may not be able to abolish all class distinctions.

The controversy between the functionalists and conflict-theorists (dialecticians) has, not without reason, been characterized as 'degenerate' by Edmund Leach (1967). In fact, efforts have been made recently by the proponents of both the theoretical views to move away from rigid positions by emphasizing points of similarity or convergence in the two approaches (see Davis and Moore 1945; Buckley 1959; Moore 1953; Parsons 1940 and 1953; Stinchcombe 1963; Tumin 1953, 1955, 1963, 1965 and 1967; Wesolowski 1966;

Wrong 1959; etc.). Now the increasing tendency is to analyse social stratification from a pluralistic conceptual frame by treating both conflict and consensus as two dimensions of the same reality.

The focus has also shifted from formulation of master theories to the analysis of social stratification with the help of a limited set of conceptual categories such as 'status', 'wealth' and 'power'. Despite some shortcomings (see Runciman 1969), this approach has theoretical viability as it can take account of the normative, as well as the economic and political aspects of social stratification. Hans Zetterberg (1965) draws a distinction between the 'prepositional' and the 'dimensionalistic' theory in sociology. The 'status-wealth-power' approach to the study of social stratification corresponds with the dimensionalistic level of theory. Indeed, most functionalist or conflict theories of social stratification too do not fulfil the strict scientific norms of theory.

It is not without significance that most functionalist theories of social stratification come from the American and the conflict theories from the Continental sociologists. It is also not without significance that the popularity and acceptance of the conflict theories of social stratification are high among the sociologists of the 'third world'. Probably, differences in the sociological perspective on stratification correlate with the diversity in the existential conditions of social scientists in different societies. These diversities set the tradition of scholarship on dissimilar lines. This fact, that the choice of theoretical frames is conditioned by social history, is now widely acknowledged by students of social stratification (see Lenski 1966; Aron 1969). This may also be borne in mind while reviewing studies on social stratification in India.

The second issue in the study of social stratification is that of the structural units through which the system of stratification may be conceptualized. Here, the emphasis is not on the 'why' of stratification which is the relevant context of theory, but on the 'how' and 'what' of this phenomenon. It is here that the issues of 'nominalism' and 'realism' in theoretical presuppositions bear relevance (see Aron 1969). The units comprising the system of stratification might range from roles to groups and categories such as family, caste, class, occupational groups and elite. In the nominalist framework which we find in the writings of most American sociologists the unit of stratification is a role or status, and these are normatively defined. This is also generally true of the functionlist theory of stratification. Even when stratification is analysed in terms of categories such as occupational types or classes, these concepts are derived inductively with the help of nominalist components. These components may consist of a set of attributes such as income, nature of role and social origin, etc. In the realist frame of analysis, the units of stratification are inclusive categories or groups such as social classes, elite and status groups or caste, and these categories are assumed to enjoy substantive autonomy and logical priority over their attributional components.

The third aspect in the study of social stratification relates to its processes. By processes we mean changes in the differentiation, evaluation, ranking and rewarding patterns in social stratification. The extent to which increased differentiation of social strata contributes to the merging, mobility and emergence of strata, classes or categories, the degree to which the system of social stratification increases or decreases social inequality, or the manner in which an entire system of stratification, such as that of feudalism or caste is transformed into class or 'non-antagonistic class' system of stratification, are problems which belong to the processual aspect of social stratification.

The sociology of social stratification, as defined in this review, implies treatment of social stratification from the perspectives of theory, structure and process, and their variations in societal and cultural contexts. This in fact is the framework in which much of the literature on social stratification can be meaningfully analysed. It offers a basis for the analysis of substantive as well as theoretical issues in social stratification.

In the context of the above discussion, the main questions that arise in a review of the Indian sociology of social stratification are: what theoretical assumptions have guided studies in social stratification in India? How far have the functional or dialectical (conflict) theoretical postulates been used either for analysis or selection of problems in social stratification? Which are the major structural foci in social stratification studies, and has the focus been comprehensive enough to cover most strategic structural units or components of the system of stratification? Or has the focus been biased for historical or other disciplinary reasons towards studies in a specific or particular direction? Considering the crucial stratification dilemmas and their urgent issues for Indian national development, have these studies been sociologically relevant? Do these studies focus upon the most strategic processes of social stratification? Have the studies highlighted in a representative manner the processes of social stratification, their causes, consequences and impact upon the overall social order and change in the Indian social system?

To analyse these we shall adopt a classification scheme related to the structural units used in various studies of stratification in India. For each structural unit we would apply an analytical frame pertaining to the questions of theory, structural adequacy and processes of change. At the end of this paper we shall also try to identify the main gaps in this field of study and suggest areas for future study.

The important structural units that sociologists have used for the analysis of social stratification in India are caste, class elite and professional-occupational categories. There are some functional overlaps between these units; but by and large, these correspond roughly with the triology of status, wealth and power as interdependent systems of stratification. We shall review the trend of sociology of social stratification in India focusing upon some of these specific structural units of stratification.

CASTE SYSTEMS AND SOCIAL STRATIFICATION*

The theoretical position of caste in the analysis of Indian social systems is highly complex. It constitutes both a

---

*Our study of caste and its changing forms and functions refers mainly to the implication of this system for Indian social stratification. It is not meant to be a review of caste studies as such. Caste system is seen here as a status principle of social stratification. For sociology of social stratification in India, the treatment of caste becomes unavoidable as a standard to measure changes with reference to other principles of stratification such as of wealth (class) and power (elite). These new principles only sometimes operate autonomously; more often these operate contingently together with the caste principle of social stratification. The reader would, therefore, find our discussions on caste to be in a comparative rather than substantive frame of analysis.

structural unit of social stratification as well as a system. The distinction between the two would depend upon the level of analysis involved. Sociologists who look across the cultural view of caste have, right from the beginning, associated it with an autonomous principle of stratification the bases of which are: institutionalized inequality, closure of social system in respect of social mobility, an elementary level of division of labour legitimized on ritual bases of reciprocity, and emphasis on quality (ritual purity or racial purity) rather than performance. In other words, caste is associated with an autonomous form of cultural system or world-view. The history of this view of caste goes far back in sociological literature (see Dubois 1906; Nesfield 1885; O'Malley 1932; Weber 1952; Kroeber 1930; etc.) and the trend still continues (see Berreman 1967; Barth 1960; Davis 1951; Myrdal 1968; etc.). The important assumption here is that the caste system of stratification constitutes merely a variant of the stratification principle which may be found operative, not only in India, but in other societies too. An important implication of this view, as we find in the writings of Davis, A.R. Desai (1966) and Bose (1968) and others is that being a structural reality caste would disappear when society in India evolves to a higher level (see Singh 1968) of industrialization. A variant of the structural view of caste is that it forms an ideal type of stratification system and as such it could exist forever, either alone or in coexistence with other forms of stratification in societies. This viewpoint is held by sociologists who take a structural-functional rather than evolutionary-historical view of social stratification.

   Thus a distinction can be made between sociologists who treat caste as a cultural phenomenon and those who define it as a structural phenomenon. Each of these positions has a further subvariation based on one's view of caste: whether it is a particularistic phenomenon, Indian in substance, or whether it has universal properties. Thus four approaches emerge as logical classes once we distinguish between the two levels of theoretical formulation, that is, cultural and structural and universalistic and particularistic. The four are: *cultural-universalistic, cultural-particularistic, structural-universalistic* and *structural-particularistic*. All the four types of conceptualization have existed in the sociological literature on caste stratification in India. Among the prominent sociologists who take a structural-particularistic view of caste we may mention Leach. He says, the 'use of the word "caste" is to define the system of social organization found in traditional India and surviving to a large extent to the present day. I myself consider that, as sociologists, we shall be well advised to restrict the use of the term caste to the Indian pheno-menon only' (Leach 1960). We mentioned above the sociologists who hold the second position where the caste system is considered as a structural-universalistic category, i.e. caste in India is only a particular case of a general phenomenon of a closed form of social stratification. The third position is of those sociologists who treat caste as a cultural phenomenon, a matter of ideology or value system, particularly that of *hierarchy* which forms the basis for ranking of persons or groups. It is maintained that caste-like cultural bases of strati-ficaion could be found in most traditional societies, where status or honour constitutes the basis for social ranking and that Indian caste is merely a special form of the general system of status-based social stratification. Formulated early by Max Weber, this viewpoint has continued in contemporary sociology. In the writings of Ghurye (1957, 1961) for instance, we find its indirect explication. The fourth view on caste is one where it is treated as a cultural but particularistic form of social reality. Louis Dumont's views on caste corres-pond to this position very closely (see, Dumont 1961, 1966).

The question is: how far do these four theoretical conceptions about caste throw light on the structure and process of stratification in India? Since the focus of this essay is on the Indian system of social stratification, the structural-particularistic and cultural-particularistic approaches have specific relevance for our analysis. Both, being particularistic, focus mainly on the Indian phenomenon of caste and take account of its structural and cultural dimensions.

The structural-particularistic treatment of caste is the pre-dominant feature of stratification studies in India. Here, caste is treated as an institutionalized system of interaction among hierarchically ranked hereditary groups for marriage, occupa-tion, economic division of labour, enforcement of cultural norms and values by caste bodies and performance of rituals based on principles of purity and pollution. The major cultural norm of caste is described as that of 'mutual repulsion' by Bougle (1958) while its other attributes are mentioned as hereditary specialization and hierarchy. From a stratification point of view, these attributes assume relevance as their operation sets a limit to the forms of allocation and evaluation of roles and status attributes of caste and perpetuates an institutionalized form of social inequality.

This institutionalized inequality and its cultural and economic coordinates are indeed the factors which render caste in India a unique system of social stratification. Structural-particularistic theory analyses the cases and forms of caste inequality and its changing patterns in various social settings. Structurally, the relevant issues that have been raised in caste stratification relate firstly to the unit components in caste ranking, such as *varnas*, caste, and subcaste; secondly, to modes of caste fusion and fission, formation of caste associations, caste federations or formation of new subcastes by Sanskritization (emulation of higher caste values and ideologies); thirdly, to aspects of caste dominance and conflict in the process of social mobility; and finally, to the extent of social mobility in the caste system.

The above structural properties of caste have direct implications for the system of social stratification. What is important, however, is the level at which the structure of caste tends to be relevant for social stratification. Many types of structural distinctions have been drawn about the reality of caste as a unit component of social structure. The distinction between caste and subcaste (Chauhan 1966; Atal 1968; Mayer 1960), formation of caste referents, such as *jatis*, caste categories, caste association and *varna* (Bailey 1963), or of caste clusters and *Varna* (Karve 1961) are examples of such distinctions. André Beteille (1965) also highlights this point by illustrating how a caste may subsume many subcaste categories (the Brahmans of Sripuram) and shows the multi-polarity in the functioning of caste in the Indian social structure.

The primary significance of these structural properties of caste to the process of social stratification lies at two levels: first, in the extent to which the new forces originating from outside the caste system such as democratization, industrialization, land reform, other social legislation, etc., affect the traditional structure of caste stratification and create cleavages in the summation of social statuses based on ritual prestige, economic rank and political power (Beteille 1965; Sharma 1974); and secondly, the degree to which castes that undergo the process of new structural differentiation through fusion and fission of forms, also bring into being new structural components for social stratification and set in conditions for the process of social mobility and change in this system.

The structural differentiation in caste results from urges for social mobility. Its first manifestation, as noted by Srinivas is found in the process of Sanskritization whereby the lower castes seek to emulate the cultural styles, beliefs, rituals and ideologies of the upper castes and give up some of their own older modes of living and cultural practices supposedly polluting, to claim a higher status in the caste hierarchy. This process, though older, started actively with the census operations following the establishment of the British regime in India (see Srinivas 1962, 1966) and it has continued in many shades ever since. The form of Sanskritization varies with the nature of the dominant caste which serves as models for cultural emulation. Srinivas' own field material refers to the lower castes emulating the Brahmanical model, but evidence from other regions reveals the operation of the Kshatriya, Vaishya, Tribal, and other caste models in Sanskritization.

The process of Sanskritization, though apparently cultural, reflects many complex motivational urges for social mobility. An important element in this process is the manifest rejection of the norms of institutionalized inequality fostered by the traditional caste stratification system. It leads, however, to a paradox: Sanskritization reinforces the normative system which is represented by caste stratification, but it also, at least in principle, violates its basic tenet—the acceptance of the principle of hierarchy. For this very reason, many sociologists have seen in the process of Sanskritization a latent form of class conflict which results because of the peculiar structural constraints of Indian society (Gould 1961; Leach 1960; etc.). Srinivas points to this process indirectly through his concept of the 'dominant caste'.

The structural constraints of Sanskritization or other forms of caste mobility are related to the closure or openness of the caste system. There is substantial evidence to suggest that, even in the past, the caste system was not absolutely closed, and mobility was possible through many channels such as migration to far-off regions, royal decrees or proclamations, raising a particular caste status, accumulation of wealth and power during economic or political crisis by some castes which eventually elevated their caste status. Thus, the caste system did offer, though in limited and exceptional cases only, changes for status mobility (see Srinivas 1966; Stein 1968; Barber 1968). The social historical studies reveal that contrary to the scriptural view of caste as a closed and stable system in which the ranking on *varna* scale coincided with that of caste or subcaste status, there existed wide divergences in the status ranking of families within the same caste on the basis of subcaste division, occupational sub-specialization and accumulation of wealth. Moreover, the position of caste in the system of ranking was itself subject to changes due to external and internal forces operating in the social system (see Silverberg 1959, 1968; Barber 1968).

The closure of caste stratification is associated with the principle of 'status summation' that a caste being high or low on one scale of ranking, say, economic, would also be high or low on political, social and ritual scales of the status system. The open social stratification is in contradistinction to the one where the principle of status summation does not operate and the ranking level on one scale, say, social or ritual, does not coincide with the ranking level (see Bailey 1963; Beteille 1966) in economic or political spheres. It may, however, be difficult to establish historically that the caste system of ranking in the above sense was ever fully closed. Indeed the changes were exceptional, but in social relevance were quite significant. Structurally, the caste system simultaneously manifests two tendencies, one segmental and the other organic. As a segmental reality, each caste or subcaste tends to articulate mutual repulsion, social distance and social inequality. But as an organic system, the caste segments are mutually inter-linked by a principle of reciprocity, through the *jajmani* system. Bailey has, therefore, rightly named the caste principle of stratification as 'closed organic stratification', in contradistinction with the class principle which is that of 'segmentary stratification'. In the former the social segments (castes or subcastes) interact through cooperation and in the latter through competition.

The distinctions between open and closed or between 'closed organic' and 'segmentary' forms of stratification are, however, relevant only as theoretical devices, because historically it is doubtful to maintain that tensions or conflicts did not exist between castes in traditional India. Such conflicts did exist, and often on a larger scale (in the form of social movements). One such instance is found in conflict among the Kshatriyas, Brahmans and Vaishyas during the rise of Buddhism and Jainism. The competition and conflict among the various caste strata continued to emerge subsequently. The thesis of the caste system being closed, or 'harmonic' is probably overdrawn by social anthropologists for two reasons: first, their perspective is on single-village studies in the framework of the functional theory; hence, integration and not conflict is the focus of their analysis; secondly, the *jajmani* system within the caste framework led them to overemphasize the element of reciprocity and underplay the inherent tensions in the system. By a curious coincidence the social anthropologists' view of organic elements in the caste stratification resembles the 'official' scriptural view of the system which tries to establish a close organic fit between the institutionalized inequality among the caste segments and its religious rationalization.

The analytical perspectives on mobility, integration and tension in the caste system have changed as studies have shifted in focus from the rural to urban realities and processes. Damle (1968) and Lynch have used the concept of 'reference group' to analyse the structural process in caste mobility. The locus of reference group behaviour is the non-membership group or other caste and subcaste whom a caste individual or the caste group as a whole seeks to imitate or identify with if its status is positively evaluated or towards which such individuals or groups develop a negative attitude of hostility and disapproval if its status is negatively evaluated. In both cases the mechanism that motivates individuals or groups to refer to or compare their existing membership position with the membership in other caste groups depends upon (a) the extent of closure or openness of the membership of groups to which reference is being made, and (b) the nature of deprivations and gratifications that individuals or groups derive from their existing membership group.

From this distinction two major types of reference groups are delineated: the positive reference groups, membership to which is aspired for, and the negative reference groups, membership to which is disliked. In the application of the reference group theory to the caste phenomenon both Damle and Lynch emphasize the significance of the concepts of role and status. Membership is a role-contingent concept. Damle cites cases of upward caste mobility by the lower caste individuals in Poona by suitable role adaptations to higher caste membership group. Lynch finds cases both of positive and negative reference group behaviour among the Agra Jatavas; in their effort to Sanskritize the Jatavas found a negative reference group in the orthodox Brahman caste. This led to conflict between the two groups. The positive reference group in their case were the Kshatriyas because of the high status attributes associated with this caste. The forces of democratization and politicization augment the aspirations for social mobility among the Jatavas. These forces bring into being forms of social interaction which have wider impli-cations. Often, mobility demands lead to mobilization. Lynch (1968) writes:

I will hazard the prediction that the model of political participation is the direction that movements for social mobility will increasingly follow in India. The danger lies in whether the more conscious and vociferous demands of these movements can be met in an economy of scarcity without jeopardizing the goal of democratic socialism that India has set for itself. (p. 237)

Both Damle and Lynch study caste mobility through the reference group approach to broaden the theoretical level of analysis. Lynch claims that it would be possible to explain the structural aspects of mobility implied in Sanskritization and Westernization, if these processes are viewed from a reference group theoretical perspective. A comprehensive and theoretically meaningful reference group approach to analyse mobility in the system of stratification should, however, focus upon at least three aspects: (1) the motivational structure, or the aspiration of the members to move upward; (2) the opportunity structure or the eligibility or ineligibility of members to move in the desired direction; and finally (3) the communication structure, or the extent of 'viability' or 'observability' of the degrees of relative deprivations in the system of stratification which might influence people's motivation for social mobility. The reference group model suggested by Lynch and Damle focuses only upon two of these three components. Damle puts more emphasis on motivation and opportunity structure and Lynch on communication and motivation structures.

The system of stratification is expected to generate tensions and conflicts if its reference group context is such that the aspiration levels and communication structures are highly active but the opportunity structure remains closed and shows dire inequalities. Social development in India corresponds, more or less, to this situation. Most other countries too would show similarity in the inter-relationship of these three dimensions of reference group process. The advantage of reference group theory in the analysis of social stratification is that it can lead to the formulation of sound theoretical propositions. These propositions can be valuable as explanatory insights both for the social scientists and social planners. So far, the studies using this approach have been of limited scope and are nowhere near formulating a set of hypotheses which could be later built into theoretical propositions. There is need to extend the application of this approach in the study of social stratification.

Another approach to the study of caste stratification in India is suggested by McKim Marriott (1968). He makes the reference group approach a point of departure for his analysis and refers to 'multiple reference' in the caste system. He argues that in order to gain fuller understanding of the stratification system in India its processes should be observed at various levels. These levels are: rural as different from metropolitan system of ranking, individual, group and corporate units in ranking and, finally, 'a series of successively wider zones of reference for the units in any local system, the several zones being distinctively characterized by distinctive values' (p. 103). Rural stratification, according to Marriot, is closed rather than open, there are limited sets of inter-group ties and in this context the reference group behaviour tends often to be dysfunctional. In the urban areas not only is the stratification system relatively open, but its character is 'attributional' and not 'interactional'. In other words, if a certain individual, group or family is able to acquire high status attributes such as education, wealth or better occupational position in the cities, the individual or group may be able to pass as a member of higher social rank. In the villages, on the other hand, the ranking depends more on the traditional evaluation of caste status. This is reflected in most forms of inter-group or inter-individual interactions. Mere acquisition of higher status attributes may not be sufficient here for elevation of caste status. Moreover, in the metropolitan settings the principle of 'corporate ranking' does not operate as it does in the rural system of stratification. In corporate ranking, status is attributed to the entire group and even if individuals or families in that group are able to acquire status-enhancing attributes, the status of the group as a whole is not changed. The status is collectively defined on cultural criteria. In the rural caste system principles of purity and pollution, hereditary occupation and kinship relations, which are more binding factors in social interaction, render the ranking system corporate. The process of status mobility through Sanskritization, in a way manifests this corporateness in the rural ranking system. This explains the tendency in the rural areas to mobilize caste, tribe or ethnic groups as a whole for advancement of social status. In the urban centres non-corporate mode of status mobility is common.

The above distinction between the rural and urban system of social stratification highlights only the main characteristic of structural patterns. It does not mean that there is a total absence of individual mechanisms of status mobility in the rural system of stratification. An important individual mode of status mobility both in the rural and the urban societies is acquisition of prestige through worldly renunciation or by becoming a *sanniasy*. This form of status mobility has been widely observed among the lower caste members (see Dumont 1970; Harper 1968; Rowe 1968; Stein 1968; etc.) both in the villages and towns. No systematic sociological studies have, however, been made on this mechanism of social mobility in India.

The third level at which, according to Marriott, the caste

stratification reflects its structural features in India is that of zones. He mentions three zones: '(1) the zone of the village community and its directly connected parts in the country-side; (2) the zone of the recognized cultural or linguistic region, and (3) the zone of the whole civilization' (Marriot 1968: 109). In the village zone, castes or subcastes are the most relevant category of stratification because of the direct and corporate nature of social interactions. In the zone of the linguistic region the relevant category for ranking is class. Classes manifest themselves through categories like 'lord' or 'servant' in northern India, or the 'waterbearing' or 'non-waterbearing' in Bengal or 'light people' or 'dark people' in Gujarat. In the civilizational zone, however, according to Marriott, the more inclusive categories, those of *varna*, ethnic origin or the cosmopolitan scheme of gradation offer a framework for understanding social stratification.

The conflicts in the system of social stratification emerge from the changing frames of reference in the ranking of castes from one level of categories to another. But this process has also contributed to the dynamics of the strati-fication system. In India, so far, there is no crystallization in favour of any one of these three levels of ranking systems and Marriott says that all of them are operating in a 'multiple reference' model.

Marriott's analysis does indicate the complexity of the social stratification system in India, but it does not offer us an insight into the mechanisms by which stratification process at one level, such as rural or metropolitan, interacts with that of other levels such as those of the three zones of the village, region and civilization. An understanding of the dialectical relationship between the stratification mechanisms at different levels can be had only through an analysis of the various social forces that operate in social stratification. Marriott's scheme offers categories for the description of the pattern of stratification in India, but is limited in theoretical viability and power. It does not offer theoretical codes for transcription of data from one level of observation to another and, finally, it fails to indicate how the scheme of categories of ranking suggested by him constitutes or does not constitute a logically interrelated set of status ranking principles through which the dynamics of social stratification could be understood and analysed. The main limitation of most contemporary studies on social stratification is this lack of theoretical concern. They have no predictive power, and fail even to establish a coherent map of the trends in the system of ranking and stratification for the country as a whole.

Mobility in caste stratification is also related to the possibility of structural changes in this system. The mobility patterns in this system, whether initiated by individual, family or corporate groups and categories, are generated by the frustrations either objectively existing or subjectively felt by various groups. This is further related to the nature of the communication system and the opportunity structure. It may be important to know the new structural pressures which contemporary changes in the opportunity structure, motivational patterns and communication system have exerted on the system of caste stratification in India. Is the caste system breaking up or taking a new form? Is the principle of hierarchy, considered pivotal to this system of stratification, giving way to new principles?

Some noticeable processes in caste in contemporary India are its changing functions and organizational forms. Caste associations, federations, and clusters have increasingly been formed, and these compete as corporate groups for access to political power, economic and cultural resources and opportunities. This has enhanced the competitive interaction of castes with other castes on a scale which never existed in traditional Indian society. These new changes are so fundamental that it is often debated if the new forms of caste are indeed a manifestation of caste or class properties. Here some important hypotheses regarding caste and its future are noteworthy.

The first is the 'mode of production' hypothesis. It is supported both by Marxist and non-Marxist sociologists. Among the non-Marxists, Kingsley Davis (1951) writes that despite the apparent resilience of caste and its consciousness as manifested by rationalization of its organizations, or fusion of its forms,

the forces now opposing caste are more numerous and definite than those favouring it. This conclusion can be reached in another way, namely, in the actual evidences of the decline of caste. Foremost among such evidences are: (1) noticeable loosening of the restrictions on interdining; (2) widespread violation of food taboos; (3) slight tendency to ignore intermarriage barrier; (4) gradual removal of untouchability; and (5) pronounced growth of social mobility. The importance that government planning must assume in the new Union of India will doubtless hasten the decline of caste there. If industrialisation proceeds rapidly in the nation, the caste system will have essentially disappeared by the end of this century. (pp. 75-6).

Davis foresees the possibility of transformation of caste into class through adaptive changes under the impact of industrialization. But he does not employ the Marxist conceptual scheme for explaining such changes. A.R. Desai (1961), on the other hand, arrives at the same conclusion but his argument is based on the Marxist thesis that the system of caste is yet another social manifestation of the forces of modes of production and ownership of property in India based on the agrarian feudal complex. Caste ranking basically inheres an undeveloped but potentially explosive class character. Desai writes:

It has been observed by a number of students of the social life of the Indian people that there is a close correlation between the position of caste in the hierarchy of the Hindu social order and the respective status of its members with regard to wealth, economic rank, class position, political power and accessibility to education and culture ... a couple of dozens of castes in India hold the monopoly of economic resources, political power, and educational and cultural facilities available.... It also raises a significant problem. Will it be possible to abolish caste system and caste hierarchy in fact without adopting measures of basic changes in the economic structure? (pp. 111-12)

A different hypothesis, which may be called 'caste resilience and adaptation' hypothesis, is based on the argument that the forces of industrialization, Westernization, growth of technology and other democratic institutional spreads tend to activate and enlarge rather than constrict the process of caste functions, and contribute to its orgnaizational mobilization, rationalization and fusion of caste ranks. M.N. Srinivas, who drew the attention of scholars towards this process (Srinivas 1964), in a later essay states that whereas caste mobility in medieval India was based on fission, in modern India it takes the forms of fusion of caste segments at adjacent grades. In this process, the nature of caste undergoes some transformation no doubt, but it would not be true to assume, as

Bailey does, that castes change their character or 'are used as building blocks in a different kind of system'. The fact, according to Srinivas, is that these building blocks themselves undergo changes (Srinivas 1962: 199), but without altering the caste system as such. The thesis of continued caste resilience has also been supported by André Beteille. He uses Max Weber's term 'status group' to characterize caste and finds evidence for the emergence of new caste-like structural forms which are both 'elaborate' and 'rigid' in structure; these 'new castes', as Beteille describes them, are discernible in the crystallization of professional and occupational groups. These maintain exclusiveness of life-style and social inter-action similar to the status groups. Logically, these new status groups may continue despite industrialization and increased political participation. Beteille writes:

Many changes are taking place in the productive organization as well as in the political system. These changes are not likely to lead to a disappearance of status groups which in any case have to be differentiated from classes. It is quite possible to visualize different patterns of status groups coexisting with a given economic or political system. Status groups derive their distinctive features not only from material elements but also from a variety of irreducible cultural and ideological factors.... In India the status groups of the future will no doubt carry the marks of the caste system which has played such an important part in the social history of the country. (Beteille 1965; also see idem 1969a)

Opposed to the caste 'resilience' hypothesis is the view that, through new structural adaptation such as formation of caste associations, caste federations and clusters, castes lose their original character and assume class-like forms (Leach 1960; Bailey 1963a; Singh 1969a; Kothari 1970b; etc.). forms. Unlike the Marxist sociologists, the proponents of this view do not link these changes with inevitable stages of transfor-mation. No statement is made about the disappearance of the caste system or its replacement with the system of class strati-fication. The treatment is more analytical than dialectical.

In the studies of caste stratification we notice that the focus on structure and process has shifted corresponding to the theoretical presuppositions with which sociologists have approached the problem. The 'mode of production' hypo-thesis is clearly based on the dialectical-materialistic view of social structure and process. It views castes as a part of the vast panorama of emerging and changing contradictions in social relationships based on the modes of production and ownership relations among the categories, castes and classes. This approach has a powerful theoretical frame. Its major limitation in objective analysis of social stratification in India is the lack of sound empirical studies.

Most studies on caste stratification postulating the resilience of caste hypothesis have structural-functional orientation for theory. They are usually based on sound field data and deep analysis of structural forms. But their theoretical concern hardly goes beyond the formulation of a conceptual scheme or typologies. Concepts like 'status group', 'class', 'segmental and organic' organizations, 'horizontal and vertical mobility', etc., are indeed used either as typologies or as continua. If the Marxist studies of stratification in India take long theoretical jumps without much empirical substantiation, the structural-functional or topological studies present rich empirical data but have little by way of power for theoretical generalizations.

Social stratification has also been analysed in some studies with statistical approaches. These studies do not aspire to establish trends for the growth of castes or classes. Their concern is to study the nature and magnitude of caste or class functions with the help of certain indices. With few exceptions, most such approaches use attributional and not interactional models. This approach can be used more effectively for macroscopic and comparative analysis of social stratification. It also makes it possible to introduce inter-disciplinary conceptual frames in social stratification studies.

One type of such studies in India has used indices and scales of socio-economic status and inter-caste distance (see Mukherjee and Misra 1955; Kuppuswamy and Singh 1967; Kuppuswamy 1962; Ruhudkar 1960; Atal 1972) for the study of stratification. With a few exceptions, especially Mukherjee and Misra, most of these studies have formulated only class indices based on selected variables. Kuppuswamy and Singh, for instance, have selected education, occupation, income and social prestige as variables for constructing an SES (socio-economic status) scale; the assumption is that these factors cumulatively merge to define the SES of a particular group.

SES measures are divided into four categories: the upper, upper middle, middle, lower middle and lower classes. These writers have assumed a cumulative causal interlinkage among the variables of their scale. They write:

education has been considered to be a deciding factor of one's occupation, occupation an important intervening variable in the translation of educational advantage into income advantage and the income a positive factor in deciding one's social prestige which, in turn, influences the educational level of the succeeding generation and possibly of the same also. (Kuppuswamy and Singh, 1967: 65)

Other scales too use sets of variables for generating class categories in the rural-urban or general social setting. Yogesh Atal has used the factors of caste, occupation and education to formulate an SES index for classification of his sample in a general election study in three communities in western Uttar Pradesh. But his scale, like most others, is also classificatory and is not formulated for developing a theoretical focus on social stratification.

Analysis either of caste or class, through SES and other scales, would necessitate that a set of theoretical propositions are first formulated. These propositions should be logically interrelated to generate a series of hypotheses which may be confirmed or disconfirmed in order to test the validity of the high order theoretical propositions. This would determine the power of the social stratification theory. After being tested with such operational devices as scales, indices and other measures the hypotheses could be verified, defining the limits of the proposed theory. A major limitation of SES and other indices used by social psychologists and sociologists in India is the lack of systematic theoretical concern. Very often, the operational devices are simply borrowed from other countries and applied to the Indian situation. The attempts thus suffer from methodological *adhoc*-ism as well as intellectual dependency. For these reasons a good deal of the value of these potentially useful methodological tools is lost to Indian sociology.

In terms of relative theoretical sophistication and relevance, the formulation of indices of caste and class 'rigidity and fluidity' by Victor S. D'Souza (see, D'Souza 1969, 1972) is relatively free from the above limitations. Formulating an operational definition of caste and class he writes:

Caste system has been defined as the integration of the interacting and heterogeneous, but internally homogeneous, hereditary groups, into a structure of status hierarchy. Not only does this concept describe the caste system as a superior or subordinate relationship among hereditary groups in a society or community, but it also explains the conditions under which such a relationship takes place. The basis for the ranking of groups in the caste system and individuals in the class system is the same. In both cases it depends upon certain properties or attributes of individuals which are evaluated by the society. But the difference lies in the pattern of distribution of these properties of individuals in hereditary groups. If the distribution in each group is homogeneous so that each group differs from the other groups and from the total population, the resulting form of social stratification is a caste system, and if it is heterogeneous such that it is more or less the same in every group and in the total population, the form is class system. In the first instance we have a rigid form of social stratification and in the second a fluid one. (D'Souza 1969: 35)

Here we find a near-formal statement about the distinction between 'caste' and 'class'. It also inheres the distinctions between 'cumulative inequality', said to be characteristic of caste, and 'dispersed inequality' that is treated as characteristic of the class system. The distinction between close (rigid) and open (fluid) social stratifications also follows logically from the above. The indices used by D'Souza to measure the rigidity-fluidity dimension in the six villages of Punjab are: occupational heterogeneity, consensus about caste status, heterogeneity about individual prestige and consensus about individual prestige. He finds significant rank order correlation between occupational heterogeneity and heterogeneity of individual prestige (0.843, significant at 0.02 level), between occupational heterogeneity and consensus about individual prestige (0.929, significant at 0.01 level), and quite notable correlation between heterogeneity of individual prestige and consensus about individual prestige (0.600, significance not reported). This proves tentatively the theoretical plausibility of his indices for measuring social stratification. D'Souza has subsequently tried to analyse caste stratification mainly in terms of distinctions between caste and subcaste in the light of set theory (D'souza 1972; Atal 1972).

D'souza's attempt at formulating statistical measures of the extent of rigidity and fluidity in caste-class social stratification

is to a considerable extent embedded in theoretical postulates. Its limitation in reaching the level of theory lies in its
dependence upon correctional measurement. Correlation
technique including factor analysis is a lower order calculus of
theoretical abstraction. Statistical models, including D'Souza's,
offer only synchronic comparisons and are essentially static.
These are based on attributional criteria alone to the
exclusion of the interactional dimensions.

Despite these methodological limitations, statistical models
offer a possibility for objective cross-regional and national-
level analyses of the dynamics of caste and class social stratification in India. Usually, as the studies in social stratification
become more scientific, advanced techniques to measure the
magnitude of mobility, normative and cultural bases of the
formation of strata, and the nature of social inequalities are
likely to be evolved and opertionalized.

*Scheduled Castes and Social Stratification**

The institutionalized inequality of caste stratification manifests
its extreme form in the growth of completely segregated set
of 'untouchable' castes in each region. The Scheduled castes,
who comprise the bulk of the 'untouchables' are, technically,
outside the four-fold *varna* scheme of caste hierarchy.
Imputed with maximum degree of ritual and social impurity,
the occupations of these castes were held to be the lowest in
normative hierarchy and this led to their ecological segregation in most villages and townships. For social stratification,
the Scheduled castes did not constitute a homogeneous
stratum. Before being scheduled, these castes were classified
as 'exterior' or 'depressed'; and a caste was so classified if it
was found subject to a set of social restrictions. In the 1931
Census the listed restrictions were:

---

*A fuller and more comprehensive treatment of the literature on the
Scheduled castes is to be found in the report by Sachchidanand. The
reference to the Scheduled castes in this report has been made mainly from
the stratification point of view. Not only do the Scheduled castes and
backward classes in India comprise a very sensitive and focal point of our
system of social stratification; it would further be observed that sociological
processes operating in this social segment provide conceptual material for
studying the transition from caste to class principles in social stratification in
India.

inability to be served by clean Brahmans; inability to be served by barbers, water-carriers, tailors, etc., who serve the caste Hindus; inability to serve water to caste Hindus; inability to enter Hindu temples; inability to use public conveniences such as roads, ferries, wells or schools; and inability to dissociate oneself from despised occupation. (*Census of India 1931*, Vol. 1, Part-I, p. 472)

These criteria admit of degrees of discrimination. Moreover, there may be region-wise variations in discrimination. It may differ also according to districts or localities. This shows not only the difficulties in visiting the 'exterior casters' but also the fact that these castes did not constitute a homogeneous social category. To the extent that the system of caste stratification was free from external challenges such as politicization, break in cumulative inequality, etc., these 'exterior casters' had no alternative but to suffer their disabilities. Occasionally there used to be reform movements or even short-term rebellious upsurges but these did not alter the entrenched status or power of the upper castes.

The nomenclature of 'exterior caste' changed to 'Scheduled castes' by 1935 through the passage of the Government of India Act. The listing of the Scheduled castes, however, continued to be on the same social criteria as were used in the 1931 Census. But the situation now had one important measure of difference—the closure of the caste stratification and the entrenched position of the caste Hindus had been challenged. The process that led to this development was the growth of movements against 'untouchability' led by Gandhiji and other nationalist leaders. A sharper edge to such efforts was also given by leaders drawn from the Scheduled castes themselves under the leadership of B.R. Ambedkar. The emergence of these movements reflected the growing self-consciousness of the Scheduled castes, which formed part of a general process of cultural, social and political upsurge in the country. Census operations made every caste self-conscious of its status and activized the process of Sanskritization and Westernization, as noted by Srinivas. But the increasing politicization and growth of communal politics in India made the Scheduled caste leaders, led by Ambedkar, acutely conscious of their separate identity. It encouraged the process of horizontal mobilization among them and the urge for solidarity replaced the urge for

Sanskritization. In the early 1930s, Ambedkar opted for communal electorate for the Harijans, the foundation of this move having been laid by the Act of 1919. This led to Ambedkar's confrontation with Gandhi who was not for complete separation of the Scheduled castes from the rest of Hindu society, and wanted radical reforms in the Hindu society itself so that the Scheduled castes could find a respectable place in its social system. One stage of this conflict ended when, after Gandhi's fast, Ambedkar relented from his demand for communal electorate and the 1932 Poona Pact was concluded.

No doubt this pact averted a major process of political and social schism in the nation's body-politic, but it did not entirely rule out the forces of segmentation and polarization among the Scheduled castes. The consequences which followed it were: first, the emergence of Scheduled castes as political groups in the country and, secondly, the pressure on the national leadership to do away with the social disabilities of the Scheduled castes and Harijans. The provision for special constitutional safeguards for the Scheduled castes after India gained freedom reflects this development. Ambedkar played a dominating role through this process.

These developments led to a series of consequences of deeper sociological significance. The first relates to the consequences that these movements had for the solidarity of the Hindu social system. We may ask: were these movements alienative or integrative (we would recall that Ambedkar stood for alienative and Gandhi for integrative ideology of the Harijan movements) for the caste system? The second issue is the extent and nature of status mobility actually achieved by the Scheduled castes either through these movements or through other measures, constitutional and developmental.

Both integrative and alienative orientations in the Scheduled caste movement have been in existence from very early times (Beteille 1969a; Srinivas and Beteille 1969; Cohn 1959; Lynch 1968; etc.). Traditionally, the Scheduled castes were integrated into the economic system of the upper castes in an extremely asymmetrical manner so that the high degree of integration also meant a higher measure of economic dependence and exploitation. The ritual and social disabilities were a 'backwash effect' of this economic dependence and servitude. Under these circumstances the urge for mobility, whenever pressing, could not ventilate itself by frontal confrontation with the upper castes but only through imitative behaviour or Sanskritization. Sometimes, depending upon the elasticity of social circumstances, the abnegation of 'old' did also follow the demand for 'new'. But the Scheduled castes always faced trouble as even Sanskritization met with the wrath of the upper castes (see Srinivas 1962, 1966; Beteille and Srinivas 1969; Rowe 1968), and they could succeed in Sanskritization either on the sly or through collective mobilization. Quite often such movements also failed (see Harper 1968). The effort to Sanskritize may be called an integrative movement mainly because it does not renounce caste as a system of social stratification. But the system of caste being organic-segmental in nature, such segmentation still used to be sociologically integrative.

The motive force for the Scheduled castes to sanskritize was existential or social and only marginally cultural. The form of these movements in free India changed radically as new alternatives for legitimation of demands came into being. It was further reinforced by the democratization process. From imitating high caste cultural models now the focus of the Scheduled castes shifted to viewing the upper caste models with disdain. This led to their horizontal level caste consolidation. Evidence of this is amply provided by sociological studies. The Vannya Kula Kshatriya Sangham was formed in Tamilnadu by the fusion of a number of subcastes into one caste group (see Rudolph and Rudolph, 1967; Rudolph 1965; Hardgrave 1968); Mahars in Maharashtra coalesced their subcaste distinctions to form a single caste group. Sunanda Patwardhan (1968) writes:

It seems that for upward mobility Sanskritization is no longer as effective and relevant as political participation. There has been set in motion a complex interaction between the traditional horizontal solidarity of the members of a caste group and the solidarity which the compulsions of political processes create. These have affected the internal structure of the Mahar community. There were 52 endogamous sub-castes within the Mahar community in the whole of Maharashtra. I found during my survey in 1963 in the city of Poona that no Mahar respondent mentioned his sub-caste, and there was inter-marriage and inter-dining between all Mahar sub-castes. Even after conversion there is inter-marriage between those who are converted to Buddhism and those who have remained Mahars (pp. 194-5)

The emergence of similar horizontal sub-caste solidarity among the Scheduled castes has been reported from other regions too. The Chamars and Jatavas in U.P. (see Lynch 1968; Rosenthal 1970), Iravas in Kerala (see Gough 1970; Beteille 1969a), Panos in Orissa (see Bailey 1963), Holerus in Mysore (see Harper 1968) and many other Scheduled castes in other parts of the country (see Rudolph and Rudolph 1967) have now become politically and socially mobilized.

The change in the strategy of Scheduled caste movements from Sanskritization to consolidation of their own positive identity as a caste group through fusion of their subcaste identities contributes to their freedom from political dependence upon the upper caste Hindus. The Scheduled caste demography is of great advantage for such mobilizations. For instance, the Scheduled castes have made an impact upon the structure of power in peninsular India. But their real independence is linked with their freedom from bondage to the economic systems of the villages and cities, over which the upper caste Hindus continue to have a near monopolistic control. This facet of the problem is significant because the demand for power is difficult to isolate from the demand for economic well-being. It is this mixed force that motivated the Scheduled castes led by Ambedkar to assert their separate identity.

In 1956, dissatisfied with the social status of the Scheduled castes, Ambedkar led great masses of them to embrace Buddhism. This was a break from the caste society, though not from the Hindu cultural tradition (see Isaacs 1964; Zelliot 1970). The roots of this movement go far back to the India Act of 1919 and the British policy for the minorities and Backward classes (see Dushkin 1961; Galanter 1961, 1963 and 1968) attempting to introduce the communal electorate system. The British policy for the Scheduled castes at the administrative level was, however, ameliorative and attuned to the demands of social justice (see Galanter 1968; Irschick 1969). But it lacked initiative to introduce major institutional changes to give this policy credible shape. The passage of the Untouchability (Offences) Act in 1955, is indeed a culmination of a series of legislations passed by the State earlier to remove the disabilities of the Scheduled castes and Backward classes.

These could not, however, keep Ambedkar's patience. He believed in the mobilization of the Scheduled castes to redress their grievances. In 1942 he had organized the Scheduled Castes Federation, in 1956 he launched the drive for the mass conversion of the Scheduled castes to Buddhism, and in 1957 he organized the political wing of the Scheduled castes known as the Republican Party. All these steps reflect alienative trends in the Scheduled caste movement with respect to the caste social stratification. Conversion as a medium for social mobility is not new to this country. There have been known instances of low castes' conversion to Christianity in parts of the country and earlier to Islam (see Zelliot 1970; Singh 1973), but the neo-Buddhist movement was an instance of conversion within the fold of the Hindu cultural tradition. As Buddhists, however, the Scheduled castes technically ceased to be entitled for benefits offered by the government. Consequently, the Republican Party had to launch a satyagraha in 1964 for the restoration of these privileges and benefits to the Scheduled caste neo-Buddhists.

A rethinking had been going on in the country for reformulating the criteria for determination of the Scheduled caste status. This was spurred not only by the mass conversion of the Scheduled castes, but also by the emergence of new dominant castes from amongst the Scheduled castes such as the Lingayats and Okkaligas in Mysore and Ezhavas in Kerala. These castes no longer suffer from older social disabilities and yet want that the criteria for scheduling should continue to be the 'pollution-purity' principle (and not socioeconomic) so that they could preserve their social benefits. It is felt incre-asingly that, in view of the secular ideology of the nation, the criteria for special social treatment of specific groups should also be secular or economic rather than religious or ritualistic. The question of scheduling new 'depressed' castes and 'de-scheduling' those who had improved their social and economic lot came up for review by the government. The Backward Classes Commission under the Chairmanship of Kaka Kalelkar had, among other objectives, also to review the question whether the list of the Scheduled castes should be modified. This commission did not, however, go into the formulation of criteria for scheduling of castes. This issue was particularly taken up by the Advisory Committee on the revision of the list of the Scheduled castes under the chairmanship of B.N. Lokur (see Lokur 1965).

This committee in its reports emphasized the need for taking only economic merit in giving preferential treatment to specific social groups. It also urged upon the government the need for periodic review of the list of Scheduled castes, and for fixing a time-limit by which the entire list of Scheduled castes and tribes could be scrapped. Government policy is increasingly veering to the economic rather than ritual-religious criteria for according special benefits to the Scheduled castes and tribes. In the meantime, the Scheduled caste movement continues to be ambivalent towards the caste system of stratification oscillating on a continuum of tendencies toward integration with (Sanskritization and reference group behaviour) and alienation from (neo-Buddhist movement) the caste society.

One may ask: how far has the lot of the Scheduled castes improved within the caste system of stratification or independently? There are no doubt some trends of upward social mobility among families and individuals. This is because reservations have been given to them for many socio-political and administrative positions. There are also favourable shifts in political and social awakening among the Scheduled castes. But these processes are more effective in regions where the Scheduled castes are dominant minorities. An analysis of the enforcement of the Untouchability (Offences) Act in various courts indicates that most cases reported under this Act are against institutions rather than individuals or specific castes. It is also revealed that enforcement is highest in states where the Scheduled castes are either politically more conscious or have higher literacy rate or where uplift organisations are more active. The highest enforcement rate (33.5 per cent) is reported from Gujarat, followed by Madhya Pradesh (28 per cent), Kerala (22.0 per cent), Rajasthan (21.1 per cent) Mysore (19.4 per cent) and Maharashtra (3.9 per cent). This indicates a rough relationship between Scheduled caste demography, their self-awareness, organizational mobilization and the demand for enforcement of the law against discrimination.

On net balance, social mobility among the Scheduled castes is far from satisfactory. Relative to their condition a decade ago, their social and economic status has improved, but relative to other castes and groups it still lags far behind (see Elder 1970; Gough 1970). This is particularly so for the Harijans, the lowest rung among the Scheduled castes. Kathleen Gough (1970) writes from her study in a region of Kerala (former Cochin State), that:

On the whole, unlike the other castes the Harijans had improved their living standards, approaching and even surpassing those of some Izavas. In 1964 only three Harijan families lived in their old-fashioned shacks. The rest had thatched cottages with verandas and windows. Harijans used soap and hair oil, drank coffee, and ate modern 'snacks'. The women wore blouses and saris; the men, shirts and long *muntus*. These improvements came mainly as a result of the fixity of tenures and minimum agricultural wages instituted by the Communist government in 1958-59. They were accompanied by greater social equality for Harijans who, in 1964, walked freely in the streets, ate in the teashops, and no longer observed distance-pollution in relation to the higher castes. At the same time, it would be hazardous to say that the Harijans had made all-round or permanent economic improvement, for during the early 1960s unemployment became more common than before and food prices were rising. Despite a bold front of modernity, many Harijans (and some families in the other castes) starved for days together during the rainy season in 1964. (p. 145)

The Harijans are thus still an exploited and subject partner in a productive system that is controlled by the upper castes and classes in the rural and the urban areas (see Rao 1970;, Galanter 1968; Gough 1970). The social improvements referred to by Kathleen Gough show only a relative position; they may even be an exception as, in Kerala, the political structure has been more responsive and more radical. We also find that status differentiation among the Scheduled castes does not conform to that among the other castes in any region. For all other castes there is dispersal of status at all levels, high, medium and low, in terms of wealth, prestige, and power. But not for the Harijans. Everywhere they are at the bottom of the social hierarchy, mostly working as labourers attached to the productive system controlled by the upper castes. In Kerala, the Nambudris formed the apex of the social hierarchy and were also the landed gentry. In

Punjab, not Brahmans, but the Jat landowners were at the top of the economic system. But both in Kerala and Punjab (as also in other states of northern India) the Harijans constitute the bulk of the labour class working on the land owned by their upper caste masters (Rao 1964).

The Scheduled caste members lag behind, despite the protective measures taken by the government, also because of poor reinforcements available to them from their family, neighbourhood and peer groups. This is so even with Scheduled caste members who have moved upward to professional and administrative jobs. Educationally, the Scheduled caste boys find themselves studying in institutions of lower standards. Even where boys from this group get admittance to professional colleges (of engineering and medicine) they are confronted with serious social adjustment problems. Thus, economic deprivation leads to and further reinforces their cultural deprivation.

The Scheduled castes have not been able to take full advantage of the reserved seats allotted to them in the services and in other fields. Of the seats reserved for the Scheduled castes and tribes in government service in 1963, only 1.30 per cent of category I, 2.20 per cent of category II, 7.47 per cent of category III and 16.36 per cent of category IV were filled. It seems easier to fill the non-technical and lower positions in services from amongst the Scheduled castes than the higher ones (see *Report of the Commissioner for the Scheduled Castes and Scheduled Tribes, 1964*). Evidently, the position of the Scheduled castes in the Indian system of social stratification should cause deep anxiety. The impact made by social legislation to remove their disability has been negligible, their position in the caste as well as class system is at the very bottom. This, coupled with their increasing political awareness and general self-consciousness, of which the alienative (neo-Buddhistic and other) movements provide one form of manifestation, are indications that steps to remedy the situation must be taken soon.

CLASS STRUCTURES AND SOCIAL STRATIFICATION

The class element in the social stratification in India is organically connected with the caste stratification although for heuristic purposes a conceptual distinction should be made. An important theoretical issue that arises in this context is of the nature of class, whether it is a universal or particularistic category. In Marxist as well as non-Marxist sociology, class is viewed as a universalistic phenomenon. The substance of class is assumed to be uniform for all societies irrespective of their historical and cultural differences or discontinuities. This assumption may not always be well founded and there is need to examine it in the Indian context. We find that a series of overlapping or intermediary structural forms exist in India that range from caste, ethnic group to class without having been individually crystallized.

There is no unanimity about the conceptual formulation of class even in the general literature of sociology. Controversies persist on the 'subjective' or 'objective' measures of class and the validity of each. It is still being debated whether class is a *component* of the system of stratification or its dialectical process (see Ossowski 1969; Wesolowski 1969); controversy also persists whether conceptual formulations of class should be 'attributional' or interactional and 'propositional'. This holds true for both Marxist and non-Marxist formulations of class. (see Dahrendorf 1966) Most studies on class stratification in the United States of America have followed the 'attributional' method. In this process, a set of indicators of status, individual or familial, are formulated and variations are measured through different scales and indices. Then a scheme of subdivision of class strata is arrived at (see Warner 1960). Here, the emphasis is on formulating a rank order of status into upper, middle, or lower categories on the basis of a set of attributes by which a population could be stratified: the interactional aspect is not taken into account. The interactional aspect may be defined as that element in the stratum which implies a certain mode of relationship with other strata. It is, unlike attributes, not a terminal quality but a sphere of predictable interactions. Interactional formulation of class is therefore theoretically more powerful. Examples of interactional class strata are: bourgeoisie, petit bourgeoisie and 'proletariat', etc., as used in the Marxist formulations; or categories like landlord, share-cropper, and money-lender, etc., as used in general sociology. Attributional criteria have a synthetic character whereas interactional ones are operational and dialectical in nature. In the former the social process is missed and, according to Ossowski, the focus remains mainly on 'order' in the class system rather than on the interactional phenomenon of 'dependence' among classes.

Continental sociology of class, being much more influenced by the Marxist and social historical traditions of class theory, focuses attention on the interactional or the 'dependence' aspects of class stratification. In this formulation the emphasis is not so much on measurement or scale presentation of the class configuration as on demonstrating the historical processes of differentiation, confrontation and mobilization of interest groups or classes based on opposition of interests and values (see Aron 1969; Bottomore 1967; etc.). It is not, however, that these approaches completely neglect the 'attributional' aspect of class. Even for Marx, Wesolowski (1969) writes:

one should remember that for Marx, classes differed in terms of a certain number of attributes interlinked with each other. The bourgeoisie enjoy a higher income, higher level of education and higher prestige. The workers have a low income, a low level of education and low prestige. The petit-bourgeoisie have an intermediate income, enjoy medium prestige and their level of education is higher than that of the workers but lower than that of the bourgeoisie. This conception of class has appeared not only in Marx but also among many non-Marxist theoreticians. (p. 28)

This aspect of status attributes, also known as 'summation of status' or 'status crystallization', has been thoroughly examined both for caste and class by the non-Marxist sociologists as well. But what differentiates the Marxist approach of class from these is that in addition to attributional elements in the class formulation, the Marxist theory postulates general sets of propositions about the direction of changes in class stratification and in the social system as a whole. This systemic aspect of class analysis renders the Marxist approach more viable, if it is duly formalized. But it also exposes itself to the danger of much speculative and ideological construction by those who are not particularly sensitive to scientific methodology.

In India, class stratification has been analysed by sociologists both of Marxist and non-Marxist theoretical disposition. The class categories as employed in the Census documents and by other socio-economic survey agencies are mainly based on attributional criteria of income, occupation or agricultural or non-agricultural modes of earning a livelihood. The terms 'maliks', 'ryots' or even orthodox Marxist categories such as 'bourgeoisie' are used by social scientists of specific theoretical dispositions (see Thorner 1956; Pavlov 1964). Compared to the studies on caste, however, the literature on class is not as substantial. The reason is partly historical; but more importantly, it is because of the continued overlaps between the caste and class status situations or interactions in the Indian system of social stratification. Often, it is difficult to draw a sharp line where the caste principle of stratification ceases and the class principle begins. Sometimes, this peculiar intermixture of status principles in India leads social scientists to make simplistic statements. For instance, caste stratification is associated with the rural and class stratification with the urban situations (see Rosen 1966). It is, however, overlooked that caste and class are two principles of stratification which have persisted in the Indian social systems in a dialectical relationship. Partly, the fallacy in such simplistic formulations arises from the social scientist's tendency to look at social phenomena through neatly formulated continua based on abstractions rather than social historical evidence regarding the functioning of our social systems in temporal depth. This focus got further reinforced by the views of Western scholars that India was a static society where not change but continuity of a primitive variety was the dominant social feature. Even Karl Marx in his early writings on India supported this viewpoint. Now, as deeper social historical insights into the past of the Indian social system are obtained the fallacies of the 'static India' hypothesis are revealed (see Thapar 1972; Joshi 1969; Cohn 1968; etc.).

The sociology of Indian class stratification, therefore, not only should take into account the present-day processes among the various class strata but also analyse them in the historical contexts of change. Studies which throw light on the class structure and its processes in the traditional Indian society reveal that class structure was related to the modes of production and ownership of property, growth of cities, markets and banking institutions and the institutions of power. Kings, feudal chiefs, priests, merchants, artisans, peasants and labourers formed the class categories. Not only the feudal and aristocratic classes, but also the merchants formed an important element of this class structure.

As in Japan, China or even the European continent, the merchants in India did not occupy the lowest rung of social hierarchy (see Joshi 1971; Singh 1973). The merchant and other classes did have their status crystallization concomitant with caste and subcaste, yet the base for their mobility and social substantialization rested in the mode of economic relationships. This introduced elasticity or dynamism in the functioning of merchant classes quite out of proportion with the system of caste stratification into which their class status was embedded. Helen B. Lamb (1959) writes:

One is puzzled by the apparent contradiction between the hierarchical view of society as contained in Indian caste and the obvious vigour of Indian trading communities. Can this be explained by the gulf between the theory and the practice of caste? Is the rationale of caste as freezing the positions of different elements of society nothing more than a myth which makes the reality of social mobility? In actual fact, the position of many castes has altered over time, and wealth and prosperity have been of crucial importance in achieving an improved status. (p. 25)

Such changes in class status of various castes, particularly the merchant class, took place with the creation of economic and political institutions through which economic surpluses could be mobilized from the villages to the cities. If the emergence of new feudal ranks under the patronage of kings constituted the political base of traditional class structure, the rise of the merchant class cemented its economic foundation. The process of social transformation of classes in India began as far back as 600 BC when

there was fusion of Aryan and pre-Aryan peoples and cultures. Kingdoms emerged embracing several tribes and centered in the rich Gangetic plain. Settled agriculture, trade, cities, the concept of private property—all came into being, and one can assume that in this whole transformation traders played a crucial role. (Lamb 1959: 27)

The period from 600 BC to the first millennium AD saw the rise of an active material cultural tradition which coincided with the development of banking, emergence of guild organizations and also the religion of Buddhism. This strengthened the growth of artisans in cities, but the spread of banking bifurcated the trading communities among those who became big urban financiers having pan-Indian net-works, and those who remained the village or small-town traders or money-lenders. The economic sphere of merchants belonging to the latter category was limited, despite their commercial links with cities. The social base of this financier class, which was created so far back in Indian history, has interestingly continued in Gujarat, southern India and Rajasthan in the form of big business houses (see Povlov 1964; Bhargava 1935; Kosambi 1956; Lamb 1959). The process of class transformation through urbanization in ancient India resulted, for some time, in the gravitation of the forces of social, cultural and economic innovations from the villages to the cities. The merchant and artisan classes on the one hand and the Buddhist and Jain princes and priests on the other, played key roles in the social movements of this time.

The first millennium AD saw a decline in the role of the business class, especially in the plain, due to the foreign invasions and re-emergence of Brahmanism. This coincided probably with the decline of cities and growth of village settlements that were economically more self-sufficient than previously. The resurgence of the business classes was now confined to some pockets in India, mainly the Gujarat area and the adjacent Rajasthan. Though limited in sphere, the active role of the business class did continue throughout the medieval period. Irfan Habib (1963) portrays this structural economic conflict between the self-sufficiency or the communal base of the village economy and its pull towards the individualistic urban market economy during the period. He says that:

though a large share of the village produce was taken to the urban market, the village hardly received anything in return from the towns. Thus the village was deeply affected by the requirements of commodity production (i.e. production for the market) and yet had to provide all its needs from within itself. Conditions of money economy, therefore, existed side by side. It was the presence of these contradictory elements that probably accounted for the social contradiction manifest in the existence of an individualistic mode of production in agriculture on the one hand and the organization of Village Community on the other. (pp. 118-19)

Despite these contradictory pulls the dynamism of the class structure of both the cities and the villages continued. Villagers were constantly responding to market demands in far off regions for new crops both for food and cash (see Habib 1963; Gadgil 1959). This implied not only the existence of agrarian classes in villages but also a stable class of merchants, middle-men and bankers in towns and cities to keep the mercantile activities going.

The British trade and commercial policies affected the bulk of Indian artisan classes, led to the decline of many towns and cities and to large-scale rural-ward migration. Ruralization had already set in with the decline of the Mughal empire and the intervening social and political unrest. The Company's policies, such as its currency regulations and banking practices, its favoured treatment to the port towns to the neglect of the vast number of inland towns, its policy of taxation and tariff, and many other biases in social and economic policies led to the decline of the traditional Indian economic structure and its former class structure (see Davis 1951; Bagchi 1970). The land settlement policy adopted by the British government in many parts of the country further altered the class structure in the rural areas and created new vested interests for agrarian exploitation (see Stokes 1970; Mukherjee 1970; Joshi 1969; Malaviya 1969). These historical factors influenced the nature of class structure as it emerged subsequently in the Indian society.

The early British economic and political policies in India led on the one hand to the destruction of many older bases of class formation and on the other created new foundations for the emergence of a feudal-agrarian class structure. In cities, a new industrial and mercantile middle class came into being and there also emerged a new bureaucratic-administrative class. The British, however, only succeeded in altering the nature of class circulation in India, and not its social base. Nevertheless, the sociology of the Indian class stratification bears a deep imprint of these historical antecedents in two respects: first, the middle classes that subsequently emerged maintained the structural continuity in terms of recruitment and social background with the previous class structure and, secondly, the British contact set a process of new cultural adaptation among the new middle classes. (see Misra 1961; Mukerji 1958)

Agrarian Class Stratification and Change

The agrarian system as it evolved during the British regime in India was based either on the zamindari or the ryotwari type of land settlements; the mahalwari system closely resembled the zamindari pattern of settlement, the difference being mainly in the mode of revenue assessment on the land. All the three systems generated more or less a similar agrarian class structure in the village. The zamindari system had the zamindars, tenants, and agricultural labourers as the main agrarian classes. The ryotwari system consisted of two types of peasants: the ryot-landlords and the ryot-peasants (see Kotovsky 1964). In fact, the landlordism which was rural in the zamindari areas had a *de facto* existence in the ryotwari areas. The agrarian class structure all over India had a feudal character; the zamindars were tax gatherers and non-cultivating owners of land, the tenants were the real cultivators often without security of land tenure and the agricultural labourers in most parts of the country had the status of bondsmen and hereditary attached labourers. With the support of the British colonial power this highly exploitative system persists despite frequent peasant unrests and movements.

The challenge to the feudal class structure emerged with the rise of the nationalist movement. Not only was a radial agrarian ideology accepted (see Joshi 1971; Malaviya 1955; *U.P. Zamindari Abolition Committee Report, 1948*) but the national leadership actively undertook the cause of the exploited peasantry and led kisan movements in various parts of the country. Following independence, therefore, land reform was introduced in most states and a beginning was made for transformation in the agrarian class structure. Most sociological studies of the agrarian structure refer to these processes of social change.

Before we take up the substantive problems as highlighted by sociological studies on agrarian class stratification it may be useful to discuss briefly the methodology implicit in most such studies about the notion of agrarian class. As we mentioned above, most formulations of class are either 'interactional' or 'attributional' or mixed. Most interactional formulations have a Marxist theoretical frame. Daniel Thorner (1956) uses the term 'malik', 'money-lender' and 'mazdur' for the chief agrarian classes; 'bourgeoisie', 'capitalist type landowners', 'rich peasants', 'landless or land-poor peasantry' and 'agricultural labourers' are the class categories mentioned by Kotovsky (1964) in his analysis of agrarian classes in India. Gadgil mentions the 'substantial landlord' and 'trade-money-lender', who according to him, dominate the rural economic system and exploit the 'cultivators'. An important feature of all these class categories is their emphasis on the processes of class interaction, dependence-independence and conflict. Especially in orthodox Marxist formulation, these categories also inhere a whole set of implicit propositions about the future course of change or revolution, but most other formulations do not. Conceptually, most of these categories are not nominalistic (that they are a name) but imply a set of propositions. To this extent these can be distinguished from the attributional sets of class categories used by other social scientists.

The attributional class categories used for the analysis of agrarian classes in India are of two types: those that use households or holdings as units for classification, and, those where regions, states or size of holdings, etc., are bases for classification. Most classifications taken from the Census records are of this type (see Gupta 1969; Ghosh 1969; Shah 1969 and Mehta 1969); the survey type of studies of agrarian problems have also usually followed this classification. Regions or states are used as units for classification of agrarian structure to analyse its bearing upon the regional develop-ment and social stratification (see *Report of the Agricultural Labour Inquiry, Rural Manpower and Occupational Structure, 1954*). Another form is found in the measurement of 'concentration ratios' of holdings for various regions to demonstrate inequalities in the distribution of land holdings. The concentration ratio ranges from zero to one; it is zero when all holdings are concentrated in one hand only. The mixed method of class categorization refers to those approaches where the categories of class are arrived at through attributional measures but each stratum also implies a mode of social interaction. Ramakrishna Mukherjee (1958) has formulated three rural class categories out of the nine occupational categories. He names these as 'land holders and supervisory farmers', 'self-sufficient peasantry' (consisting of the cultivators and artisans), and the group of 'share-croppers, agricultural labourers, service holders and other'. These, according to him, roughly correspond with the categories of 'sub-infeudatory landlords', 'self-sufficient peasantry' and 'agricultural labourers'. The chief characteristic of Mukherjee's classification is that he works through attributional classification of occupational groups and formulates on that basis three categories of interactional class strata.

The significant trends noted by the students of agrarian class structure in India following the 'interactional' methods are that: (1) there is a wide gap between the land-reform ideology projected during the freedom struggle and thereafter and the actual measures introduced for land reform. Consequently, socialist transformation in the class structure of the villages has not taken place; (2) this lag could partly be explained by the class character of the Indian political and administrative elite, who are resistant to the needed radical reforms; (3) the existing land reforms have initiated a process by which the security of tenure and economic prosperity of the rich peasantry has increased but the condition of the small peasant both in respect of economic level and tenurial stability has deteriorated; (4) the feudalistic and customary types of tenancy have declined and they have been replaced with a capitalistic form of lease-labour or wage-labour agrarian system; (5) a new class of rich middle stratum of peasantry has come into being, not all of them from among the ex-zamindars; (6) inequalities between the top and the bottom levels of the classes have increased rather than decreased; (7) the benefits of land reform have gone not so much to the agricultural workers or even to the ex-zamindars as to the emergent middle peasantry; (8) these contradictions in the agrarian class structure have increased the tensions in the rural social system and the tensions are bound to increase further; and finally, (9) the sociological process dominant in the current class transformation in the village involves 'embourgeoisiement' of some and 'proletarianization' of many social strata.

The gap between precept and practice in the land-reform ideology in India is said to have resulted from the Indian ruling elite's concern to tread a 'middle path' away from the extreme policies of revolutionary land redistribution, with emphasis on providing security of tenure. With this in view, soon after independence intermediary rights in land were abolished and ceilings on land holding were imposed. The result, however, was that this created owner-cultivators and also capitalist farmers who cultivated through hired labourers. These land reform policies were, of course, elite-sponsored (Joshi 1971) and did not emerge from strong peasant movements or organized unions, unlike in other countries. Ladejinsky (1964) writes:

The peasants themselves while discontented have not developed a movement, whether in the form of tenant-unions like those of Japan before the reforms, or peasant political parties like those of Eastern Europe after the First World War.... For the most part the peasants behaved as if any change in their condition depended upon somebody else. By their apathy they disproved the reasonable assumption that in an agricultural country a government must have peasant support. The fact is that the national and state legislatures in India do not represent the interests of the peasantry; if they did, reform might have taken a different character altogether. The reality is that even when voting is free the peasantry in Asia is not yet wooing its own interest. (Quoted in Joshi 1971)

The impact of land reform on the agrarian class structure has been uneven. It led to the eviction of smaller tenants, as is evident from the decline in the percentage of holdings reporting land-lease. For the years 1953-4, 1960-1 and 1961-2 the corresponding all-India figures of land-lease are 39.85, 27.33 and 23.52 per cent. The declining trend is confirmed for Hyderabad by A.M. Khusro's study (1958), which revealed that land reform led to a marked decline in tenancy and growth of owner-cultivators. In this process the eviction of share-croppers and oral tenants caused hardship to the rural poor. Smaller tenants received much less protection and suffered more by evictions than the bigger ones. Dandekar and Khudanpur in their study of Bombay State (1957) came across cases of extensive resumption and continued dominance of landlords over their tenants. In Gujarat, the study of M.B. Desai and R.S. Mehta (1969) reveals that if land reform gave ownership of land to some tenants these also created the new phenomenon of 'concealed tenancy' and occupancies which perpetuates the agrarian class differences. Similarly, in West Bengal the *baragader's* fate remains uncertain for getting an opportunity to cultivate land. It depends upon the landlord's assessment of the 'political situation'. Even when the *baragaders* are allowed to cultivate land the same is continually shifted as not to allow any permanent interest of the *baragaders* to develop over the land. The situation is the same in the states of Bihar and Andhra Pradesh (see National Sample Survey Nos. 30, 122, 146, etc.).

The uneven impact land reform has had on the agrarian classes leads one to question: who has benefited from the land reforms and developmental changes in the agrarian system in India? Has the landlord benefited most or has a new class of beneficiary peasants emerged? There is a view that the landlords have come off best (see Warriner 1969), but the comparative data show that the real beneficiaries are the intermediate peasants, who have replaced the older zamindars in economic as well as political power. In Uttar Pradesh, for example, the traditional zamindars, who were mostly Rajputs, Brahmans or Bhumihars are being increasingly overwhelmed in economic as well as political competition by the middle class peasants belonging to the Ahir, Kurmi and other intermediate castes. The power of the feudal families is, of course, on the decline all over the country.

The trends in the agrarian class structure and relationships have been summarized by P.C. Joshi (1971) as

(1) the decline of *feudalistic* and customary types of tenancy and its replacement by more exploitative and insecure lease arrangements; (2) the increasing importance of commercial tenancy based on the rich and middle strata of the peasantry who are part owners and part-tenants and possess resources and enterprise for dynamaic agriculture; and (3) the decline of feudal landlords and the rise of commercially oriented landlords either functioning as owner-farmers or utilising the mode of a new, non-customary type of tenancy for the puruit of agriculture as a business proposition.

The emergence of commercial peasants has led to two important socio-economic consequences in the country: first, it has increased the efficiency and productivity of agriculture and has led the country to what is popularly called a 'green revolution'; but, secondly, the process of agricultural capitalism in villages associated with the decay in the fortunes of the poor peasantry and agricultural labourers has also accentuated class conflicts and tensions in various parts of the country. In fact, the agricultural prosperity of a few magnifies the poverty of the many and leads to social discontent. This is further enlarged into class movements and radical political mobilization. Thus, a cumulative or 'value-added' process of agrarian unrest tends to operate which has far-reaching social and political implications.

The process of class mobility and transformation following agrarian reform and other measures has been variously described by sociologists. The rise of the middle-class peasantry into new landlords in parts of the country is described as 'embourgeoisiement' of these social strata. K.L. Sharma (1968) studying six villages in Rajasthan from the viewpoint of changes in social stratification has found that, in some villages, not only the agricultural labourers but quite a few of the ex-landlords have slid down in class status, almost to the state of what he calls 'proletarianization'. The neo-rich peasantry has replaced the older landlords, emerging as the new rural bourgeoisie. Kotovsky (1964) also observes the increasing proletarianization of the peasantry in villages. He says: 'with the agriculture developing along capitalist lines the process of ruination and proletarianization of the bulk of the peasantry is growing more intensely all the time' (p. 160).

Using a mobility model for analysing the changing class position in villages, Beteille observes that as opposed to the past summation of the class, caste and power elements of status in the same group, there are now signs of these attributes being dispersed among different groups in a non-cumulative fashion. It is not unusual for a member of the upper castes to have a lower class status today. The change from 'cumulative' to 'dispersed' inequalities represents an important element in the changing social stratification. Beteille also uses the terms 'harmonic' and 'disharmonic' as two models or paradigms through which the system of social stratification in India and the West could be compared. In the harmonic system, e.g. the traditional caste stratification in

India, there was a close fit between the ideology of inequality (*dharma* and *karma*) and the reality of inequalities. In the disharmonic system (of the West) the two diverged, although according to Beteille pre-industrial West also had a system of stratification closer to that of traditional India.

As heuristic terms, harmonic and disharmonic systems may be of some utility; but as operational concepts, the sense in which Beteille uses these terms might pose serious limitations. It is doubtful if the stratification system of the traditional Indian society was ever 'harmonic', unless one identifies the ideology of social stratification with its reality.

Another important change in social stratification is marked by industrialization. As industrialization proceeds, not only does the ratio of working forces engaged in agriculture relative to those engaged in industrial activities go down but the process of social mobility is also accelerated. This may not lead to a drastic reduction in social inequalities, as some sociologists have maintained (see Mayer 1964), but the scale of inequalities is reduced. The number of workers engaged in factories also increases over those engaged in agriculture. Michael Young (1961) rightly says: 'The soil grows castes: the machine makes classes.'

India is still a peasant society. The number of persons engaged in registered factory employment in 1954 was only 2.6 million. In 1961 it was estimated to be 3.9 million. Class awareness among the Indian industrial workers, if measured through union membership or participation, is not quite strong. The trade unions are generally weak in financial resources, although most of them are supported by political parties. Many sociological studies of the industrial workers in India show that caste stratification does influence the nature of the industrial working class; it affects its class character. Industrial workers maintain continued and close relationship with their caste and kin groups, villages and regions. Almost all caste groups are represented in the working population. Recruitment to the industrial class is more on the basis of particularistic ties than free individual motivation (see Lambert 1963; Mayer 1960; Giri 1958; etc.). These characteristics reduce the sociological impact that an industrial force could have had on the system of social stratification.

Elite and Social Stratification in India

The elite form a crucial analytical category for analysis of changes in the system of social stratification. Definitions of the elite are far too many but most of them agree that this sociological category comprises members most influential or powerful in their respective fields of activities. Lasswell, Lerner and Rothwell (1952) postulate a hierarchy of elite based on the principle of 'agglutination' of influence and power. According to them, each type of elite commands excellence in its own sphere of 'valued outcome'; 'skill', 'respect', etc. When a maximum number of these specific attributes combine either through skill or command of power into a single category of elite, they constitute the 'power elite' in society. In this sense, 'power elite' may be distinguished from the political elite. The power elite constitute the elites *par excellence*, as they command power over all other types of elite.

Dynamism in the elite structure comes through constant circulation from one elite rank to another. According to Pareto and Mosca this circulation operates through conflict, intrigue and competition by which each section of the elite tries to overthrow the power elite and occupy its position; the competition is between the 'governmental' and the 'non-governmental' elite of varied categories. A serious limitation of the Pareto-Mosca approach to the theory of the elite is its incapacity or inattention to analyse the extent of mobility and circulation from the non-elite to elite strata in a society. In contradistinction, the Marxist approach is focused more closely on analysing the relationship between the elite and non-elite in the system of social stratification. It posits a permanent conflict between classes which have command over power and wealth (feudal lords, capitalists and rulers), and those who do not possess them (workers and peasants). Marxist theory is basically non-elitist, but agrees with the Paretian view of the universality of conflict for succession to power and the Paretian assumption that the power elite are self-seeking and stick to power for exploitation of the people unless thrown out by force. For a comprehensive analysis of the role of the elite in social stratification, however, it may be necessary to draw from both, the 'elite circulation theory' of Pareto and the 'class struggle theory' of Karl Marx. In the

Indian context particularly, both the processes apply.

Both sociologists and political scientists have studied the elite phenomenon in India, and recently historians too have shown interest in this phenomenon. Just the same, studies on the elite phenomenon in India are few. Whereas the sociologists and the political scientists have focused more on the structure, recruitment, socialization and enculturation processes of the Indian elite, the social historians have analysed the pattern of social mobility and circulation of elite in the traditional, medieval and British periods of Indian society. In terms of substantive orientations these studies could be grouped into the following four categories:

(1) Studies of the structure, recruitment and social bases of elite. The elite may be classified in structural terms for their being rural, regional or cosmopolitan, which are eco-structural categories, as functional categories such as the political elite, business, professional, bureaucratic and intellectual elite, etc.

(2) Studies of the values and ideologies represented by the elite and their socio-cultural impact on the social system in India.

(3) Social historical studies. These portray the changes in various periods of Indian history in the structure and function of the elite and their pattern of social mobility. They also study the extent to which the past of the Indian elites bear relevance to their present-day structure and function.

(4) The role of the elite has also been studied for their contribution to the policies of social and cultural change in India and their impact on the processes of modernization, political democratization, and social growth in Indian society.

It may be necessary to refer to representative studies of each of these types to have a balanced review of the contribution made by the sociology of elite to the analysis of social stratification.

Traditional Elite

The category 'traditional' or 'charismatic' is used for elite in Indian society well up to the beginning of British rule (see Park and Tinker 1959). The elite role in many studies is related with the caste structure and the theory of *varna*, and especially the charismatic role of the Brahmans, is emphasized. This hypothesis is taken as confirmed by demonstrating the wide extent to which the Brahmans continued to hold predominant elite roles during the British period of the Indian political and cultural movements and after independence.

The image of the traditional elite is deeply coloured by the view of the Western historians and ethnographers of the nineteenth century. The elite are, in their studies, identified successively with the Brahmans, the landed aristocracy and the educated middle classes, that emerged through Western education. European Orientalists such as William Robertson, sociologists like Max Weber and historian James Mill, were all overwhelmed by the Indian caste system and the supreme role of the Brahman as elite. James Mill wrote in 1820 that

the Brahmans among the Hindus have acquired and maintained an authority, more exalted, more commanding and extensive, than the priests have been able to engross among any other portion of mankind. As great a distance as there is between the Brahman and the Divinity, so great a distance is there between the Brahman and the rest of his species.... The Brahman is declared to be the Lord of all the classes. He alone, to a great degree, engrosssed the regard and favour of the Deity;... Their influence over the government is only bounded by their desires, since they have impressed the belief that all laws which a Hindu is bound to respect are contained in the sacred books.... (James Mill, 1920. *The History of British India*, London, Vol. I: 159-62, quoted in Inden.)

William Robertson and Max Weber held similar views, almost completely derived from the Hindu scriptures and texts, rather than from the reality of Indian social history.

Next to the Brahmans, the traditional elite in India were identified with the 'aristocracy'. British administrators like Mountstuart Elphinstone, Charles Metcalfe, John Malcolm and Henry Lawrence sponsored this idea, and during the post-mutiny period, the British administrators tried to strengthen this 'Indian aristocracy' as a counterforce to the rising nationalist educated elite. Mention may specially be made of the despatch of Viceroy Lytton to Queen Victoria saying: 'Your Majesty's Indian Government has not hitherto, in my opinion, sufficiently appealed to the Asiatic sentiment and traditions of the Native Indian Aristocracy. That aristocracy exercises a powerful influence over the rest of the native population' (quoted in S. Gopal, 1965. *British Policy in India, 1858-1905,* Cambridge: 115; also see Inden). Lytton desired to convert Indian aristocracy into feudal nobility on the European pattern and considered them as the 'natural leaders' of society.

In the later nineteenth century the British began to recognize a new clite class, that of the educated middle classes who imbibed in their style of life Western culture and ideologies, including those of nationalism and liberalism and of religious and cultural reform. Many British writers and admistrators described them as 'Babus'. Inden writes:

The standard picture of elite formation shows India as a caste society which was stable if not static, before the impact of British rule. Elite status traditionally rested in the Brahman, as the centre and head of the caste system and the monopoliser of ritual influence and power. Alternatively, and to some extent concomitantly, elite status also rested in the aristocracy, defined as the descendants of pre-British royal houses and the substantial land-holders. The stability of the society was shaken, but not destroyed by the consequences of British rule; and particularly through the introduction of English education, and the new occupational opportunities for the educated in the modern segment of the society, a new Western educated elite arose. (p. 5)

True, the Brahmans have comprised a pre-dominant section of the elite category through the British period up to now. It is also true that the elite structure in India bears a deep imprint of the traditional form of caste stratification. But it would be an exaggeration to locate all structural processes of elite structure and change in traditional India into the systems of caste and charisma. Such formulations result from neglect of the eco-structural and existential forces that have contributed to the formation of the elite from time to time. Control over the mode of production, wealth and power by varying sections of leadership in India constitutes an organic component for understanding the character of the traditional elite.

The aristocracy and the educated classes did form the elite category during the eighteenth and the nineteenth centuries. But what the Western scholars miss about the traditional elite during this period of Indian history is the constant process of mobility and transformation. They also do not clearly bring out the structural forces that influenced the processes of elite formation all through this period. For instance, most of these treatments of the traditional Indian elite completely omit the rise of the Persianized elite during the medieval period of Muslim rule in India. By about the early sixteenth century a new style of elite had taken shape through the patronage and employment offered by the Mughal courts. Persianized in style, it consisted of Brahmans, Kshatriyas and Kayasthas. Akbar's introduction of the 'mansabdari' system had already introduced a new elite element in the Indian social system. During Akbar's time about 15 per cent of high 'mansabdars' were Hindus, mostly Rajputs, and some Brahmans and Khattris. Aurangzeb introduced Marathas to the 'mansabdar' ranks (see Spear 1970: 9-10). The 'mansabdars' formed a social category and not a social group; they did not possess a 'principle of unity amongst themselves, no cohesive spirit which could on occasion produce united action' (ibid.:13). On the elite status of the 'mansabdars' Percival Spear adds:

Looking not at the *manasbdari* system as an elite it seems clear that it can only be so described in a rather special sense. First comes the question of relationships. Can it be called an elite in itself or was it itself the product of an elite?... My conclusion is that the *mansabdars* constituted a genuine elite but one which was of a secondary type. They never developed a personality of their own and owed their effectiveness to the control of the emperor. They derived from a larger class from which they were selected. They were, in fact, a selected cross-section of the landed aristo-crats of India. (pp. 13, 14)

An important implication of the findings on the elite structure during the Mughal rule and after is that identification of traditional elite status exclusively with the Brahmans, as done by many Westerners, is proved wrong. Non-Brahman elite, did exist in India long before an influential and sizeable Western-educated elite came into being. Similarly, the landed aristocracy as an elite class underwent many vicissitudes of social transformation both during and following the Mughal rule. This becomes evident when we analyse the rural, regional and cosmopolitan dispersal and interaction of elite ranks during the eighteenth and nineteenth centuries. This evidence substantiates the view that the traditional elite did not consist of a unitary changeless class, but their formation depended upon the changing empirical situations of Indian society from time to time.

The traditional structural base for elite formation in India was the peasant society. The elite substratum even at the bottom of the hierarchy did not lie in the village but in the town-fort, which was not only the basic or elemental centre of political life and urban life-style but also a place for the formation of elite nuclei. Eric Wolf (1966) has characterized this 'eco-structural' unit as the 'patrimonial domain' or the little kingdom controlled by a lineage. Here the members of the domain, who ruled over the adjoining territory, collected the agricultural surpluses. This supported a higher style of life as well as many specialized functionary classes such as the crafts-men, priests, scholars and various other specialists. The same rural elite during the Mughal rule also imbibed court-culture and the Persianized sub-cultural nuance (see also Inden) Another set of elite were the local chiefs, who did not belong to a lineage; here not a corporate group but an individual inherited the 'domain', who used to be a local raja or chief. These local chiefs often directly emulated the Mughal court by appointing *divans,* military officers and court priests, etc., who formed the elite of the domain on the basis of their office. Finally, there were 'probendal domains' formed through grants to officials who drew tribute on behalf of the state. Granted only for a limited period, probendal domains in course of time became hereditary. Unlike the patrimonial domain, the elite of the probendal domain often did not have any social or kinship links with the territory over which they ruled; a Muslim, might, for example, rule as an elite of the probendal domain in a predominantly Hindu area.

The regional and cosmopolitan elite grew around these rural elite of the various domains. The process of the formation of the regional elite was linked with the emergence of a number of regional cities (Murshidabad in Bengal, Lucknow in Oudh, Poona in Maharashtra, Baroda in Gujarat and Mysore in the south) during the eighteenth century following the decline of the Mughal courts. The regional cities grew up around the courts of the regional *nawabs* and rajas. Around these courts also grew up the functionary elite, who later were transformed into the Western-educated elite.

The commerical elite also developed in association with the patrimonial and probendal domains, but it is not correct to asssume that they were always subordinate to the landed regional elite. In Ahmedabad and in Maharashtra the commercial elite had independent dominant position. In Murshidabad they worked in close association with the ruling officials and had considerable say in governmental affairs (see Gune 1953; E. Washburn Hopkins, (1901) 'Ancient and Modern Hindu Guilds', *India Old and New*, New York in Inden). In course of time, these commerical elite established their independent equations with the British administration.

The element of social mobility in the structure of the traditional elite of the eighteenth century would be evident from the fact that,

Scindia, the great Maratha chief of the mid-eighteenth century, came from a shepherd family and his father had been the slipper bearer of a local chief. Murshid Kuli Khan, the founder of the Bengal State, was believed to have been a Brahman who was purchased as a small child by a minor Mughal official and brought up as his own son.... The family of the Rajas of Banaras derived from petty landlords in the beginning of the eighteenth century who made in one generation from this relatively low status to rajas of a major part of Oudh. (Inden: 11)

By the nineteenth century this process of mobility and circulation in the elite ranks gathered new momentum.

In the rural segment, the main source for the traditional elite structure and mobility in its rank were the land and revenue policies of the British government. By then, with the exception of Oudh and Panjab, in most other parts of the country 30 to 40 per cent of land was possessed by a handful of landlords and 70 per cent was held by thousands of petty landholders. In Bengal, the number of estates progressively increased from 1790, when there were only 46 estates, to 122 in 1793, and 4,408 in 1875. Of these 4,408 estates 133 large estates paid over Rs. 1,000 annually as land revenue (*Statistical Account of Bengal, Vol. II, 'Jessore'*, London, 1875; quoted in Inden). The emergence of landed elite class was also a fact in the ryotwari areas where the settlements were supposed to have been made with the 'peasants'.

In all of Madras presidency (which includes several permanently settled districts, 804 Zamindars paid over Rs. 1,000 revenue annually and held 40 per cent of the land. Close to three million ryots and *Inamdars*, most of whom paid less than Rs. 10 annually controlled the remaining 60 per cent of the land. (see Baden-Powell, 1892: Vol. III: 142.)

Throughout much of Bengal, Bihar, United Provinces and parts of south India many new landed elite came into being as a result of the British land revenue policy. Inden writes:

In 1895 in four of the Eastern Districts of United Provinces, 134 revenue payers paid about one-third of revenue of the districts: well over 100,000 others paid the rest. The largest number of these large revenue payers can be termed 'new': 29 owed their rise to economic prominence to government service under the British, as subordinate officials (head clerks) and judges; 36 of the new men owed their origins to commercial activity. Out of the 75 families, few came from landed families in the areas. Most came from the outside or from towns or elites. (p. 15)

Eric Stokes, analysing the nature of the traditional elite in the rebellion of 1857, also confirms this view regarding the dispossession of the old and the rise of new landed elite as a result of the revenue policy of the British administration. He mentions the role of a 'magnate leadership' which existed in the villages and townships and played a crucial role in either augmenting or controlling the rebellion. Analysing the land circulation that took place in the western districts of U.P. as a result of revenue policies, Stokes notes two patterns of land transfer: from village proprietors to 'magnates', and from one section of proprietors to another. In Aligarh, 50 per cent land changed hands during 1839-58, and the money-lending classes registered considerable gain in the process. They increased their grip over land in the district from 3.4 per cent in 1839 to 12.3 per cent in 1868. Amongst the landed classes themselves, 40 per cent of land changed hands. Similarly, in Hathras district 66 per cent land changed hands during 1839-68. Of this 34 per cent land circulated among tthe land-owning classes, a large chunk of it going to Bohras and Banias (see Stokes 1970: 16-32). The transfer or auction of land took place as a result of rise in the revenue demands or, as in Hathras, due to direct settlement with the Village Communities (the anti-taluqdar settlement by Thornton) in 1839.

The question arises: how far did these changes in land

holding lead to the emergence of a new elite and the withering away of the older landed gentry? On this point the evidence suggests that although the transfer of land did often create new landed classes, it did not necessarily lead to the extinction of the older landed magnate classes. Stokes (1970) writes: 'high cultivation and high land revenue demand had generated a quasi-commercial market in land titles, while at the same time part of the traditional elite had transformed itself into a successful magnate element and more than kept its footing alongside the trading classes' (p. 29). This point is also borne out by other studies. In the Banaras region during 1795-1850, 70 per cent of buyers of auctioned land indicated urban residence—absentee landlords, evidently. The older resident elite probably continued to cultivate as tenants the land from which they were dispossessed, after adjustments with the new owners, their dominant social position in the villages they formerly controlled remained untouched.

Through this process of mobility and dispossession of the landed rural elite in interaction with the urban elite, who as we mentioned above, were money-lenders, speculators, traders and professional persons like judges, lawyers and clerks, slowly the Western-educated elite, who engineered the cultural and political renaissance in India, came into being. The traditional elite of the patrimonial and probendal domains right from early eighteenth century had a liasion with or offered patronage to various ranks of the professional elite. In course of time, during the nineteenth century these professional elite differentiated from the commercial or business elite on the one had and the landed rural elite on the other. In this process of interaction both caste and class factors played a role.

This interaction in the rise of the new elite can be observed in Calcutta during the early nineteenth century (1815-38). Here too, as elsewhere in the country, the British administration helped to create a new middle class through its settlement policies by which land passed from the 'ancient families' to the new moneyed class; it also helped to create a Hindu middle income group while many Muslim elite lost their positions. S.N. Mukherjee writes: 'If the British rule brought misery to the Muslim "nobility" and the high-ranking Hindu officers, the misery was shared by the old zamindars, and the old bankers. The men who gained most in the New World were small traders, brokers and junior administrators, *pykars, dallals, gomasthas, munshis, banyans, and dewans'* (Mukherjee 1970: 43). Caste and kinship factors influenced this process of the rise of the new elite. The path to the elite status in Calcutta during the eighteenth century was through the 'caste cutcherries' but in the nineteenth century, the 'cutcherries' were replaced by *'dals'* or *de facto* social factions. A hierarchy of elite emerged through the operation of these *dals*. Mukherjee divides them into two categories: the *abhijat* (aristocratic) *bhadralok*, and the *madhyabitto* or *grihastha bhadralok*. The distinction between these two types being vague there was considerable circulation between the two elite categories. The *abhijat bhadralok* consisted of

aristocratic families, Debs, Tagores, Deys, Ghoses, Mallicks, whose descendants claimed leadership in Calcuatta society during the nineteenth century. They were the first urbanised social group in Bengal, who transformed their Calcutta *basas* (temporary residences) into *baris* (permanent homes) in the eighteenth century, long before any other social groups. (ibid.: 45)

The *abhijat bhadralok's* permanent settlement in Calcutta from their former temporary abodes does indicate the link beween the landed aristocracy and the new educated and urban elite.

The *madhyabit* elite consisted of 'large shop-keepers, small traders, small landholders, and white-collar workers in commercial houses and government offices, teachers, "native-doctors", journalists and writers'. These elite followed the lead of the *abhijatas,* but circulation between the two ranks was quite common. The ranks of the elite of both categories kept on increasing. It is found that during 1822-7 in Calcutta while 6,000 huts disappeared, over 3,000 brick buildings were added, which must have belonged to the elite classes (ibid.: 60). In fact,

the nineteenth century *abhijat bhadralok* were new men: not only did they move into the city during the second half of the eighteenth century, they rose to high social status in one or two generations. They were of humble origin, small traders, junior administrators and small landholders, who made money working as junior partners (*banyan*, or *dewan*) of English officers and free merchants (ibid.: 48).

In Madras and Bombay as well, the rise of the new elite

was from the ranks of the middlemen for the English traders, commercial speculators, junior officials of the Company or the British Raj (see Misra 1961). The elite structure which thus emerged was new in function, ideology and social recruitment. The traditional elite of the landed aristocratic type also climbed to the new elite status; but the circulation and mobility among them being of the magnitude we have described, the structural possibility for the emergence of the 'new educated elite' is more than substantiated.

With the emergence of the 'new elite' there also took place a functional differentiation among the various types of elite. The political, business and cultural elite did exist in the traditional social structure, but their ideology and function in society was more tradition reinforcing than oriented to structural changes or cultural innovations. The nationalist ideology which the new elite imbibed from the West along with the ideology of economic, social and technological modernization implied a radical departure from the hierarchical, patrimonial and feudal types of elite ideology of the past. The new nationalist elite were the product of cities rather than villages and belonged to the professions (journalists, lawyers and social workers) more than landed aristocracy; the new elite constituted a new middle class which grew as a result of English education, and the expansion of administration, judiciary and teaching profession. Raja Ram Mohun Roy was a journalist and scholar, Ishwar Chandra Vidyasagar and Keshab Chandra Sen were educationists and teachers, Dayanand Saraswati and Vivekanand were social and religious reformers, Ranade and Gokhale were social workers and teachers, Madan Mohan Malaviya was an advocate and educationist, B.G. Tilak was a journalist and teacher, Motilal Nehru, Jawaharlal Nehru, Rajendra Prasad, Lajpat Rai, Ambedkar, Vallabhbhai Patel and above them all Gandhi were trained in the legal profession.

Functional Differentiation of Elite

As a result of the social, historical and economic forces that governed the structure and mobility of the elite during the eighteenth and nineteenth centuries, the elite structure as it emerged in early twentieth century got substantially differentiated. The political, business, bureaucratic and professional-intellectual elite roles developed autonomy of functions and social organizations, though the source of their recruitment remained localized to the upper segment of the social stratification. While this marked a kind of structural continuity in the elite category in India from its traditional social moorings it also reinforced the predominant role of the established classes and higher castes in the country's structure of power and privilege. What relationship these new elite bear with the system of social stratification would become evident when we analyse the salient features of their functional types.

Political Elite

The new political elite in India emerged through the process of the establishment of Indian nation-hood and consolidation of its political freedom. A plurality of structural background characterized the nature of these elite from the outset, although the elite of the nineteenth and early twentieth centuries were functionally diffuse. They led not only political but also social and cultural movements. Career politics, giving rise to functionally specific political elite came into being probably after independence. The important structural phenomenon which influenced the nature of political elite before independence was the multiplicity of ethnic and cultural traditions, of Islam, Hinduism, Christianity and other minority traditions. The major political consequence of this plurality of historical experiences and structural demands was partition of the country through polarization of the ideologies. The process of this polarization has been very complex but it could be related with the growing sense of loss and scepticism of the Muslim elite in India ever since the fall of the Mughal empire and establishment of the British regime, and the fact that they could benefit least from modernizing institutions and services that the British established in India (see Kothari 1970a; Mukherjee 1970; Singh 1973). The conflict was not only ideological but also structural.

Structurally, the political elite before independence came from the upper rung of social stratification, irrespective of the variations in their ideologies and ethnic-religious backgrounds. Ideologically, however, there was no such uniformity except that most of them shared a broad modernization ideology (see Myrdal 1968). This modernization ideology, of which political ideology formed an important part, was divided into various shades based on whether the elite professed the Western rationalist ideology or were for a synthesis between the Western and the Indian tradition. It is indeed difficult to draw a sharp line between these two divisions (see Dalton, 1970), yet relatively speaking a distinction on these two lines can be maintained. Both these ideologcial shades had many sub-variations. For instance, the rationalistic ideology had its manifestation in the Marxist and liberal-democratic ideologies and the synthetic ideology reflected itself into both secular and revivalistic forms. These divisions the of elite on ideological grounds did lead to significant segmentation in the elite structure on the lines of political parties, but more importantly, the process of segmentation in India due to the predominant role played by the Indian National Congress was from within this party. For instance, the Congress was led both by Gandhi, a proponent of synthesis ideology and Nehru, a rationalist liberal; the socialist ideologies could also be found to have been represented in the Congress party which led to various stages of segmentation in its form.

The Indian National Congress, therefore, in a way repre-sents the plurality of most types of ideological traditions of the Indian political elite. It also fully represents the structural background, recruitment and socialization processes of these elite. Structurally, the Congress like most other political-ideological parties in its initial form was composed of the 'new elite' of the urban educated middle classes.

Of the total of 13,839 delegates who attended the various annual sessions [of the Congress] between 1892 and 1909, as many as 5,442, or nearly 40 per cent, were members of the legal profession. The other important groups were those of the landed gentry with 2,629 delegates, and of the commercial classes with 2,091. The rest of the total was made up of journalists, doctors and teachers.... (Misra 1961: 353)

The predominance of urban sections in the Congress is revealed by its membership composition and leadership of the active members of the Congress. In 1958, only 28.1 per cent were agriculturists; in the AICC during 1956 only 20.6 per cent were agriculturists; and the Working Committee of 1946-54 had no representation from the agricultural occupation, whereas 72.5 per cent membership was from the professions (see Kochanek 1968: 347-58). The background of members of Indian professional groups, which we have analysed below, being mainly upper caste and upper and middle class, the structural continuity of this elite structure with that of the past can be easily observed.

Indeed, even political parties professing radical ideologies have most elite coming from the upper caste and class background. An analysis of the social origin of the Communist Party elite in West Bengal, Kerala and Andhra shows that the left-wing Communist leadership in the three states is made up to a much greater extent of individuals of lower class and caste than is the right-wing leadership. In West Bengal all nine right-wing leaders are Brahmans, Kayasthas or Vaishyas, the three dominant castes in West Bengal, whereas none of the three left-wing leaders about whom information is available belong to any of these castes. Two of the left-wing leaders are Muslims. In Kerala, there are proportionately more Ezhavas than Nairs in the left-wing Communist leadership. The left-wing leaders in that state—and in others—tend to be lower class, less educated, and without a fluent command of English. The right-wing leaders are high class, much better educated and more fluent in English. It is symptomatic that almost all the English-educated Communist graduates of Cambridge, Oxford, and the London School of Economics belong to the right wing of the party. Many of these, who come from prosperous middle class and upper class families, are resented by their lower-class 'comrades'. As one disgruntled Communist put it, 'You have to have a Cambridge degree to get anywhere in the Party' (see Zagoria 1969: 120-1).

The process of fission of the Communist Party into right and left wings based on changes in the elite recruitment is also confirmed by changes in the composition of the Congress elite. The agrarian interest groups have gained more ground slowly in the subsequent compositions of the Lok Sabha (see Dutta 1969; Kochanek 1968; Rosen 1966). The lawyers' share in the first, second, third and fourth Lok Sabhas has been declining from 35 per cent to 30, 24.5 and 17.5 per cent respectively. While lawyers have been losing ground the agrarian classes have increased their representation in the first to fourth Lok Sabhas from 12.4 per cent to 31.1 per cent (see Dutta 1969). Structurally, the important changes that have taken place in the recruitment and social background of political elite following independence are, first, that there has been a regionalization and ruralization of the elite structure; secondly, greater differentiation has now taken place between the political elite and intellectual and professional elite since more and more of the agricultural groups have entered into this role; thirdly, among the agricultural groups that have found representation in the ranks of the political elite, the dominance has shifted from traditionally upper-caste landlords to the intermediate-caste, rich landed peasantry (see Kothari 1970b). The pattern does, however, differ from state to state. For instance, in Rajasthan it is reported that the former feudal lords, businessmen and large landholders still dominate in the political elite role, even in the villages and districts (see Narain 1964). Similarly, studies in Maharashtra also reveal the dominance of the upper classes as rural political elite. V.M. Sirsikar (1970) concludes in his study of the rural elite that 'there is a perceptible trend toward concentration of socio-economic and political power. The democratization of power involving a democratic society has yet to take place.

The pluralistic character of Indian society and the feudal nature of the political system impinge upon the functioning of the political elite at all levels, national, state and village. There are consequently, both integrative or organic and divisive or segmental forces working that build themselves up as contradictory demands on the functioning of the Indian political elite. Irrespective of party affiliations, the political elite have to reconcile these two types of demands while performing their roles. The two contradictory demands provide scope for the political elite and those from tribes and the backward groups. Despite the narrower orientation of the objectives of the minority elite, an important feature of their functioning so far is their reconciliatory character. This is true of the movement led by the DMK regional political elite as much as of the Sikh and Scheduled caste and tribal elite in various parts of the country.

The reconciliatory character of minority political elite as also of other elite in India is probably derived from their social background and their place in the social stratification. The Muslim elite, for instance, also come in higher proportion from the upper classes; have typically higher educational level for their community (about 50 per cent of the elite have college education whereas only 23 per cent Muslims are literate); most of them originate from the medium size cities (here the process of ruralization noted by Myron Weiner and others for the elite from other communities does not seem to operate); and most of them belong to the Congress party (see Wright 1965). The tribal and Scheduled caste elite also come from relatively higher status groups from within their community.

An important issue regarding the functional differentiation of the political elite is related to their professional institutionalization as a category. This question is linked with their political socialization. Systematic studies have not been conducted in this area, but the indications are that particularistic loyalty rather than ideology commitment matters more in the growth of political affiliations and stances for most of our political elite. This attribute among the political elite became probably stronger since independence and assumed specially epidemic proportion in coalition governments in the states. This probably reflects the fact that the political elite in India, having been recruited to most political parties from a single type of social base, are not existentially committed to varying or alternative political ideologies. Interest groups thus do not in reality fully reflect themselves through political parties. Percival Spear (1970) associates this trait in the Indian political elite with the tradition of *Khidmat* or service rather than personal allegiance *a outrance* to a person, a tradition which has continued from the Mughal times. He writes:

Mughal rulers often took the supporters of a rival into service immediately after a decisive battle and it was common for such an event to lead to an avalanche of changed allegiances. It was *khidmat* or service, which was honourable, rather than allegiance ... to a particular person. This tradition of Indian public life may perhaps help to explain the epidemic of changing sides which has recently occurred in some Indian legislatures. It was no disgrace to join the winning side provided it really won. (p. 10)

Spear's interpretation tends entirely to be cultural, that is perpetuation of the service norms in the elite role. He does not seem to recognize the significant structural feature of these elite, that is, their essential homogeneity in terms of recruitment irrespective of ideologies. This indeed is the factor that reinforces this type of cultural attitude. It also omits the more mundane or pragmatic considerations, rather than altruistic *khidmat* values, that are often motivating factors in changing sides.

To sum up: the important features of the political elite in India are: their social structural homogeneity with a nascent tendency for differentiation; their essentially upper middle class background of recruitment and political socialization; the tendency to constantly reconcile rather than mobilize the political demands and interests through various sets of networks through levels of political echelons; their progressive functional differentiation from other elite forms, but lack of professionalization; and, finally, their capacity for continual conversion of political interests into emotive symbols through which a path for political bargains and reconciliations is laid out.

Business Elite

We have noticed the extent of structural continuity in the recruitment of the political elite in India. In the case of business elite, this continuity has been far greater. Firstly, most business elite come from the traditional merchant castes, and many among them have maintained their occupational continuity over a long historical period (see Ito 1966; Misra 1961; Hazelhurst 1966; etc.). There is yet another sense in which the business elite did succeed in maintaining their links with the traditional social structure. Quite often they had simultaneous links with the village, despite their dealings in the cities (see Das Gupta 1970; Bagchi 1970). There is yet another difference in the nature of the business elite and the 'new political elites'. The life-style of the former was not Westernized in most cases until very recently whereas the latter types of elite are highly Westernized not only in ideology and skills but also in style of life and living. Mobility from lower trading occupation to the status of business elite or even industrial entrepreneur has been, no doubt, quite common. There are many cases of status mobility from a position of petty trading or money-lending class to that of industrial entrepreneurship (see Pavlov 1964: 383).

The role of the business elite in the struggle for independence has been more nationalist than that of the landed aristocracy. For a very short while, if ever, the interest of these elite coincided with that of the British regime. Otherwise contradiction always existed between the interest of the business elite who wanted a greater share in industrial investment and that of the colonial regime which favoured British business interests and wanted to use Indian business-men merely as a tool for commercial exploitation (Bagchi 1970; Desai 1969). This made the business entrepreneurs join hands with the leaders of the national movement.

This historical event had two consequences: first, the business elite, unlike the feudal and aristocratic elite, succeeded in establishing a working relationship with the political elite and evolved a method of response and recon-ciliation to the industrial policies being followed after independence (see Weiner 1963). This probably also softened the attitude of the political elite towards the business elite. They were allowed to play an important role in the industrial economy of free India. This development contributed to the growth of the economic power of the business houses and elite entrepreneurs in course of the years, following the two five year plans.

R.K. Hazari's study (1966), covering approximately 1,000 public and private companies and twenty corporate groups from within these companies reveals a definite trend during 1951-8 towards concentration of economic power in these corporate groups. The growth of this power has not been strictly monopolistic since most of these groups have control over more than one industry. The managing agency system through which a few business houses extend their control over the organizational structure of companies, contributes to the concentration of their economic power. *The Report of the Committee on Distribution of Income and Levels of Living*, Part I states:

The data we have given in the previous paragraphs do indicate the presence of concentration of economic power within the economy in terms of income, property and especially of control over the non-

Governmental corporate sectors. There can also be no doubt that, in part at least, the working of our planned economy has encouraged this process of concentration by facilitating and aiding the growth of big business in India. (p. 53)

The concentration of economic power in a few business houses also resulted from the licensing policies that the Government pursued to augment the industrial sector. A committee that inquired into this says:

The licensing system worked in such a way as to provide a disproportionate share in the newly licensed capacity to a few concerns belonging to the Large Industrial Sector. The maximum benefit of all this went to a few Larger Houses. Our conclusion, therefore, is that the licensing system was not properly organised, for the purpose which it was expected to achieve, the authorities concerned were not clear about these objectives and no clear guidelines for their attainment were ever laid down. The result has been that the licensing system has not contributed adequately to the attainment of the social and economic objectives of the Industrial Policy Resolution and Plans. (*Report of the Industrial Licensing Policy Inquiry Committee, Main Report:* 184)

Hence, obviously, the business elite in India not only has enjoyed a structural continuity in terms of recruitment but has also kept on growing in economic power and social influence. This inegalitarian process has combined with yet another dysfunctional aspect in the growth of the business elite—the lack of dispersal of entrepreneurial role in various social groups and strata. Only a limited number of middle-level entrepreneurs from traditionally non-business communities have emerged so far (see Berna 1960). This, of course, is the pattern in most developing countries. It is said that:

the middle classes in the newly developing nations today are not entrepreneurs, but are more likely to be lawyers and teachers, political bureaucrats, military officers, and members of the clergy. The composition of this class differs from that in the West because the international economic scene has changed sharply in the past 200 years. The entrepreneurial role is not so pivotal for the new nations as it was for the West; and other skills, chiefly political and diplomatic, are more important.... The entrepreneurial role is being fulfilled by governments or through government sponsorship rather than by individuals acting independently. (Reissman 1967: 262-3)

Professional and Bureaucratic Elite

This brings us to the role of professional elite in the system of social stratification. Sociologically, the distinguishing characteristics of the professional elite are: (1) their sustained training to acquire a certain minimum level of skill for performing the professional role; (2) their functioning in formal organizational set-up and the complexity of the nature of their work; (3) the need for their commitment to universalistic values, particularly to those of rationality, objectivity and pragmatism; (4) the specificity of their roles; and (5) the existence of legal procedures and legitimizations for the performance of their duties and evaluation of their functions. The bureaucratic elite are specially governed by this last attribute of the professional elite. Indeed, on this basis often a distinction between the professional and bureaucratic elite can be drawn. The professional elite like doctors, engineers and lawyers deal in their work more through the normative standard of skill and knowledge, which is not closed, but open and constantly expanding. The bureaucratic elite, on the other hand, lay more emphasis on conformity to the formally established procedures and rules. Despite this, the distinction between these two types of elite is often difficult to maintain. The significant role that a professional elite plays in a country's system of social stratification is twofold: first, it reflects the degree to which the country is undergoing social structural differentiation, or changes from tradition to modernity in the fields of occupation, industry and economy; secondly, professional elite assume relevance for the analysis of social stratification also as indicators of social mobility in the class system. For the latter, the structure of recruitment of these elite and their class background may offer significant insights into the processes of social stratification.

According to one estimate, the number of members in professional employment (employees in medical and health services, teachers, journalists, lawyers) in the 1960s in India was 770,000; this increased by 1961 to 1,220,000. Similarly, the category of administrators, excutives and technicians (including clerks) increased from 2,700,000 in the 1950s to 3,100,000 in 1961 (see Rosen 1966: 178). Compared to other Asian countries, however, the professional classes in India constitute a lower proportion of all workers. The number of professional employees per 10,000 of all workers in India is 171 as compared to 489 in Japan, 349 in China, 446 in Sri Lanka, 314 in Malaysia and 294 in the Philippines (see Madan and Varma 1971: 18). Another significant attribute of the professional persons in India, relatively speaking, is the lowest representation of females compared to the other Asian countries.

The unevenness in the growth of professions comes clearly to light when we analyse the recruitment patterns and the origin of professional elite. Irrespective of the types of professional elite chosen, it is revealed that the recruitment is heavily biased in favour of the upper castes, urban dwelling groups and males. A survey of bureaucrats, managers and intellectuals shows that among all the Hindu members recruited to these classes (which is 85.0 per cent) the upper castes constitute 81.5 per cent, middle 6.8 per cent, lower 3.5 per cent and the Scheduled castes only 1.1 per cent. From the viewpoint of social origin, 59.02 per cent of the IFS and 47.45 per cent of the IAS come from upper middle class families; if we include other middle classes also for calculation, then 88.53, 95.57, 82.20 and 84.85 per cent of the IFS, IAS, IPS, Accounts and Customs and Postal Services recruits respec-tively come from the middle classes. Very few administrators come from the farmer and artisan-workers' families (see Navalakha 1971). The same pattern of social origin and recruitment exists for other professional elite. A study conducted recently reveals that 84.3 per cent of university teachers come from the upper castes, and only 0.4 per cent from the lower and the Scheduled castes; of all university teachers 67.7 per cent come from the urban areas and only 31.4 per cent from the villages. Also, 84.2 per cent university teachers come from middle class families and none from the lower classes. These studies, though not very comprehensive (in sample size) do broadly indicate the unevenness in the distribution of professional elite in terms of various social strata. Evidently, the upper-middle and middle classes dominate over most of the opportunities and positions in the professional sector of our society.

Functionally, the professional and the bureaucratic elite constitute a new component of the social system. The Indian bureaucracy developed in response to the needs of the East

India Company and later of the British government to consolidate their colonial regime. It was not an importation of a developed bureaucratic model from Britain to India, since rational methods of recruitment of bureaucrats developed there almost simultaneously with those in India (see Tinker, 1966) or even later. The characteristics of bureaucracy such as 'open entry based on academic occupation; permanency of tenure irrespective of party political changes; a division into grades or classes according to whether the function is responsible or merely routine; a regular graded scale of pay; and a system of promotion based on a combination of seniority and selection by merit' (Tinker 1966) did not exist in the Civil Service of the U.K. in the eighteenth century. Most appointments were political on the basis of patronage.

The demands for rationalization of the patronage system in the appointment of the Company's offices arose for historical reasons and the establishment of the Crown's rule accelerated this process. The Indian Civil Service Act, 1861 reflects this attempt to rationalize the bureaucracy. The Indian bureaucracy may seem to have passed through three major stages in terms of its dominant orientations:

First, at the inception and during the early phases of the Company's rule (1600-1740) the 'ethos of trade' was dominant in the civil service. Second was the period of the Company-Crown rule (1740-1947) when the civil service was guided by the 'ethos of professional career' and the psychology of 'masters and guardians'. The third stage, following Independence (1947-) is when the ethos of Indian bureaucracy became professional and developmental. It tends now also to be imbued with nationalistic values and aspirations. (Tinker 1966)

This functional transition in the organizational goals of Indian bureaucracy has, however, not been followed by structural transformation of this class of elite. As mentioned above, the bureaucratic elite are still drawn mainly from the privileged sections of society. The demand for them to now work progressively under the control of the political elite who come from a different cultural and ideological background generates varieties of stresses. These relate to their commitment to (and sympathy with) many egalitarian and ameliorative policies of the government, in carrying them out, and in the nature of their dealings with the public at large (see Park and Tinker 1969). The bureaucratic elite in India have, despite these many sources of tension, given stability to the administration, and as a class represent an active agent of modernization. Interestingly, like the business elite the bureaucratic elite too have been reconciliatory with the aspirations of the Indian political elite.

Intellectual Elite

The intellectual elite share many characteristics with the professional elite. Indeed, many professional elite categories, such as scientists, doctors, engineers and university teachers and lawyers are treated as part of the segment of the intellectual elites. It is difficult, however, to define intellectual elite. The category becomes too broad if we define it as consisting of all those who earn their living by doing creative mental work. The term creative itself is ticklish for definition. In science, most discoveries have a cumulative quality; in literature, arts and humanities, symbolic-creative work is said to be not entirely original or unique but synthetic in nature. Nevertheless the intellectual elite must in the ultimate analysis consist of those who succeed in assuming a lead in society as also in their group by creative symbolization through writings, scientific discoveries and artistic creations. Edward Shils (1961) identifies the intellectual as: 'independent man of letters, the scientist, pure and applied, the scholar, the university professor, the journalist, the highly educated administrator, judge or parliamentarian'. This list should also include other categories of artists such as the creative painters and sculptors.

In structural terms, the transition from the traditional to modern intellectual elite category may not be highly remarkable. The recruitment of most modern or new intellectual elite continues to be from the traditionally established communities of castes that threw up intellectuals all through Indian history. However, the intellectual elite that emerged during the eighteenth and the nineteenth centuries in India did mark a basic change in ideological orientations. Their emphasis on civil liberty, democracy and social justice was an entirely new development. These ideological traditions no doubt existed in varied shades, but these did provide a catalytic force for setting the pace of modernization.

There are few systematic studies of intellectual elite in India by Indian sociologists. Edward Shils in his study of Indian intellectuals covers many important sociological problems. His analysis of the existential base of intellectual elite in India and their problems is mainly derived from the Euro-American frame of reference. His evaluation thus tends to be rather coloured, although it has at another level—the empirical level of reporting—substantial objectivity. His conclusion that the intellectuals in India suffer both from existential deprivations and ambivalence in respect of primordial and civil ties is one that should be examined not in absolute but in relative and comparative terms. It may then appear that many elements, structural, existential and cultural, that Shils attributes to the intellectual elite in India might cease to be unique. Others might justify alternative propositions.

Other sociologists have discussed the problems of the intellectual elite only in a discursive and non-systematic style (see Mukerji 1958; Desai 1965; Bottomore 1967; etc.). These studies touch upon selected aspects of the structure and ideology of the Indian intellectual elite, such as their mode of Westernization, their rise from the traditional middle class and their ideological bases. There is need to examine in depth the various sociological issues related to the intellectual elite, their social structure, function and social responsibilities in India today. Nirad C. Chaudhuri, a litterateur, has also dwelt upon the nature of Indian intellectuals. His treatment is based partly on individualized empathy and partly on a personal viewpoint. Its sociological value in terms of the logic of proof is, however, limited (see Chaudhuri 1967).

There is thus a need for systematic studies on not only the intellectual but also the professional elite in India. The political and bureaucratic elite have been studied in some depth but many emerging facets in the field also need closer examination.

The issue which as a whole emerges in the sociological treatment of the elite and social stratification in India is the rather exclusive nature of their recruitment. It is reflective of the lack of status mobility in the system of social stratification. It does not, however, bias to the same extent the elites' modernization ideologies or their goals of social change. In this respect the Indian elite have shown a remarkable responsive quality. Another feature of the elite in India is their mediatory role between the primordial and civil levels of social operation on the one hand (see Khare 1970) and their capacity for micro- and macro-structural levels of negotiation on the other. This quality of the elite has worked in India as a shock-absorber in the social and political system against the continual demands and frictions from the varied pressure groups. This feature, especially of the Indian political elite, is one that tends to successfully manage most tensions that otherwise would have threatened the very base of the Indian system of social stratification. It has, of course, both positive and negative consequences for the direction and ideology of social change in India.

The structural exclusiveness of the elite in India tends to pose many questions: How does it reconcile with our goals of socialism and social justice? How does it bear upon the ideology and strategy of social change being adopted since independence? And, finally, how does it reflect upon the social role or commitment of the Indian elite?

Lamentably, scientific studies have not been conducted to analyse the various dimensions of these questions. A few studies have argued that though there is a contradiction bet-ween the social background of the political and administrative and other bureaucratic elite in India there is no reason to anticipate a conflict in their orientation to the goal of moder-nization or social change (see Bottomore 1967; Beteille 1969c; Singh 1973). Most studies on the nature and functions of elite strata in India bring out not only the element of structural continuity but also the responsiveness of the Indian elite. This characteristic has also been indicated by the study of Donald B. Rosenthal (see Shils 1961; Rosenthal 1970). In his study of the municipal politics in Agra and Poona, Rosenthal finds that the elite in the two cities simultaneously respond to the rational demands of individualistic freedom of choices and to demands of the primordial status groups. He writes:

Despite the numerous frictions which arise from these newer forms of intergroup relations, the presence of some freedom of choice for individuals as individuals or for members of previously excluded political groups in selecting the kind of goals which they may pursue presumably provides them with a 'stake' in democracy. Thus, while occasional fears have been expressed about the potentially disintegrative effects of the 'politicization of caste', it may well be the case that the sense of participation associated with this politicization is actually one of the factors working for the successful maintenance and continuity of the System. (Rosenthal 1970: 283)

Such adaptive changes in the role of the elite and their facility to respond to different levels of interaction, such as the primordial and the civil in different idioms, is highly significant. This is why the Indian elite, despite their upper-middle class origin are able to elicit responses from all sections of society. Not many deeper studies, however, have been done about this phenomenon and the pattern of social mobility among the elite strata. Whatever evidence is available goes to show that whenever there is a break in the upper or upper-middle class dominance in the elite roles, it is the castes or classes at the middle level that tend to replace the older order. The ruralization of the political elite also conforms to this pattern.

GAPS IN STRATIFICATION STUDIES AND PRIORITY AREAS FOR RESEARCH

On the basis of the above review of studies in the Indian sociology of social stratification some gaps that come to light can be analysed under two headings: (a) theoretical-methodological and (b) substantive. Theoretically, as we discussed above, most studies of social stratification in India have focused on caste and social mobility in this system; sometimes occupational strata have been analysed or class stratification has been formulated on the basis of the Census data through a set of attributes for classification. In theoretical terms most such studies of caste or class stratification operate at the level of nominal scales. Their one major limitation is their inadequacy for generating general or even middle-range hypotheses or propositions regarding social stratification. This is true not only of caste studies but also of most efforts at classification of classes on the basis of *ad hoc* sets of attributes. Such studies add to our insight into the nature of some problem and trends of change at an impressionistic level, but are devoid of 'theoretical power'. There is need, therefore, to undertake studies in social stratification having macro-sociological perspective. Such studies may use 'real' definitions of caste, class and other categories and be conducted through a systematic research design with a battery of significant assumptions and hypotheses. The results of such studies could be tested and compared for precision and relevance at cross-regional or cross-national levels. The criticism that stratification studies that tend to be methodologically very sophisticated are sociologically least relevant is true only when attempts to measure the structure and process in social stratification are made purely on 'attributional' criteria. Such studies are mere statistical catalogues of social strata. Theoretically these do not form even proper 'taxonomies', to say nothing about their explanatory power.

The descriptive-analytic type of studies have, of course, enriched Indian sociology. Indeed, these studies have offered us much needed insight into the structure and process of social stratification. Despite the richness of observational data and analytical insights, however, these studies lack in propositional or nomological qualities necessary for formulating statements about the nature and direction of changes in stratification that could be confirmed or disconfirmed within a certain limit of probability. Yet, the studies of descriptive-analytic type could be valuable sources for formulating the designs of research, conceptual and definitional frames, assumptions and hypotheses, for social stratification studies with greater theoretical power.

Substantively, the areas in the sociology of social stratification which need attention on a priority basis can be the following:

(1) Study of the nature and direction of social mobility in caste and class systems of stratification and its impact on the social system.

(2) Study of agrarian class structure, peasant economy and the processes of conflict and integration in the social systems.

(3) Professional class structure, professionalization and social development in India.

(4) Studies in the continuities and discontinuities in the elite social structure in India, and its role in the growth of an egalitarian society.

(5) Levels of elite strata, their social networks and communication.

(6) Status mobility among the Scheduled castes and tribes, its problems and processes.

(7) Entrepreneurial classes, social mobility and development.

(8) Patterns of interaction between the agrarian and non-agrarian class system, social change and development.

(9) Family socialization, kinship-linkage and social stratification.

(10) Cultural bases of class formation, class mobility and social stratification.

(11) Patterns of social inequality, social stratification and nation building.

(12) Economic development, social mobility and social stratification.

(13) Ideology, symbols and systems of social stratification.

(14) Social stratification, social integration and nation-building.

Specific research projects may be developed in each of these areas for analysis of the system of social stratification. Each problem suggested above has intercontingency of a set of variables related to social stratification. This is suggested in order to maintain the needed systematic character of such studies.

2
Sociology of Social Stratification: II

INTRODUCTION

The decade of the 1970s has contributed richly to the emergence of new substantive and theoretical concerns in the study of social stratification. This has resulted from the consolidation of self-awareness of Indian sociologists in respect of theory and methodology. To a very large extent, it has resulted also from the interplay of social forces in Indian society released by social, cultural, political and economic developments. The national ideology of social stratification has come under sharper evaluation. The consciousness among caste, class and ethnic groups on issues such as social mobility, justice and equitable access to socio-political and economic resources has increased manifold.

These developments have marked the social stratification studies of the decade with an imprint of self-criticism, and search for relevance. It is a sign of maturity as well as of enlargement of interest in the studies of this period that its interests have crossed the disciplinary confines of sociology and social anthropology. Contributions from economists, historians and public men have enriched the literature on social stratification during this decade. These developments have no doubt exerted pressures on the paradigms of study, issues of their theoretic and policy relevance and their anchorage in ideology.

Some identifiable new trends in the studies of social stratification during this period were: increased debate on the ideological moorings of concepts and theories, efforts to re-schematize conceptual systems and their presuppositions in the light of shifting paradigms, new substantive concerns of study, and fruitful convergence of multi-disciplinary interests, both substantive and theoretical.

IDEOLOGICAL DEBATE

The prominence of ideological debate in the studies of stratification during the 1970s was a result both of historical forces and the tensions towards reorientation and replacement of paradigms. Historically, this period marked a global disenchantment with sociological positivism (entrenched in the 1950s), the ascendancy of phenomenology and Marxism in theory, and of ethnomethodology in the operationalization of concepts and tools of research. The structural-functional paradigm for the study of social stratification came particularly under attack.

In India, as in most developing countries, these developments could not be dissociated from the historical forces such as the colonial background of the methodological and theoretical legacy of the social sciences, the quest for indigenization of paradigms and for relevance. The studies thus assumed a broad framework of the sociology of knowledge for establishing the identity of Indian social science in the global context.

The impact of the colonial foundation of sociology and social anthropology in India on the conceptual-theoretic evolution and its ideology can be witnessed at two levels. First, there was underpinning of categories such as rural-urban, caste and class, community and tribe, etc., which constituted the basic elements in the analysis of social stratification into analytic formats which were helpful in enlarging the segmentary rather than the organic character of Indian society. In this effort conducive to the perpetuation of colonial rule the categories were rendered deliberately mystifying.

The abstracted and ahistorical detachments of caste from tribe, the attribution of exaggerated autonomy to systems of religion and village community (see Y. Singh 1976) and the omission of the exploitative and alienative role of colonialism in India on its society and economy from most sociological analyses of its institutions, prove adequately the ideological foundation of such theorizing. The demand for the indigenization of social science paradigms, now so widely voiced by social scientists in India, is a product of such historical conditioning of concepts and theories (see Dube 1976; Y. Singh 1979a, 1979b), and their ideological grounding.

The second context where the ideological issues were in the forefront was that of the sociology of knowledge. Here, the social background of sociologists, their class character influencing the choice of problems and paradigms for research constitute the theme for evaluation. It is said that the professional training of sociologists, their grounding in Western theory and ideology along with their narrow social experiential background delimits the reflexivity of their observations. In several recent studies of social stratification such issues have been raised. It is held that the sociologist's perception of the structure of relationships, the degrees of felt deprivation or exploitation within the caste or class system in a village or community, his theoretical formulation of the problem or identification of its existential coordinates is determined by the nature of his own social origin. This has led to appeals for an 'upside-down' rather than 'top-down' perspective in the study of caste and social inequality (Mencher 1974; Saberwal 1979b).

The allusion to intrinsic relationship between the sociologist's choice of conceptual and interpretive categories and the cultural and economic groove he himself comes from is not recent. Edmund Leach had raised a similar point about Srinivas's formulation of the concept of Sanskritization (see Srinivas,1966; Leach 1960). In a review of Srinivas's *Caste in Modern India* (1962), Leach holds that the fluidity in the principle of caste hierarchy that the process of Sanskritization seems to reflect appears odd. He writes: 'that such fluidity exists has been clearly demonstrated, but that it should be seen as arising from an emulation of the Brahmins seems to me odd—a specifically "Brahminocentric" point of view!' (Leach quoted in Srinivas 1966: 148). In a more recent review symposium on Srinivas's *The Remembered Village* (1976), C. Parvathamma (1978) has reiterated the element of Brahmano-centrism in Srinivas's contributions. She writes: 'A degree of subjectivism is inevitable in all social science writings. Srinivas's point of view is that of a South Indian Brahmin and it is important to understand how this influences his work' (p. 92).

The logical implications of such propositions are constituted in the antinomy between ideology and theory—a fundamental problem in social sciences. The issues involved are those of comparison, objectivity, empathy, and reflexivity which constitute the cognitive bases of social science understanding and its symbolic universe. There is scope for fresh debate on these problems in Indian sociology.

Another factor contributing to the prominence of ideological issues in studies of stratification emerges from the application of non-Brahmanical models for the study of caste. This model inverts the purity-pollution paradigm of caste. The Dalit movement, the resurgence of neo-Buddhism amongst the so-called 'untouchables', and particularly the growing ideological divide between the Brahmanical and non-Brahmanical models of the Indian social system, as postulated by Phule, Ambedkar and some 'materialist' historians, have contributed to this new orientation. The explanation of caste and class relationship from the perspective of this model focuses more upon the understanding of the forces which, in order to perpetuate the caste model of society in India, tended to mystify the feudal and authoritarian structure of economic and social exploitation in Hindu society.

By implication it is held that the caste model of society obscured the intrinsic class relationship both in the cultural and economic domains of social interaction. The new thinking on the Ad-Dharma movement in Punjab in 1926, Ambedkar's movement (with Mahars) in Maharashtra in 1924, the Namashudra movement in Bengal, the Adi-Dravida and Adi-Andhra movements in Tamil Nadu and Andhra respectively, and the Adi-Hindu movement in Kanpur in U.P. in the early 1920s reflected the ideology of revolt against the Brahmanical caste model. Patankar and Omvedt (1979) have sharply focused on this element of the ideology when they write:

Ideologically, in spite of their very diverse origin, it is remarkable how many themes the dalit movements shared in common. Central to their thinking was the *adi* theme, a definition of themselves as the original inhabitants of the country, a claim that their own inherent traditions were those of equality and unity, and a total rejection of caste (*chaturvarna, varnashrama dharma*) as the imposition of the conquering Aryans who used this to subjugate and divide the natives. Very often this went with a rejection of Hinduism as the religion of the invaders and the main support of caste society. Ambedkar's movement was the most important one that did not stress such an *Adi* identity, yet the theme was still a strong one among Mahars. (p. 427)

The bases of such ideological assertion are both historical and textual; in the latter case a new exegesis of scriptures and traditions has been attempted by scholars. The emphasis on the '*Bali* mythology' by Phule invoke the theory that the Aryans pushed the indigenous population to the bottom of the social hierarchy. It is based on textual exegesis. It has been reiterated recently that the philosophies of India are not divided between materialistic and idealistic systems, but between a-Brahman or *nastika* (anti-transcendentalistic) and Brahman or *astika* (transcendentalistic). *Sankhya* (later tradition classified this as Brahmanic), *Lokayata* (materialism), Jainism and Buddhism are a-Brahman, while *Purva-Mimansa*, *Vedanta*, *Nyaya* (logic) and *Vaisheshika* are Brahman. All these non-Brahmanic philosophies had their own monastic orders called *gana* or *sangha* (tribe) which were casteless (i.e. classless). It is well known that these were against the caste system and *karmakanda* (see Patil 1979: 287).

One would observe that the resurgence of the non-Brahmanic ideology in the Dalit movement simultaneously also implies a shift of paradigms for the study of caste from function origin, from hierarchy to power, from consensus to exploitation and from tradition to history or historical materialist forces in society. In contemporary literature, such a paradigmatic shift also implies a Marxist or quasi-Marxist approach to the study of social stratification (see Omvedt 1976).

This brings us to the relationship between theory and method in studies of social stratification and its linkages with the new wave of ideology. The dichotomies of Brahman: non-Brahman; insiders: outsiders; cultural: materialistic; *nastika: astika;* pure: impure; caste: class; etc., could be interpreted as binary tensions both from a structuralist and historical-Marxist theoretical perspectives. R.S. Khare (1978) associates the insider-outsider or Indian-Western distinction in the approaches to the understanding of Indian reality—on which most thinking for indigenization of sociological models is based, and of which Louis Dumont's contribution is a representative one—as indicative of the incipient tendencies towards structural analysis, wanting, however, in establishing fully the 'relational' or 'transformative' dialectics, essential to structuralism.

It is transformative logic in structuralism which bridges the gap between the binary segments of reality and their apparent contradistinctions. Comparisons would be impossible otherwise. Satish Saberwal (1979b), on the other hand, associates the construction in the value premises of the social stratification studies in India with the colonial roots of the institutional foci from which the ideology of equality and hierarchy has emerged in social science as well as public policy. The British-American influences on theory and methodology in such studies were historically produced. These, together with the narrow experiential grooves which social scientists come from has, according to him, led to the distortion of theoretical perspectives and substantive concerns.

The studies of stratification during the 1950s and 1960s too had their grounding in ideology. The supremacy of the Brahmanical model of hierarchy in the theoretical framework of the structural-functional paradigm, however, tended to keep ideology muted. The contribution of Louis Dumont (1970) served to bring the ideological ramification of the concept of hierarchy in the system of social stratification to the forefront. Nevertheless, most of the debate in his work *Homo Hierarchicus* reflects a methodological rather than *critical* or ideological concerns (see Madan *et al.*, 1971: 1-81).

The emphasis on ideology has its moorings primarily in *praxis* and not in structural foci or their facticity. Leach commenting on Dumont's method justifiably writes:

Levi-Strauss 'recognises' that history as an operative force in the present cultural situation, is a mythology encapsulated in the mind of the actors. Dumont's view of the past is much more ambiguous, and indeed it is his attitude to history which creates the greatest difficulties for his more empirically oriented sympathisers. This is of course a general worry about 'structuralist' interpretations. Levi-Strauss maintains that the practice of the economic fact and the praxis of ideology do not interact directly as is often maintained by Marxists, but are 'mediated' by a 'structure' in the mind, but whose mind? (Leach in Madan *et al.* 1971:16)

Hence, one notices a basic mismatch between existential and normative levels in Dumont's interpretation of the Hindu caste society. This is identified by Berreman implicitly when he states that Dumont's principle of hierarchy is merely an extension of the Brahmanical model of caste; hence, its own roots in ideology.

There is one common normative foundation on which both Dumont's notion of hierarchy and structural-functional paradigms of social stratification during the 1950s and 1960s were based (under the British-American influence). This is the ideology of a harmonic or consensual society. Looked at from this frame of analysis, caste automatically becomes a system based on 'cooperation' and class on 'competition' or 'conflict'. The non-Brahmanical model challenges this ideology and locates the essence of caste in the historical foundation of class exploitation and domination in society. The relationship between the normative and existential levels is thus reversed. The cognitive map of the two ideological systems of social stratification is grounded in dissimilar constructions of Indian social reality. The high-pitched ideological resonance in the sociology of the 1970s came both from within the profession that got increasingly differentiated in respect of the recruitment of sociologists and their commitment to theoretical traditions and from the varied social movements of the depressed castes and classes, who were increasingly exposed to cross-currents of politicization and cultural self-consciousness, for status mobility.

This awakening of social consciousness led to a reiteration and reworking of the Dalit ideology of the early 1920s. The support these movements received from political parties also contributed to ideological self-consciousness. It is evident how during the decade of the 1970s caste increasingly came to be seen as a useful ideological resource by political parties for mobilization and support. Even the left parties saw the need to take notice of this reality. Thus, the ideological debates in the area of social stratification had their bases both in the cognitive and existential dialectics of the processes of social change and development during the decade.

CHANGING THEORETICAL ORIENTATIONS

This decade witnessed substantial differention in theoretical approaches and substantive concerns in the studies of stratification. During the 1950s there was dominance of the structural-functional theory. Towards the end of this decade, structuralism and Marxism made their entry, the former led by Dumont and D.F. Pocock and the latter by A.R. Desai, Daniel Thorner and Charles Betellheim. The decade of the 1970s saw a sharpening of the diversity of theoretical interests of the Indian social scientists in general. Indeed, the structural-functional studies of stratification have continued, but specific substantial thinking and research has been undertaken from a historical perspective in which both Marxist and non-Marxist paradigms have been used. Hence, one might categorize the theoretic concerns in the stratification studies of the 1970s as (1) structural-functional, (2) structuralist, (3) structural-historical and (4) historical materialist or Marxist. These are considered below in some detail.

Structural-Functional Approach

The basic premises of the structural-functional studies of social stratification in India have implied a systemic teleology based on the Brahmanic or 'hierarchical' model of caste society, assumption of harmony or consensus as the system state from which status mobility, differentiation of roles of power structure and of factional ties, and processes of fusion and fission in the caste structure were studied, and the emphasis on a micro-structural or communitarian scale of reality. All expressions of conflict in the caste structure were treated as adaptive tensions resulting from the structures outside of it, such as polity, economy and technology. Such tensions, the theory assumed, would be eventually absorbed in the system with adaptive changes, without changes of the system as such.

A logical corollary of caste-class relationship as observed from this perspective was to treat class relations within the caste framework as a deviant though manageable expression. Thus, any departure from the traditional summation of status attributes such as status, wealth and power in the caste system was equated with the emergence of class relationships or its sub-structures. Mobility within the caste system was interpreted often through a reference group theory which itself was deeply anchored in consensual ideology (see Y. Singh 1973; Damle 1968). A curious feature of all such treatments of changes in the caste structure was a lack of historicity.

Studies based on the structural-functional method during the 1970s have shown two tendencies, namely, (1) deeper substantive and theoretical concerns about processes of change, such as social mobility, class-caste relationships and comparison and (2) a notable increase in the diagnostic orientation. Substantively, these studies reiterate the continuity in the dominance of the upper and middle caste groups over the other strata of society. However, some new stresses in the functioning of caste stratification have been observed, such as evidence of downward mobility and proletarianization of some sections of the upper castes, selective upward mobility of sections of the middle and lower castes, and crystallization of new awareness among the lower castes, where caste-class consciousness seems to have a fused existence (see K.L. Sharma 1980; Y. Singh 1977; Jha 1970). The processes of fusion and fission in the structure and ideologies of caste continue to prevail (see Chaturvedi and Shah 1970; Moffatt 1975; Wiebe and Ramu 1975). These studies have generated data which refute the necessary relationship between religion and caste (cf. Wiebe and Ramu 1975) and establish the resilience of caste as a process of structural evolution even in tribal society (see Reddy 1973).

An evolutionary structural perspective on caste emerges from these studies, which establishes its probable origin in the indigenous institutions and principles of inclusion and exclusion, through rules of connubial, commensal, occupational and ritual segregation. Studies of equality and inequality in the social system resulting from caste-class stratification, but within the overall hierarchical model of society have reinforced the functional orientation in stratification studies (see D'Souza 1975; Beteille 1977; Srinivas 1979).

In his analysis of the future of caste in India, M.N. Srinivas clearly postulates how the principle of hierarchy prevails despite the Dalit-Hindu ideological asymmetry, the growing self-consciousness of the Scheduled castes and backward classes, and the increasing attack on caste from the sections at the bottom of its hierarchy. Consolidation (fusion) rather than differentiation (fission) of identities within caste seems to characterize its process during the 1970s according to Srinivas.

Similarly, Pauline Kolenda's review (1978) of *Caste in*

Contemporary India, which in conformity with her earlier writings (see Y. Singh 1973) treats caste as localized social structure comprising the endogamous birth-descent group or *jati* as its basic unit, confirms that the solidarity of caste remains intact, although the danger of splitting 'organic' loyalty in the caste system exists. She has, by highlighting the segmentary character of caste or *jati* and its localized existence, postulated that the theory of organic solidarity in the Indian caste system has been exaggerated and is founded upon thin empirical proof. The continual emergence of caste movements for status mobility, access to economic, cultural and political resources and growing conflicts in the system are proofs of this. Kolenda's emphasis on 'beyond organic solidarity', her explanations of conflict or incongruity in its structures, true to her functionalist orientation, is contained within the system properties of caste which continues to be defined in consensual rather than dialectical terms.

There is yet another variety of functional studies of caste and class, which are based not on the observation of these structures as interactional patterns, i.e. caste as status group or community but on their construction or analytical abstraction, as statistical-mathematical indicators, or as analytical typologies. The properties of the concepts here are constructed analytically either using statistical survey data or by introducing heuristic typologies. Such studies were initiated during the 1960s themselves, but in the 1970s they gained both theoretic sophistication and innovation of range and scope.

Victor D'Souza's treatment of caste-class relationship and problems of inequality (D'Souza, 1972) offers a good example of the application of the mathematical-statistical model, generating analytical typologies of caste and class to study inequality and caste-class principles of stratification. He applies set-theory to postulate relational typologies which determine the structural features of caste and class. However, instead of locating the structural reality of these entities in the specificity of cultural or regional contexts, his model accords the concepts operational universality so that they are rendered comparable, and theoretically powerful. Ramakrishna Mukherjee (1970) has offered a methodological strategy for the construction of indicators of social structure.

Another variety of the use of analytical typologies to study stratification has its focus on the comparative relationship among a set of variables that may constitute its indicators. This trend emerged in the late 1960s. It undertakes to analyse stratification using a set of conceptual categories as analytical variables. Since Beteille's typologies of 'caste', 'class' and 'power', a series of studies using analytical typologies have been undertaken (Agarwal 1971; Bhatt 1975; Aurora 1972; Pocock 1974; Fox 1971; etc.), not all of them using these typologies in a truly theoretical context.

The caste-class relationship and degrees of structural differentiation are usually analysed in these studies in terms of hierarchy of relationships among the chosen variables, may be religious, political, jural or others. The logical boundary for the analysis of change in these studies is ahistorical and set in terms of changing intra-systemic relationships measured through conceptual typologies. The focus here, thus, remains on the 'closedness' or 'openness' of the system of stratification as such, even though the relationships are analysed from a host of multidimensional variable sets. Theoretically its focus, therefore, remained structural-functional even though the typologies may often appear neo-Weberian.

The use of analytical typologies has for long attracted theoretical attention in India for understanding the emerging phenomenon of class. Caste studies did not meet with a similar demand. For unlike class, caste constitutes a community, a status group where the people's own model bears direct relevance to its understanding. Class, on the other hand, constitutes a category and its conceptual scheme has of necessity to be located at a higher level of abstraction.

The use of class typologies in Marxist theory implies a definite system-property, but in functional theory emphasis is on the categorization of classes in terms of abstracted variables such as income, occupation, power, psychological identification, etc., which do not imply a definite system-property. The term class is operationally defined and scalar measures are used for its classification (see Kurup 1971; D'Souza 1975). Similarly, studies of 'peasantry', 'agricultural labour', 'entrepreneurs' and 'industrial workers' using such operational methods for generating conceptual categories (see Sharma 1970, 1976; Bandopadhyaya et al. 1975) have been undertaken contributing to the observations on variability and differentiation in the class-caste structure.

Structuralist Approach

Beyond the structural-functional studies the decade of the 1970s saw significant contributions to the growth of the 'structuralist' approach. The lead in this direction no doubt came from Louis Dumont, particularly his *Homo Hierarchicus* (1970). The pivotal notions of structuralism, such as *ideology, dialectics, transformational relationship* and *comparison,* through which a unity of principles among a variety of societal or civilizational forms is established, were brought to bear upon the analysis of caste stratification in India. Dumont's treatment of the ideology or 'principle' of caste following Bougle is posited in 'hierarchy'; the opposition between pure and impure defines its binary tension, its dialectic. He writes:

This opposition underlines hierarchy, which is the superiority of the pure to the impure, underlies separation because the pure and the impure must be kept separate, and underlies the division of labour because the pure and impure occupation must likewise be kept separate. The whole is founded on the necessary and hierarchical coexistence of the two opposites. (p. 43)

Hierarchy also inheres in the relationship of 'encompassing' and being 'encompassed'. As postulated in the caste system the pure or the status principle encompasses the impure, the principles of power and economy. Hence, the superiority of the priest over the king, of the transcendental values over the utilitarian values of gratification—in other words, of *dharma* and *artha,* in Indian society.

The principle of transformational relationship in Dumont's contribution is postulated in his conception of social change, which he essentially equates with ideology. He asserts: 'One thing is certain: the society as an overall framework has not changed, there has been change *in* the society and not *of* the 'society' (ibid.: 218). Hence the significant role of comparison which to him constitutes the principal sociological task. Dumont rejects sociological particularism or the thesis of the uniqueness of the nature of social realities in different civilizational settings. Overemphasis on the thesis of the uniqueness of culture, he asserts, would terminate in cultural solipsism.

Comparing the Indian principle of 'hierarchy' with that of 'equality' in the West, or the 'collective' principle as against that of the individual in the two civilizations, he postulates structural equivalences in the two civilizational types. He says: 'The point is important for comparison with the West. We are not dealing with a solid opposition, as if in one case there was nothing but the individual, in the other nothing but collective man. For India has both distributed in a particular way' (ibid.: 186). The principle of 'renunciation' in the Indian tradition, according to him constitutes the equivalent of the individual in the West. As within a cultural system, so between cultural types the comparison is possible, according to him, through the dialectical juxtaposition or conjuncture of logically opposite cultural types.

The symposium on *Homo Hierarchicus* led by T.N. Madan (1971) projects a mixed response to Dumont's structuralist theory of stratification. Though his work is universally applauded for its scholarship and brilliance it is faulted on theoretical and substantive grounds. Within a structural scheme, Dumont's opposition between pure-impure is questioned on textual and substantive sources. The pure and impure, it is said, instead of being disjunct are fused together (see Das and Uberoi 1971) in many rituals in India. It is suggested that the opposition between 'sacred' and 'non-sacred' would be more inclusive and appropriate than one between pure-impure. Similarly, the notion of 'reciprocity', it is suggested, should be introduced together with 'hierarchy' in the analysis of the caste system.

In Dumont's conception of history, according to Leach (1972), one finds his most intractable difficulties, especially if one is his more 'empirically oriented sympathiser'. Leach adds:

What real standing are we to attribute to Dumont's long discussions of the role of kingship in caste ideology? Kautilya's king was surely, like Machiavelli's prince, an idea rather than a fact? But Dumont often writes as if he thought otherwise. On the other hand his view of the relevance of Kautilya for 20th century ethnography is quite clear.... Dumont plainly assumes that it is the structures implicit in the *Arthashashtra* working themselves out in the collective mind of the Kallar, which have produced this correlation across the centuries. An alternative possibility, which is bound to worry Dumont's colleagues, is that it is the operation of the *Arthashashtra* on Dumont's own mind which has led him to make this kind of analysis. This is, of course, a general worry about the 'structuralist' interpretations. (p. 16)

Criticism of Dumont's structuralist treatment of caste has been made on empirical grounds. T.N. Madan observes the limited nature of the ethnographic evidence on which Dumont has based his major propositions, together with his neglect of the politico-economic dimensions of Indian reality (see Madan 1971 and 1972). He is explicitly supported by Heesterman, Kautowsky (see in Madan 1972) and Edmund Leach. To Dumont, however, most such problems arise out of the confusion of levels between the substantialist and structural modes of thinking. This is where he draws a distinction between dialectics and hierarchy, between the principles of contradiction and complementarity. In a diachronic process complementarity produces *differentiation*, by which the universe of discourse as it existed in its unity gets split into two complementary opposites. Contradiction is on the other hand a process of development in time in which, he says,

a substance (thesis) develops by creating or becoming first its contradictory (anti-thesis) and further on a synthesis which unifies the former on a superior level and which is thus assimilable in a manner to the 'universe of discourse' in this first case, but with a change, a transformation of it. There is a change of level, a leap to a superior degree of complexity which brings Hegelian dialectics closer to our hierarchical model. Regarding the latter, we observed that in hierarchy something that can be called analytical contradiction (or a complementarity) is encompassed with the unity of a higher order. There is thus between hierarchy and dialectics a formal homology but a basic difference. The homology consists of the presence of two levels, one of which transcends the other, but there it ends. (Dumont 1971: 71)

We have commented elsewhere on the relationship between the growth of the structuralist method of sociological analysis, particularly Dumont's contribution to this theoretical orientation and the profession of sociology in India (see Y. Singh, 1979b: 298-9). In our view Dumont's approach succeeded more in creating high self-consciousness among Indian sociologists rather than in offering a widely acceptable model for interpreting the reality of caste and class in this society.

The sociologists who have applied structuralist orientation in their studies, too, have not shown a clear imprint of Dumont's model in their studies (see Das 1977); others have found Dumont's structuralist ideas narrow and inadequate.

A few sociologists have indeed published studies on social stratification where they claim to have followed Dumont's approach (see Carter 1975; Marglin 1977; Holmstrom 1972). The evidence brought forth by these studies does not, however, fully and in all cases support Dumont's postulates. Anthony Carter's study suggests that the caste system is not based solely upon the principle of hierarchy. Status in the caste system is determined by a cross-influence of ritual hierarchy and the principle of kinship unity (Carter 1975: 123-37).

Mark Holmstrom's study (1972) of a Bangalore village supports the continuity of caste ideology but not without significant changes. No longer are all valued statuses defined in and through caste; formally, the symbolic universe of caste remains the same but the meanings have changed. Holmstrom suggests that if change implies revision in categories, this is taking place indeed but not in terms of economic determinism. Ideas and values too have pre-eminence.

F.A. Marglin's study (1977) demonstrates a correspondence between hierarchy and power but contrary to Dumont's postulate, power is not found to be encompassed in hierarchy. Dumont, according to Marglin, does not take into account the differentiation in the extent of power. The correspondence between hierarchy and power, according to him, goes only to the extent that hierarchy coincides with certain privileges in terms of access to women, occupation and wealth.

A few studies using the structural-linguistic approach have also been conducted (see Den Ouden 1979; Rocher 1975), but these are confined either to a textual analysis of the principle of hierarchy in caste (Rocher 1975) as expressed in a series of binary divisions in norms or they seek to analyse the linguistic usages and styles by various strata in an empirical setting (Den Ouden 1979). Such studies, however, take a very narrow view compared to the whole system of structuralist postulates which Dumont has adumbrated.

These developments have indeed contributed to the awareness of the theory and practice of the structuralist model for the study of society (see Uberoi 1974; Das and Uberoi 1971; Khare 1978; Jain 1977). Studies using this model in the analysis of social stratification in India attempt either to improve upon some of the schemes of binary concepts, such as 'hierarchy and power', 'pure and impure' and 'complementarity and contradiction', or they attempt comparisons of structures in a systemic boundary devoid of history. The structuralist's (including Dumont's) treatment of dialectics is dissociated from history. History links essence to existence, form to content, superstructure to infrastructure and theory to practice. Devoid of such a sense of historical conjuncture, 'structuralism' amounts to a set of conceptual schema, devoid of a basis in evolutionary changes in societies. Its transformational relationships, being ahistorical, abound in tautologies.

Structural-Historical Approach

The shift in the paradigm of study relating to social stratification during the 1970s may be witnessed in the growth of structural-historical studies. Unlike structuralism, studies undertaken from this standpoint are grounded in history. Such studies have grown in two directions, the non-Marxist and Marxist. The non-Marxist historical studies are further theoretically differentiated. We find in such studies a variety of theoretical perspectives, structural orientation, historical evolutionary typologies, and processual analysis of structures as social movements. Curiously, some of these studies have rekindled interest in the 'origin' of caste and class, long forgotten after the rise of structural-functional theory. Now we find the problem of origin being analysed both by Marxist and non-Marxist sociologists. Such shifts in the paradigms of social stratification serve as indicators of the changing theoretical and ideological ethos of Indian sociology.

Unlike the studies of social stratification which follow the structuralist approach, the structural-historical studies have been pervasive not only in sociology but also in other disciplines, especially economics and history. One may observe some convergence of theoretical and substantive interests among these disciplines on issues vital to the understanding of the processes of social stratification in India. The historian's treatment of the colonial anchorage of structures and processes of agrarian and industrial forces of stratification, the debate on feudal-capitalist modes of production and its stratification correlates on the one hand and, on the other, the economists' studies of the emerging agrarian structure, its relationship with modes of production and their operation-alization of the notion of class, and treatment of caste-class relationships, have reinforced this outcome.

In this process massive empirical data have been generated, which offer scope for cross-fertilization of ideas and hypo-thesis from a multi-disciplinary perspective. Such a theoretical linkage of sociology and social anthropology, with other social sciences was indeed lost during the 1950s and '60s probably due to the over-arching influence of functionalism. It has now revived during the 1970s.

The question of the origin of caste social stratification has resurfaced in the context of the distinctive features of South Asian society. The controversy over the 'Asiatic' mode of production in this regard is of long standing and by no means fully settled. It offers a theoretical scheme through which enduring Marxist propositions about the nature of caste in Indian society have been postulated (see Namboodiri-pad 1979, Ranadive 1979). From a non-Marxist perspective, the origin of caste has been analysed using an eclectic theoretical approach, a synthesis of structuralism and evolutionary economic anthropology (see Klass 1980). Effort has also been made to seek the origin of caste with evidence from the philosophical and ritual traditions of Hinduism and Buddhism (see Patil 1979).

Using eclectically a variety of theoretical notions, Morton Klass (1980) has speculated about the origin of caste in South Asia. Following Marvin Harris he views the surplus as the basis of the emergence of stratification. With this he combines the evolutionary cultural biologism of Leslie White and Michael Harner's proposition that surpluses generate popula-tion growth, contribute to dispersion of population (due to scarcity of land resources), leading to the structural comple-mentarity and antinomy between clan and caste, between the 'bear and the Barber' as Levi-Strauss postulated. Putting all these different theoretical perceptions together, he hypothesi-zes that caste in South Asia has evolved historically from an equalitarian clan-based society. In course of time, due to natural differentials of ecological advantages or inventions of technology which create uneven opportunities for the generation of surpluses, hierarchical relationship amongst the totemic clans emerged. This hierarchy marked the beginning of caste stratification. This process took place all over South Asia, and both migration and relative ecological advantages to clans in their ability to generate or command surplus played a role in this process. Hierarchy thus emerged as a payoff for achievement by the more fortunate clans. Its cognitive or ideological crystallization has roots in the interactional milieu through which it got institutionalized.

Klass's hypothesis derives its support from several logically autonomous strands of theories and substantive findings. His effort to establish a convergence of all these elements in order to establish caste origin may appear a *tour de force*. He is unable to explain the factor which historically contributed to the transformation of clan into caste, or why this happened only in the South Asian subcontinent: why not in other parts of the globe where too the clan-dispersed ecosystems with uneven benefits of natural resources or abilities among men existed? Apart from the weakness of theoretical eclecticism which he admits, the difficulties of theoretical integration, and lack of plausibility in his substantive evidence render his effort a matter of mere exercise. The significance, however, of such an effort lies not in what he contributes but in what he represents in the context of the study of social stratification. His contribution is symptomatic of paradigmatic tensions, probably in response to challenges of Marxist anthropology, which have revived interest in the origin and evolution of structures and societal forms.

Ideological formulations, too, have reinforced thinking on the origin of caste. The revival of Phule's theory of caste in the Dalit movement, discussed earlier, has contributed to a new exegesis of texts and mythologies (see Patil 1979). Not only is the ancient root of the separation between the Brahman and non-Brahman traditions highlighted, it is also reinforced with textual evidence of how caste did not exist as a birth-determined social group during Vedic times. At this time, caste was determined by initiation only. During 850-600 BC the *sangha* and *gana* of a Brahman did not have any major role for the Brahmans, except in the ritual of bath. The

Brahmans could, however, deny initiation and thus create new ritually segregated groups leading to hierarchy. The evolution of caste society is thus a consequence of the evolution of Brahmanic ideology and their class domination in a disguised form (Patil 1979; Omvedt 1971).

In addition to the origin theme, the historical perspective in the studies of stratification has grown in two other theoretical directions. First, the studies of caste and class structures have been undertaken in terms of their evolutionary transformation, linkages with kinship, social and political organizations and the contradictions emerging in the pattern of relationship as a result of new socio-legal and economic policies. The changing relationships in structures and processes of class-caste mobility and domination are analysed in these studies in historical contexts. Attention has been paid particularly to agrarian structures and their relationship with caste and class during the colonial and post-colonial periods. These studies have been influenced by works of historians (see Stokes 1978) who have been sociologically oriented. The second direction in the structural-historical studies is where the social movement approach is employed by sociologists to study the agrarian caste-class and tribal mobilizations in the wake of demands for status mobility.

As mentioned earlier:

In this theoretic orientation not only do the number of conceptual schemes for comparative studies increase, but also the relationship between concepts and social reality undergoes a new formulation. This is evident in the replacement of studies of villages, so dominant in the sixties, by those of 'agrarian structure' and 'peasantry' in the seventies and eighties. The focus on the study of agrarian structure and not the village, takes sociology into the macro-analytic domain. It introduces a theoretical rather than a territorial orientation in sociological thinking and also brings the Marxist and functionalist formulations of sociological theory face to face, challenging each to test and verify its relative theoretic power. It also introduces a new dimension in the study of change, through emphasis on the sociology of social movement and revolution. These innovations in concepts and theory have also led to a new methodological awareness in sociology. Sociologists now increasingly use the historical method and archival and documentary data to formulate their propositions. This has brought history and sociology closer together, and there is a possibility of one reinforcing the other. (Y. Singh 1971: 303)

The changing historical relationship between caste and class as embedded in the agrarian structure, its historical conditioning by the British policy towards the feudatory classes and landownership, the contribution these factors made to shape the cultural and economic foundation of social inequality at the village and in the region have been studied both systematically and also as social movements (see Rajendra Singh 1974 and 1978; Jain 1977; Shah 1977; P.N. Mukherjee 1977; Pouchepadass 1980). The relationship between status and power and the role of stratification in the institutionalization of polity have been empirically explored (see Stern 1979). Indepth studies of changes in the agrarian structure, their implication for broader issues of social stratification and social change (see Beteille 1970, 1974), the role of the colonial experience in the formation of class and caste relationship (see Saberwal 1979a) and the problems of categorization of strata have been undertaken. Empirical studies of caste and class have followed with the conscious objective of testing theoretical propositions. These studies combine both the historical and the fieldwork traditions.

In a study of two villages in south India, S.S. Sivakumar and Chitra Sivakumar (1979) have observed the changes in class and caste relationships during 1916-76, and have concluded that neither the Marxist nor the empiricist analytical premises hold enough explanatory value for the understanding of their data. 'The role and function of caste are not explainable in material or dialectical terms alone.' They add: 'Our view is that conventional Marxism treating caste as a super-structural reality is not fully attentive to its significance, and empiricists have not fully explored the economic significance of *jati*.' The authors conclude:

Notwithstanding the evolution of class structure since 1916, and notwithstanding the drastic changes in production relations since the 18th century, we find that the cognitive world is not characterised by 'class consciousness'. The consciousness, if we may hazard the use of such a value-loaded term, is highly complex with elements of awareness of the consequences of the distribution of income, inter-mixed with a reinforced awareness of ritual distinctions pertaining to *jati*. This element of cognitive dualism manifests itself particularly strongly among the 'have-nots'. (p. 283)

The historical perspective has also been introduced in the

study of caste movements in different regions of India. These studies generally introduce the element of time in analysis of structures of caste and class and the manner they underwent changes due to ideological, social, economic or political demands. Such studies employ both a theory of movement as well as of structure in their treatment of data. Movements are seen as a series of interventions in the established structure of relationships of caste and class, giving birth to conflicts and contradictions and their successful and not so successful resolution.

The studies of the Yadava and SNDP movements (see Rao 1979) in Uttar Pradesh and Kerala, of the Kurmi Sabha, a caste association of the Kurmis in Bihar (see Verma 1979) and of the national profile of caste-class movements in different regions of the country (see Rao 1979) have strengthened this tradition of research. Most of these studies of social movements have a historical narrative style, but in their treatment of ideas and interests governing the strategies of mobilization they do identify dialectical moments in structures of caste, class, ethnicity and region. In this fashion these studies also contribute to the understanding of the processes of stratification.

Marxist Analysis of Social Stratification

The treatment of stratification in Marxist theory has distinctive features: it is systemic; it is dialectical; it treats structures (stratification) as a historical product; it locates historical forces in the mode of production, and also in the reflection of the species nature of man, which under certain historical conditions creates contradictions of classes; it is essentially evolutionary and developmental, since the mode of production and the relationships that it generates are endowed with the dialectical quality of self-transformation. The mode of production is the centre-piece of the Marxist theory of social stratification. Indian sociology has a long history of Marxist sociology, but its application to the indepth empirical study of structures is of relatively recent origin. Studies of agrarian structure (see Hira Singh 1979), ˜ social movement (see Dhanagare 1974, 1975, 1976 ˜ough 1974), regional movements (see Gupta ˜nal and cultural institutions (see Nirmal

Singh 1979) have been conducted through degrees of operationalization of the Marxist model. The debate on the 'Asiatic', 'feudal', capitalist' and 'colonial' modes of production has engaged historians, economists, and sociologists in their effort to operationalize Marxist categories for the analysis of social structure and stratification in India.

Kathleen Gough (1979) offers a clear case of the application of Marxist theoretical categories in the study of rural social stratification in the Thanjavur villages, the colonial economics of this region, its kinship structure and peasant movements. She has started from the traditional Marxist premises of the succession of the 'Asiatic', 'feudal' and 'capitalist' modes of production in India within the overarching system of colonialism. In a comparative study of kinship and modes of production in Thanjavur and Kerala, Gough postulates her approach on the modes of production as follows:

The Marxist concept of modes of production seems to be the closest we have to the concept of general and specific evolution used more widely by anthropologists. It must at once be admitted, however, that there is much disagreement about this concept: disagreement about how many modes of production at the state level have existed so far, what they are, which past states have been predominantly characterized by which of them, and whether any or all of the modes of production that have been outlined are general or specific evolutionary forms.

Although I could not go into this intricate subject in any detail, I chose in my lecture to refer to three modes of production—Asiatic, feudal and capitalist—because it did seem to me that they hit upon essential differences between the states of Kerala and Thanjavur in the 15th to 18th centuries, and between them and the modern period. Thus, I have argued that the 'Asiatic mode' was formerly dominant in Thanjavur because of the joint possession of land, cattle and slaves by village communes and peasants and gentry based on kinship and because of the direct appropriation of surplus by a bureaucratic state-class in the form of both kind and labour. I have called the Kerala state 'feudal' because land was owned privately by gentry, noble, royal or priestly households or by temples, because serfdom and service-tenures based on households characterized production relations in the countryside, and because government was conducted through private lord-vassal relations which combined military, judicial and economic rights and obligations. I have argued that both regions have become predominantly capitalist in their mode of production in the modern period because of their absorption into the world market and because of the prevalence of commodity production and wage labour, but that the dominance over India's economy of such 'core' countries as the United States, Western Europe and the USSR requires us to view India as a country in the periphery (or perhaps more recently, semi-periphery) of world capitalism. (pp. 286-7)

We have quoted Kathleen Gough at some length because her formulation of the modes of production in India also inheres in the evolutionary stages in the transformation of social stratification. In her other studies she has examined the political economy of Thanjavur from 1749 to 1975 passing from the Asiatic mode of production through feudalism to the capitalistic mode, which after independence links India's economy to that of the nations of the 'core' in a neo-colonial relationship. Traditionally, Thanjavur economy had all the characteristics of the Asiatic mode of production, before it evolved into the feudal mode, under the Chola kings, whose exposure to British mercantilism (through the East India Company and British rule) brought in economic decadence and dependency. It led to de-urbanization, fall in foodgrain production and its export, pauperization of the artisans and peasantry and emigration of labour to East Asia. The Asiatic mode of production of Thanjavur, which had passed slowly to the feudal mode under the influence of the north Indian Muslim empire, due to the growing importance of cavalry, gunpowder and the formation of the ruling administrative feudatory chiefs and private property in land, passed thereto to the capitalistic mode during Company rule. This rule caused the economic decline and dependency of the region in place of its former self-sufficiency owing to predatory revenue exploitation.

In the stratification system the capitalist mode of production brought about class polarization as the richer sections such as the bigger landed estates and commercial entrepreneurs benefited, at the same time that the smaller landlords, peasants and artisans suffered a decline. Colonial rule, on the one hand introduced modern technology and institutions and, on the other, strengthened exploitative processes with the help of these very institutions. A latent function of this historical process was the emergence of the national bourgeoisie who succeeded in achieving freedom from colonial rule, but not from neo-colonial exploitation which, according to Gough, continues as a consequence of political and economic linkages. The experience of Thanjavur, such as the emergence of the new bourgeoisie, the polarization of the peasantry, and the pauperization of the working classes owing to historical transformations in the modes of production point out to the totality of contradictions in social stratification which continue even to this day (Gough 1977, 1980).

In her studies, ranging from kinship organization to political economy of colonialism and rural social structure, Gough has consistently maintained a Marxist theoretical approach. She has also the distinction among Marxist sociologists of having studied India by combining a historical approach with intensive field observations. Of course, she admits the variety of ways in which mode of production as a concept has been defined and operationalized in Marxist literature leading to complexity in its uses (Gough 1980 and 1977: 286). Her usage of this notion, however, connects it to issues of origin, structure and change in caste and class in India, which is closer to the perspectives of the Indian Marxist thinkers (cf., Namboodiripad 1979; Ranadive 1969).

The role of caste and kinship in social stratification is analysed within the framework of the evolving modes of production of which these structures tend to be products. In other words, the class relationship in stratification constitutes the domain assumptions in the treatment of caste and kinship in India. An interesting exegetic view on caste, its origin and structure, using Marxist methodology is that of Claude Meillassoux (1973) who locates the origin of the institutions of caste such as *varna* and *jajmani* system in the class relations as embedded in the mode of production. He also does not treat caste as a culturally specific reality, but only as a variant and not a universal manifestation of class relationship.

There have been several other sociological applications of the Marxist approach to the study of stratification at the village and regional levels. At the village level, the use of observational data in the theoretical framework of the mode of production, periphery-metropolis linkages, class stratification in relation to infrastructures based on production relationships and exploitation have been attempted (see

Djurfeldt and Lindberg 1975). Attempts to view the changes in agrarian structure in a region from feudalism to its new transformations, and analysis of caste in terms of class relationship have also been undertaken (see Hira Singh 1979).

Daniel Thorner has contributed richly to basic thinking on the application of the mode of production approach, its limitations and required innovations. He considered that the mode of production approach as applied to developing countries should be flexible as it is highly differentiated in form. He felt strongly in his later writings about the need for innovating on the Asiatic, feudal and capitalist modes of production derived from classical Marxism, in order to capture the specific historical developments in societies, particularly India (see Thorner 1969 quoted in Y. Singh, 1977: xii-xv; Braudel 1980).

A variant of the Maxist approach has been used in the study of caste and class movements. Here, the focus is mainly upon the linkages between caste and class structures, their role in stratification and the evolution of their ideology in historical phases (see Omvedt 1971 and 1976; Patankar and Omvedt 1979). A basic contradiction between the caste ideology of the dominant and the 'dalit' castes is drawn in the context of their class origins under the conditions of 'caste feudalism'. Caste relations are here, as in Gough, treated as encapsulated class relationships existentially as well as ideologically.

In several studies the evidence on caste-class exploitation, its emerging contradictions in the economic and agrarian structure, and specially its impact on the rural working classes and the Scheduled castes have been highlighted (Mencher 1970 and 1974; Breman 1967a and b). We come across studies on the emerging structural and economic profile of India, indicating increased polarization of classes and its growing contradiction, reviewed from a conceptual-theoretical perspective (see Kamat 1979).

As mentioned above, the use of the Marxist theoretical approach in the study of stratification has a systemic quality. Most interactional patterns of caste and class and their significance to social stratification are in this approach derived almost deductively from the properties of the formulated system. This essentially deductive nature of Marxist theorizing, despite a new emphasis on fieldwork and historical data, not only does not forcelose but also inspires counter-interpretations of reality, especially in the Third World countries where its relevance is recognized as very high. There is a postulate of systemic thinking that not empirical *activities* but *relationships* constitute the prime data for the analysis of reality. 'Relationships' is not an empirical but constructed social reality in Marxism, derived largely from the modes of the production system. This exposes the theoretic formulations of caste-class and other categories in the Marxist approach to social stratification to the charge of formalism to which it claims to be antithetical.

We find an example of the application of systemic logic in a writing of I.P. Desai (1971), who is otherwise a pragmatic empiricist. In the context of occupational mobility Deasi argues that taking 'activity' and not 'relationship' as the indicator of change obviates basic structural changes in Indian society which have already taken place in the emergence of capitalist society. The significant changes seem to be disguised when activities are observed as indicators, since most of them may be of the same kind as in the past. What is significant is that relationships governing these activities have now fundamentally changed, such as money wages, market relationships and the new organizational setting in which these obtain. A formal-deductive analysis of this kind has many limitations (see Y. Singh 1977), yet this formulation raises some basic questions to which Marxist theory in general must address itself.

The deductive nature of categories in Marxist theory has been a matter of debate for long. A proper epistemological response to the question does not lie in speculative history pertaining to the origin of caste or feudalism, etc., but in the empirical grounding of its conceptual categories in concrete structures and historical forces. The contribution that the Marxist approaches have made through the studies of social stratification during the 1970s have successfully demonstrated such a methodological control and rigour in their theorizing. This has logically contributed to rethinking and reformulation of categories and methods in non-Marxist sociology. This process has indeed been aided by contributions from other social sciences in India, especially economics and history.

The mode of production, its location in the infrastructure-superstructure relationship, internal contradictions, the transformation of these contradictions into class struggle and finally political mobilization leading to the revolutionary overthrow of the State, are essential elements of a Marxist paradigm. Studies have, however, indicated that in India the mode of production is highly differentiated. Several modes of production—primitive, semi-feudal and capitalistic—coexist and cooperate in a complex relationship of interpenetration in the same time span; the superstructures like caste and kinship enjoy relative autonomy and consequently persist in a refracted form of existence, not fully yielding to the logic of class contradictions.

This tenacity in caste relationships has led some scholars to view caste relations as another expression of class relationships (Millassoux 1973). The autonomy of the superstructure in India, it is said, has deflected the nature of contradictions from their total subsumption in the class structure; there are levels of contradictions, ethnic, religious, tribal, sexual, territorial, occupational, etc., having nuances of class but not isomorphic with it in Indian society (see Lieten 1979: 313). Thus, it is increasingly realized that prototypical Marxism needs to be modified to find application to the Indian reality. So also the reductionistic logic in Marxist theory needs a redemption resurrection (see Meszaros 1971; Hall 1977, etc.).

The debates in Marxist theory and its application to Indian society have enriched sociological insights into the structure and process of social stratification. There has been an increased conceptual and methodological cross-fertilization between Marxist and non-Marxist theoretical approaches. The role of other social sciences in this process has been highly sensitizing if not directly catalytic. This calls for a short review of the role of other social sciences in the contribution to studies in social stratification.

OTHER SOCIAL SCIENCES AND STRATIFICATION

An important development in the 1970s has been the rich input into the study of stratification, both into its conceptual and methodological schemes by history and economics. As the studies of social stratification through the mode of the production model have gained popularity, both historical and observational data have been adduced to test a series of related propositions, around the theme of colonialism and social and economic modernization in India (see Chandra 1970; Banaji 1972). It is held that from the Indian experience, colonialism should be better treated as a distinct social formation, as a 'well structured whole' which intervened in the process of passage from the semi-feudal to the capitalist stages of development. It is obvious how this formulation puts into the process of the emergence of classes and institutions in India a new historical meaning, a new context which should occupy a pre-eminent place in historical studies. It is said:

The recognition of colonialism as a distinct social formation would not only enable historians of modern India to draw up a better 'structural model' of their researches, but also enable them, by analysing the evolution of the basic characteristics of colonialism, to contribute to the prevention of slide back. (Chandra 1970: 40)

The focus on colonialism shifts the emphasis from the classical formulation of the developmental stages of the modes of production to the analysis of a new historical phenomenon—the colonial mode of production, a process which emerges in the context of burgeoning world capitalism, centre-periphery relationships or neo-colonialism, and exploitation of the Third World nations by the metropolitan countries constituting the system of world capitalism. This approach has a wider appeal, but a significant consequence of its application is that it directs the analysis from concrete to abstract, from specific to realistic and from national to international structures. In this process the treatment of the concrete structures and their contradictions in individual societies is sacrificed. A debate on the merit of this model of Marxism in India as well as in Latin America is, therefore, going on. In the meantime, modifications of the colonialism model have been suggested. It is suggested that the colonial mode is not necessarily a distinct social formation but a transitional one (see Patnaik 1972) or that it could be treated as an abortive form of capitalism, etc.

The essential issues from a Marxist theoretical perspective are the extent to which this model offers a treatment of social stratification as determined by the relationships of the mode of production, structural contradictions, class struggle and revolutionary mobilization within a historical social system. Otherwise, the analysis of dependency relationships between nations measured through categories of economic relationships in abstraction within the framework of world capitalism deflects the attention of social scientists from the study of concrete structures. Is world capitalism a concrete structure, as a national society is, for the observation of the processes of social transformation in a society? This is the basic question when one tries to evaluate the 'colonialism' hypothesis as a conceptual tool for the analysis of social stratification.

The rethinking, therefore, about the colonial mode of production has not so much been in respect of its definitional formulation as about the ways it could be operationalized to help in understanding social processes in specific historical settings. To analyse the processes within a social system the usages of the 'Asiatic', 'semi-feudal', 'capitalist', 'colonial', and 'neo-colonial' modes of production have been put to intensive empirical verification. In this exercise, the propositions of classical Marxism for explaining the dialectic of social structure and stratification have been reinforced. Therefore, much of the substantive discussion in the areas of social stratification in India is based on empirical studies related mainly to the agrarian structure or colonial economy, its historical penetration into the contemporary economic structure and policy and its impact on social stratification.

In the agrarian context, the studies have led to a debate on the feudal *versus* capitalist mode of production in Indian agriculture, its implications to caste-class relationships and emerging contradictions. Some of these studies (see Alavi 1975) are critical of the postulate of the colonial mode of production, and reiterate the relevance of the feudal 'capitalist' modes of production in the study of the Indian socio-economic reality. In the judgement of these writers the social structure of Indian agriculture too continues to be at the developmental stage closer to the developmental stage of the feudal mode of production. A series of studies by Marxist economists (see Prasad 1974, 1975 and 1976; Sen Gupta 1977) have attempted to confirm this proposition.

The proposition that the semi-feudal mode of production still dominates Indian agriculture (which determines the modality of social stratification in the country) is based on the prevalence of usurious loans for consumption, bonded-labour relationships, and exploitation of the landless and the poor peasantry by rich peasants and landlords. The absence of manufacturing industries to absorb surplus manpower is claimed to reinforce the feudal pattern of exploitation, rural poverty and persistence of the traditional institutional foci. This hypothesis is contradicted on the basis of contrary findings. It is observed that non-usurious productive loans are advanced to crop-sharers by landlords for increasing productivity and that interest-free consumption loans are also not uncommon; these are results of the 'green revolution' which has already ushered in the capitalistic mode of production in Indian agriculture (see Rudra 1970, 1975a, 1975b, 1978; Bardhan 1970a, 1970b, Bardhan and Rudra 1978). However, the methodological basis of identifying the capitalist farmer approach continues to be debated (see R.S. Rao 1970). An attempt has been made to operationalize the notion of 'class' in the agrarian structure from a Marxist conceptual scheme of peasant capitalism (see Patnaik 1976; Shanin 1980).

In substantive terms, these studies confirm the process of class polarization, increasing status differences, and the emergence of the middle peasantry as a dominant class in rural stratification. The exploitative nexus, it is observed, has now expanded beyond landlord-tenant relationships to that between bigger and small tenants (see Nadkarni 1976; Bhalla 1976, 1977a, 1977b; Blackenburg 1972; Swamy 1976; Saini 1976a, 1976b) contributing to the process of proletarianization. In some studies, the hypothesis of proletarianization (increasing proportion of landless agricultural workers to the total workforce) is, however, discounted (Vyas and Mathai 1978) and optimism is shown about an integrated agricultural development.

These economic and historical studies of social structure have introduced an inter-disciplinary orientation in the conceptual and methodological treatment of stratification. One can see how directly the Marxist sociological contributions to the understanding of caste and class relationships in India, their role in the processes of change and continuity have been benefiting from the findings of the economists and historians in this field. This is obvious in studies both of the structural and movement orientation, mentioned earlier.

The theoretical problems which studies in the sociological and other social sciences fields have encountered are also of an organic nature. The contributions to the debate on the modes of production, the operationalization of their structure of relationships and the concomitant institutions and also the relevance of micro and macro structural units of observation in the generation of data have led to the enrichment of theoretical awareness. Social stratification studies during the 1970s, therefore, have advanced theoretically and the inter-disciplinary input augurs well for further conceptual and methodological innovations.

SOCIAL STRATIFICATION IN NON-HINDU COMMUNITIES

There have been a good number of studies of stratification in non-Hindu communities during the 1970s. The number of those on stratification among the Muslims has been substantial, with some also of the Christian, Sikh and tribal segments of society. The decade also showed evidence of growing self-consciousness among sociologists from the non-Hindu segment of society. As in the 'dalit' ideology, the sociological categories employed here also tend to question the relevance of the Brahmanical model of culture for the analysis of 'caste' in these communities. Accepting, however, the need to look at various segments of the social structure in India from a composite perspective, it is said that 'intellectual preference or bias partly explains the historical development of Indian sociology as an academic discipline. The pronounced tendency among sociologists to equate Hindus society with India, though sometimes explicit, often remains an unstated assumption (Imtiaz Ahmad 1972: 175). A fundamental question in such debates, as mentioned above, is the relevance of comparative theoretical analysis. The postulate that the theoretical issues are grounded in the unity of conceptual systems rather than diversity of social forms merits closer examination in this context.

The social stratification studies of Muslim society in the late 1950s did have their grounding in theoretical problems.

Leach's treatment of caste as a cultural system and the debates on comparison had their moorings in theory. The earlier studies of Ghaus Ansari and Frederick Barth did establish the existence of caste-like status groups among the Muslims. In the 1970s, however, more extensive and systematic data on the principles of social stratification among the Muslims have been generated. Not only the internal patterns of ranking such as the Ashraf-Ajlaf dichotomy (see Imtiaz Ahmad, 1965, 1966) but also the cultural and ideological basis of stratification in this segment of society have come under closer examination.

T.N. Madan has studied the religious ideology both of the Pandits and Muslims in Kashmir as it bears upon the stratification principle. Apart from establishing the reality of *zat*, his study reveals that images of this entity in the two cultural orders differ significantly. He writes:

Dependence in deference to a principle characterizes the relationship of the Pandit with the Muslims. He cannot continue to retain his ritual status without the crucial services of at least some of the principal Muslim occupational groups. The dependence is absolute: as well as in practice. To put it differently: the Pandit keeps the Muslims out of the *sanctum sanctorum* of his cultural universe, but has to let him into his social world; hence the strain and anxiety that he experiences. Muslim, on the other hand, considers the Pandit as outsider, both ideologically and empirically. (Madan 1972: 135)

This cultural dualism indicates the tensions that the caste-like ranking systems among the Muslims encounter in their functioning and adaptation, especially as the ideological pressures from Islamic fundamentalism increase.

Empirically, however, studies indicate continuance of the caste-like existence of status groups among the Muslims. Selecting a set of conceptual attributes of caste, such as endogamy, occupational specialization, hierarchical ordering of caste and ideological-religious basis involving restrictions on social intercourse and commensality, Imtiaz Ahmad (1973) finds that a series of empirical studies of the Muslims, with few exceptions, prove the existence of the first three attributes of caste with the exception of one observation (see Bhattacharya 1976) that Muslims may have 'inter-ethnic stratification' rather than caste stratification, to which it is only analogous. Thus, a comparative similarity is confirmed.

On ritual purity the studies suggest contradictory evidence (see Leela Dube 1973; Siddiqui 1973). A basic incomparability between caste and status groups among the Muslims in Tamil Nadu is observed (see Mines 1977) and it is contended that different Muslim subdivisions are not ranked hierarchically; endogamy occurs, not to maintain the exclusiveness of blood but due to the tendency to match spouses who share the same economic background.

More recent studies of Muslim social stratification reinforce these findings. Zeyauddin Ahmad's study (1977) of Bihar suggests that despite the notion of 'community of equals' in Islamic ideology there does exist ranking among Muslims in Bihar, with *Ashrafs* at the top, the *Ajlafs* below them (Carpenters, Darzi, Dhunniya Manihar, Kujra, etc.) and the *Arzals* (Halalkhor, Lalbegi, Bediya, in some parts only) at the bottom of the stratification ladder. He also confirms the existence of caste endogamy. In the wake of new Islamic reform movements, however, a process of homogenization in the horizontal direction is taking place, according to him. The Wahabi, Deobandi and Bareilvi movements of puritanism in Islam have initiated this process, which P.C. Agarwal had reported for the Meos in Rajasthan way back in 1971.

There is also evidence of downward and upward mobility in some Muslim classes. The former landlords have been seriously hit, as they did not hold to personal cultivation—being absentee landlords—and did not take to new trade and commerce after the abolition of zamindari. The middle rank commercial Muslim castes have benefited with the new opportunities for trade and commerce; they are the new ascendant classes. So the saying: 'Last year I was a Jolaha, now I am a Sheikh, next year if prices rise, I shall be a "Sayyad"' (Zeyauddin Ahmad 1977: 20). This process is also putting pressure on the rule of endogamy, which in future may weaken under the economic pressures on the upper Muslim castes.

The social stratification studies among the Sikhs (see Inder Paul Singh 1977; Harjinder Singh 1977) indicate that ranking exists between the Sardar and the Mazhabi (scavenger), more on dualistic pattern as the caste elaboration in this region (as pointed out by Marriott) is low; but caste endogamy exists. The status of Brahman in Sikh villages is below that of the

Sardar. But caste cuts across religion, as the Jats marry across the Sikh-Hindu religions. The mobility processes indicate decline in the status of Brahmans as Sikhism renders many rituals inoperative; the Mazhabis of course, are observed to improve their status by becoming *granthis* or wrestlers in the village. Occupational mobility also is taking place in their favour. In this context, also, religion has not been able to fully prevail upon the hierarchical principle of caste, though it has introduced new adaptive transformations.

Some studies of caste among the Christians of south India have revealed that its presence dates back to the sixteenth century when mass conversion took place after the arrival of the Portuguese. In Kerala the Nayar Christians were in the middle hierarchy, with Brahman converts at the top, the Izhavas and Mukkavas ranking below them, and the Pulayas being placed at the bottom of the hierarchy. Scheduled caste privileges subsequently motivated some low-caste converts to return to Hinduism. Reform movements in the Christian churches followed, for example, the New Religious Church by Parayas and Prattyaksha Raksha Daiva Sabha by Syrian Christians. It is observed finally that conversion to Christianity has not been able to obliterate the caste disabilities of converts, nor has it led to their complete withdrawal from former ritual and social practice.

Status mobility, if any, has come through economic and educational advancement rather than by conversion alone. In Tamil Nadu, the study by Wiebe and Peter (1977) suggests that among about 83 per cent of the converts coming from the former 'untouchable' castes, caste considerations prevail. It is concluded that

> though today the caste system is undergoing many changes, it seems to retain much of its strength as an organising feature of social life in both rural and urban India. In any case the system largely has absorbed the challenges that non-Hindu religious systems have posed and, in turn, has rendered them relatively impotent. (ibid.: 47)

TRIBES AND SCHEDULED CASTES

The force of social mobility, change and contradictions in the social segments in contributing to new processes in social stratification has been observed by sociologists and social anthropologists. Studies have shown the formation of caste-like endogamous status groups among the once homogenous tribal groups with the emergence of restrictions on inter-dining and other caste-like interdictions. Some studies show that such changes result through endogenous structural differentiation (see Reddy 1973) or historical contact through con-quest and colonization (see Chauhan 1980; Singh 1978).

Such contradictions in the tribal social stratification follow different directions, depending upon the context of their origin. If the caste-like structures emerge in the natural course of the occupational differentiation and its cultural rationalization, the contradictions remain dormant, to which attention has been drawn. But where the class or caste strati-fication emerges through the economic expansion of the dominant castes from the non-tribal society and the control or exploitation of the tribal society, the contradictions are compounded leading to protest movements, in political, economic and ideological forms (see Sengupta 1977; K.L. Sharma 1976).

The differentiation of new strata and the fusion of the strata into communal ideological entities in tribal society recur almost simultaneously. Development efforts have in this context played both a positive and negative role. They have created a class structure where none or little existed, and have offered scope for ideological mobilization by the ascendant tribal classes of the sections lagging far behind. In this process a large-scale displacement of symbols, emotive, cultural and political has taken place; new symbols have been created, and the older ones resurrected to encounter the economic, political and cultural forces released in and tribal society as it gets increasingly differentiated, and confronts the wider segments of society to safeguard itself from exploitation and loss of identity.

The issues relevant to social stratification in relation to the Scheduled castes have been examined in the 1970s both in respect of ideological and structural changes. I.P. Desai's study (1976) of untouchability in Gujarat analyses both the ideological and behavioural changes taking place in the pollution-purity matrix of interaction. The study finds a significant weakening of the ideology of 'untouchability' in the utilitarian domains of interaction. It continues, however, in the ritual domain. The obliteration of untouchability in the utilitarian domain, as it now turns out (in the wake of caste riots in Gujarat) was primarily rooted in the structure of interests, and access to resources (see Bose 1981). P.K. Bose finds that caste riots in Gujarat are most virulent in those areas where the Scheduled castes have advanced economically and educationally and where they are more concentrated. It would thus seem that the ideology of 'untouchability' had all along its roots in the class interests of the dominant sections of society rather than in 'hierarchy'.

This aspect of the ideology of 'untouchability' has been reiterated and confirmed by several studies in the 1970s (see Omvedt 1971, 1976; Patankar and Omvedt 1979). The emergence of the counter-ideology of caste in Phule's recons-truction of Hindu mythology finds its new expression in the Dalit movement, giving a sharper edge to the social contra-diction of the place of the Scheduled castes in Hindu social stratification. The sharpness of the ideological schism increases as two-way contradictions are emerging in the Scheduled caste social stratification: first, the benefits earmarked for the Scheduled castes are not as yet reaching most of them or the most needy amongst them; secondly, the demonstration effect of the status mobility by a few Scheduled caste families and that too in limited sectors of opportunities is being exaggerated by non-Sheduled caste strata, creating larger than life negative images, and a back-lash rooted more in emotion than reason.

Studies of educational opportunities to the Scheduled castes show that though there is marked progress where facilities have been institutionalized generally, inequality persists. New inequalities have arisen in addition as Scheduled caste students get access only to poor schools and poor colleges because of the cumulative effect of their poor enrolment and retention in the school system (see Chitnis 1972). Occupational mobility too is low among the Scheduled castes (see Ramaswamy 1974). The land allotted to them under State welfare measures is alienated from them (see Murdia 1975); the Scheduled caste share in the services, in banks and new public institutions remains below the expected norm (see Mankidy 1976) and the poverty of their overall socio-cultural and economic conditions keeps them at the fringe of the development processes despite decades of planned efforts (see Chandidas 1969; Agarwal 1977). A sociological outcome of this uneven change, and its resultant contradictions is the increased ideological and structural tensions between the Scheduled caste and the caste-Hindu societies.

The impetus to ideological movements and protest results from these contradictions. Recent studies indicate that attitudinally Scheduled caste youth reject the caste model of social stratification and the Karma ideology of Hinduism (see Paranjpe 1971). Only a few among them think that prestige in society depends upon caste. Other studies confirm this observation (see Agarwal 1977). The ideological rejection of caste, however, does not harmonize with the empirical reality of the social stratification of the Scheduled castes, which is still embedded in the caste system. Hierarchy is as much a value system among them as among the caste Hindus (see Moffatt 1975; Fiske 1977). One finds grades based on caste segregation among the Scheduled castes deriving from the ideology of caste purity and pollution.

The ideological rejection of the caste model, therefore, although powerfully and widely articulated at one level involutes the emotional and psychological ambivalence towards caste at another level. Neo-Buddhism is one result of this process; but conversion to Buddhism contributes only to psychological succour and not to the improvement of social status (see Fiske 1977). The roots of caste ideology, therefore, would seem to disguise the class contradictions of Indian society, and the nature of economic exploitation which now increasingly gets exposed as the pressure of social stratifcation on the system increases.

SOCIAL STRATIFICATION, SOCIOLOGY AND SOCIAL CHANGE

The process of social stratification is a pivotal element in the dialectic of change in a society. Its sociological features in India, as evident from the above review of selected literature, raise issues both in the theoretical and substantive domains. Theoretically, the 1970s marked some new orientations in studies of stratification and some innovations in methodology.

Substantively, the decade was marked by a process of (i) concretization of class-caste contradictions as a result of the emergent economic and political forces, and (ii) polarization of caste-class identities through the crystallization of the middle class-caste dominance in the rural society. These forces have sharpened the schism in the ideological consensus about the system of stratification. This development has significant consequences for the paradigms used for the study of social stratification in India.

The new theoretical and methodological directions in the study of stratification can be seen in the emergence of Marxism as a widely used paradigm, with a methodological shift in favour of historiography and historical anthropology. The re-emergence of the 'origin' theme in the analysis of caste both in Marxist and non-Marxist studies is yet another indicator of the shifting paradigmatic interests. The non-Marxist structural studies, too, have gained in sophistication of analytical conceptualization and historical depth. A keen interest in such studies seems to have emerged in order to conceptually make use of the relationships between infrastructures, such as economic and existential institutions and kinship and primordial identities, in the analysis of the superstructures of caste and class, and their ideology. This trend in historical-structural studies has been supplemented by an innovation of structuralism as a method of understanding social stratification. Added to these tendencies are the interdisciplinary or multi-disciplinary contributions to the studies on stratification during the decade, which directly and indirectly enrich sociology.

In the substantive domain, studies have remained enclosed in the concerns of caste-class structure and their overlap in stratification, and its emerging dialectics. The professional classes, business entrepreneurs, and the elite have been studied, but the over-arching framework has remained that of caste and class. Studies have been conducted on the culture of entrepreneurs (see Nandy 1973; Spodek 1969), their recruitment and background (see Panini 1977; Bandopadhyay et al. 1975; Saberwal 1976), their policy-related role in the Indian economy (see Guha 1970; Van Der Veen, 1976) on the one hand, and on the other the structure of the industrial working classes and professionals (see Gandhi 1978; B.R.

Sharma 1976; King 1970). But the major substantive orientation in the analysis remains that of the caste-class nexus. This is particularly true of the studies of agrarian structure and the peasant economy. In order, however, to analyse the dynamics in these structures some studies have applied a social movement approach.

The processes of ideological schism, class consolidation as well as polarization, heightened self-consciousness among the strata coming from the poor and exploited segment of society, uneven growth between sections and sectors of society (rural-urban; regional-national) and the ideological demand for high status mobility, all these forces combine in present-day India to bring the forces of social stratification face to face with a scenario of emerging contradictions. The capitalist-feudal structure of society, which defines the limits for reconciliation in social policy and implementation of social policy, also constrains the options for change. The contradictions today have, therefore, a new sharp edge, being a product of development as well as of underdevelopment. Simultaneously with this increasing contradiction, there is a rush for the revival of primordial identities, values and relationships which encapsulate the emerging class consciousness. The hierarchy principle thus coexists in India with the ideology of class. Rituals are adhered to by those who denigrate the Brahmanical model of stratification.

This amalgam of contradictions, this ambivalence of will, and this coexistence of contra-cultures and role-sets delimits the possibilities of a more radical outcome to the forces of contradiction in Indian society in the near future. Anomie and resentment might continue to prevail, the haves may have to part with more of their privileges to pacify the have-nots, and to mystify their dominance. The emerging model of social stratification, however, despite mounting contradictions, does not seem to be moving towards imminent collapse, not soon, in any case. The possibilities of new theoretical explorations in the study of these challenging processes of social stratification, however, are immense and are sure to prove viable. Indeed, the new directions in the theory and methodology of stratification augur well for the growth of sociology in the coming decades.

3

Concepts and Theories of Social Change

INTRODUCTION

Social change is a widely discussed subject but its theoretical position in sociology remains controversial. Interest in this area has also fluctuated because of many vexed theoretical problems, especially those relating to explanation or prediction of the course and content of social change. We may find a periodicity in the literature of Western sociology about its theoretical concern with change. In its formative phase (roughly 1875-1920, see Sorolkin 1965: 833) sociology was deeply attached to historical reconstructions and generalizations about social change. Such theoretical postulates were also reinforced by those from social anthropology and ethnology. The contributions of Spencer, Comte, Marx and Pareto about social and cultural evolution and its laws were oriented to historical reconstruction similar to those of Henry Morgan, McLennan, Bachofan and Henry Maine. Social change was, however, the central concern of sociology at this time. It also had a nascent ideological bias, that of universal progress of mankind, and unilinear course in social evolution for all societies following the Western model. There were slight variations on this theme, but by and large, this assumption permeated the sociological literature of the time.

This over-concern with social change got a setback in sociology roughly during 1920-58. The focus shifted from evolution of social forms to their function; the speculative and scholastic approach was replaced with an emphasis on field studies and collection of first-hand empirical data. Macro-sociological generalizations gave way to small-group studies and micro-sociological theorizing; system change remained no more the dominant focus of sociology; instead, the interest shifted to system integration and boundary maintenance functions of social forms. This trend, which too had its origin in the West, also reflected the growing methodological sophistication in sociology. Theoretically, the implied isomorphism of social system with organic system and of social process with biological evolution (especially the irreversibility of evolutionary forms) of the earlier phase could not be sustained on empirical and historical grounds. Existentially, the social cost of industrialization and the two world wars dispelled the optimism about the universal evolutionary progress of mankind, and the invariable laws postulated by utilitarian positivism.

During the decade following 1958, however, a revival in the study of social change can be observed in Western sociology. The theoretical presuppositions of functional analysis came increasingly under fire during this period (see Dahrendorf 1958; Wright Mills 1959; Hampel 1959; Homans 1964). Moreover, the sociologists of functionalist orientation are now seen making heroic efforts to demonstrate the effectiveness of their model for the analysis of social change also (see Smelser 1959 and 1963; Parsons 1964). The urgency for revival of interest in social change probably emerged also because of the process of decolonization of Asia, Africa and Latin America where, not continuity, but revolutionary change was the dominant national aspiration and ideology. Concern with change became a necessity for Western sociologists as they confronted a new younger generation in their own country which defied the *status quo* in quest of new values and a new social order. Consequently, the analysis of social change once again became a central concern of sociology. It rather assumed the overtones of sociological ideology (see Dumont 1964: 10) for the developing nations.

SOCIAL CHANGE THEORIES IN INDIA

The theoretical growth of sociology in India has been deeply influenced by its development in the West, particularly the UK and the USA. The fluctuations in the study of social changes and its relevant theoretical formulations as seen in the West, however, existed only partially in Indian sociology. Analytic descriptive studies of various social and cultural systems in India engaged the interest of British and European scholars right from the eighteenth century, but alongside studies about the processes of social change went on. In contrast, the Indian sociological tradition does not seem to have undergone theoretical fluctuations such as evolutionary, functionalism and neoevolutionary, for analysis of social change. One might discern some correspondence with these three major orientations in the sequence of Indian sociological studies but the concern with social change was always present. Even the functionalist studies were mainly focused on the analysis of social change in India, as we shall see later. In fact, some of the most discussed concepts of social change in India have been developed by sociologists who are clearly oriented to the structural-functional method. Indian sociologists have been more concerned with the processes of social accommodation and adaptation rather than with abstract theory building, so much in evidence in Western sociology, past and contemporary. Most sociological writing in India tends to be substantive rather than theoretical. The only clear exception, where a systematic effort is made toward abstract theorization or model-building, are the writings of Radha Kamal Mukherjee. Consequently, the analysis of change is inherent in one form or another in most sociological writing right from its early days.

Our objective in undertaking a survey of literature on social change in Indian sociology is to review the salient conceptual and theoretical formulations about social change. We shall be mainly interested in analysing the nature of theoretical presuppositions and conceptual schemes that have grown through substantive studies of the structures and processes of changes in Indian society from time to time. We would review the theories of social change and their implicit forms and formulations with regard to major sociological studies in India. We would also like to evaluate the conceptual formulations of these theories for their power and relevance.

Sociology as distinct from historiography and social philosophy emerged slowly during the first quarter of the twentieth century in India. The pace was set by early British and European 'orientalists', 'missionaries' and 'administrators' turned ethnographers and cultural historians, (see Cohn 1968: 3-28). In the Indian tradition itself one finds a metaphysical rather than sociological treatment of change. The major categories of thought that comprise the Indian tradition are 'hierarchy', 'holism', 'continuity' and 'transcendence' (see Y. Singh 1973); change as such forms less than a central category in Hindu metaphysics and social philosophy. The concept of change has in this tradition an organic link with the differentiation of the Timeless and the Eternal. We find this reflected right up to the twentieth century in the writings of Aurobindo Ghosh, who cherished faith in the possibility of the emergence of the 'Perfect Man' following the battle against the evil (Kurukshetra) and thus rendered the specific concept of 'Avatar' into a diffuse category, a 'work-form' that would permeate the human condition.

Obviously, such formulations of the process of change in the Indian tradition, not without parallels in the West (see Stark 1958) have their limitations from a sociological point of view where the existential reality by rule of correspondence forms an essential component for verification in each postulated categorical or conceptual model. This rule of correspondence seems to be lacking in the traditional formulations of social change in India.

Indian sociological formulations of the concepts of social change find a beginning in the writings of British and Indian scholars following the last quarter of the nineteenth century. Gradually, these concepts and formulations got differentiated and a variety of approaches emerged. For a brief survey these approaches could be classified as: (1) evolutionary approaches; (2) cultural approaches: Sanskritization-Westernization; little and great tradition, and multiple traditions; (3) structural approaches: differentiation and mobility analyses; dialectical-historical approaches; cognitive historical approach; and institutional approach. This classification is purely heuristic. It represents the dominant theoretical or conceptual orientations in the writings of the sociologists concerned.

EVOLUTIONARY APPROACHES

The village community, caste and family were the three themes which social ethnographers and sociologists studied in the late 1890s and early 1920s. Whereas a few students of these realities were struck by continuity in the Indian social system and tradition (see Charles Metcalfe's *Minutes of the Village of Delhi* of 1830 and Dumont 1966), most others, influenced by the evolutionary approach, concentrated on the stages through which institutions like caste, family, marriage and kinship and village community passed. Cohn writes:

The data and their organization implicitly reflect the work or Morgan, McLennan, Lubbock, Tylor, Stracke and Frazer. These men were concerned with the use of 'customs', for example, marriage by capture, polyandry, or the levirate—to infer: something about the origin of culture or as they termed it, 'civilization'. Similarly, religious practices were utilized as disparate bits of information to develop stages of the development of religion. The 'customs' were reported and studied out of their context as hard facts which could be compared and classified as to the stage of development. (Cohn 1968: 17)

The origin of caste and its racial composition formed frequent themes for evolutionary speculations (see Crooke 1896; Ibbetson 1916; Risely 1915; Dutta 1931; Ghurye 1945; Guha 1937; Hutton 1955; etc.). In these studies emphasis was uniformly on the factors which contributed to the origin of the caste system. Even in comparative analyses, the evolutionary perspective remained, that is, effort was made to find out institutions similar to caste in other societies based either on the racial, occupational, ethnic or other socio-cultural attributes. Data derived from myths, epics, history and folklore were adduced to confirm many speculative generalizations about the origin of caste and its future form. An evolutionary perspective was thus built into general statements about caste. One may, of course, find elements of departure in the writings of Hutton and Ghurye, but they too were more concerned with hypothesizing about caste origin and not only about its structure and function—the aspect of study which later replaced the evolutionary orientation.

The studies of villages and land systems were similarly oriented either to finding out the historical stage of growth or their comparative evolutionary sequence and succession of forms (see Maine 1890; Baden-Powell 1892 and 1908). Maine was particularly concerned with placing the Indian village into an evolutionary scheme through which its linkages with the village communities in the West could be established. As Dumont rightly says, Maine 'hardly ever looked at the Indian village in itself, but only as a counterpart to Teutonic, Slavonic or other institutions'. India was to him little more than 'the great repository of veritable phenomena of ancient usage and ancient juridical thought' (see Dumont 1966: 830). In his treatment of the process of 'feudalization' Maine clearly postulates a transition from 'village community' to Manorial Group which succeeds in an evolutionary sequence universally. Baden-Powell too is concerned with the 'origin' and 'growth' of the village communities in India, and both in his treatment of the land systems and forms of village communities he comes very close to formulating an evolutionary process by which villages emerged in India from a communal ownership to that based on joint sharing and single landed ownership. The severality, joint zamindari and jagirdari types of villages, according to Baden-Powell, could have evolved through a process of succession of dominant groups of conquest and settlement.

We thus find a continuity in theoretical formulations about change in Indian sociology of the nineteenth century. Such evolutionary formulations also implied that the social forms and traditions in India were at a lower stage of growth than the Western forms and structures. The writings, despatches, Census and Gazetteer reports of this time disclose sometimes overt and sometimes hidden slant on this type of inter-pretation of the Indian social system and culture, evoking resentment among many Indian scholars. Sir Brijendra Nath Seal severely criticized the attempt of British anthropologists and Western ethnologists to classify Indian culture and social institutions at a lower level of evolution, through a phylogenetic method. He took an anti-evolutionary viewpoint in his lectures at the Calcutta University during the first quarter of the twentieth century (see Y. Singh 1967). Radha Kamal Mukherjee responding to this issue wrote: 'The attempt to force systems and methods of industrial organi-zation, economic arrangement and institutions which have admirably suited a different geographical environment would always be futile' (see ibid.). These developments set a new trend in conceptual formulations about social change which coincided with the rise of the functional method in Western sociology.

Cultural Approaches

During the second quarter of the twentieth century Indian sociology and social anthropology became essentially empirical. The analysis of field-data replaced speculative generalizations. Thus the focus shifted from the process of change to that of integration and functioning of the system. Cohn says,

By 1940 the study of Indian society cumulatively had the following components: (1) a broad-scale humanistically oriented tradition which emphasized the relationship between textual studies and a static model of contemporary Indian society; (2) an administrative tradition centered on the census for the study of caste which sought to see Indian society as a collection of discrete entities whose traditions and customs could be classified and studied; (3) a tradition of economic study which sought to describe the working of village economics, with some attention to the social structure of villages; (4) an anthropological tradition centered on the study of tribal peoples; and (5) the historical administrative strain which centered on the general theory of village organization in a broad comparative framework, but without an intensive ethnographic base. (see Cohn 1968: 23)

Mann's surveys of Deccan villages and Wiser's studies of the *jajmani* system and rural social structure in U.P. were the beginnings of a new orientation in the Indian sociological analysis (see Mann 1921; Wiser 1936).

Analysis of change in these studies ceased to be macroscopic and assumed a strictly empirical character, that is, change was analysed strictly in terms of observed deviations in the forms and functions of the systems concerned between two points of time. Such analysis had no significant conceptual category to offer for describing the processes of change. Even the diachronic element in the analysis was in fact merely 'double synchronic', to borrow Dumont's phrase (see Dumont 1964: 9). The concepts of Sanskritization and Westernization as formulated by M.N. Srinivas were the first systematic attempt to define the processes of change taking place in Indian society.

Sanskritization and Westernization

A comprehensive theory of social or cultural change assumes that sources of change lie both inside and outside the system. The concepts of Sanskritization and Westernization postulated by Srinivas define these two types of sources of social change.

Sanskritization represents actual or aspired for cultural mobi-lity within the framework of the established 'Great Tradition' and stratification system of caste. Westernization implies change resulting from cultural contact with the West, parti-ularly Great Britain. Srinivas (1966) defines Sanskritization

as the process by which a 'low' caste or tribe or other group takes over the customs, rituals, beliefs, ideology and style of life of a high and, in particular, a 'twice-born' (*dwija*) caste. The Sanskritization of a group has usually the effect of improving its position in the local caste hierarchy. It normally presupposes either an improvement in the economic or political position of the group concerned or a higher group self-consciousness resulting from its contact with a source of the 'Great Tradition' of Hinduism such as pilgrim centre or monastery or proselytizing sect. (pp. 67-8)

This definition of Sanskritization is by far the most comprehensive that Srinivas has postulated. Earlier he used the term 'Brahmanization' for this process wherein the castes lower in hierarchy imitated the cultural and ritual practices of the Brahmanas (see Srinivas 1952), but later on he found that for emulation there may be many models other than the Brahman model as reported by various sociologists (see Shah and Shroff 1959; Cohn 1955; Pocock 1957; Rowe 1963; Kalia 1959 and others). Accordingly, Srinivas changed the contex-tual meaning of Brahmanization to Sanskritization first on the basis that 'certain Vedic rites are confined to the Brahmans and the other "twice-born" castes' (see Srinivas 1962: 42) and later broadened its reference context to any group higher in caste status, particularly the 'twice-born' castes.

Sanskritization as a concept not only identified a crucial aspect of the process of change in Indian culture and its institutions but the use of this term soon led to a debate in Indian sociology which has not yet concluded. Here was a concept which had an equal appeal for the Indologists, historians of Indian culture and sociologists and social anthro-pologists. It also satisfied those who had a special fondness for developing Indian concepts for analysing national socio-cultural phenomena. The historical context of Sanskritization received special attention by many scholars (see Raghavan 1959; Chanana 1961; Harper 1959; Staal 1955-6). These historical evaluations not only provide additional confirmation to the reality of the process of Sanskritization but also reveal contextual gaps and limitations in the formulation of this concept. Chanana (1961), for instance, mentions that in Punjab not only the Hindu but also Persian cultural contact characterized the model for imitation. He also expressed doubts about Westernization as such. He says: 'as regards the present [situation in Punjab], it would be better to say that Indianization is at work; by this we mean Westernization to a large extent in externals and the reassertion of largely Indian values, mingled with the humanitarian values of the West in matters of spirit' (p. 414).

Similar suggestions have also been offered by other social scientists, for example, that Sanskritization as a process should be analysed in the context of the nature of socio-economic deprivations experienced by various groups in the social structure (Gould, 1968: 945-50). The urge to Sanskritize may be a disguised attempt to raise social status ritually as a result either of a closure of economic means for status mobility or as a consequence of it. There is also a view that the imitation framework that Sanskritization suggests based on the hierarchy of the Great and Little Traditions or of levels of dominant cultural traditions might function in a circular rather than linear form. McKim Marriott (1955) observes that there is no clear process of Sanskritization 'at the expense of' the 'non-Sanskritic' traditions. Instead of there being a borrowing, he finds 'evidence of accretion and of transmutation in cultural form without apparent replacement and without rationalization of the accumulated and transformed elements ... Sanskritic rites are often added on to non-Sanskritic rites without replacing them'.

Sanskritization is also a term with many connotations. Srinivas writes that 'Sanskritization is an extremely complex and heterogeneous concept. It is even possible that it would be more profitable to treat it as a bundle of concepts than as a single concept. The important thing to remember is that it is *only a name* for a widespread cultural process' (Srinivas 1962: 61, italics added). No doubt, the considerable literature that has grown on this subject reflects this fact. Sanskritization is given varied interpretations. Not only have social scientists understood Sanskritization differently but they have appreciated or criticized it for contradictory reasons. Edward H. Harper (1959), for instance, treats Sanskritization as a 'functional concept' as distinct from a 'historical' concept. It is, according to him, an interpretative category to understand the relationship among the changing elements within the tradition, than its historical construction. J.F. Staal writes, however, that Sanskritization describes a process and is a concept of change. It is not a concept at which synchronic analysis could ever arrive in order to explain material obtained by synchronic analysis. Sanskritization is a meta-concept in this sense, and *all historical concepts are meta-concepts in that they are based upon concepts of synchronic analysis* (Staal 1955-6: 15, 23-36, italics added). Here the natural implication is that Sanskritization is a historical concept or belongs to the concepts of the same species. Many more examples reflecting the contradictions of meanings associated with the term Sanskritization could be mentioned.

As Srinivas himself acknowledges, the concept of Sanskritization helps one to identify the cultural or 'positional' and not the structural forms of social change. Sanskritization, however, presupposes the existence of structural constraints on pressures in the social system. That is why it is related to another important notion of Srinivas—that of 'dominant caste'. A dominant caste is one which enjoys a relatively predominant position in the caste hierarchy ritually, economically, numerically and educationally or—as it really obtains—on the basis of the combination of any of these four variables of dominance. Srinivas's formulation of the criteria of dominance has been critically examined by many social scientists. No doubt, the complex nature of the term 'dominant caste' and its relationship with the power structure of groups is such as might call for further modifications (Dube 1965; Oommen 1970) but the phenomenon of dominance does render the concept of Sanskritization much more dynamic. It is the dominant castes or groups that offer themselves as models for Sanskritization by the groups lower in hierarchy. Thus cultural mobility is seen as a function of power.

Associated with Sanskritization are Srinivas's concepts of 'Westernization' and 'Secularization'. Westernization refers to all cultural changes and institutional innovations in India as this country came into political and cultural contact with the Western nations, primarily the U.K. Secularization is a counterpart of the process of Westernization specially as it emerged after independence as a national ideology. This ideology calls for a spirit of religious and cultural tolerance and coexistence amongst the religious groups. It also refers to various legislative and constitutional provisions that have been made in India to reinforce its foundations. Srinivas has thus attempted to portray the most important processes of social change in India through these three concepts.

Little and Great Tradition

The process of social change in India has also been studied and analysed with the help of the concept of tradition and its social organization. The approach emanates from the works of Robert Redfield in Mexico. For societies having deeper historical past and civilization maturity, Redfield postulated a series of cultural and social organization. Each civilization consists of traditions, one of the elite or the reflective few where it is formally articulated, and the other of the folk or the unlettered peasants. The former he called 'Great' and the latter 'Little' tradition. Each tradition has its own social organization, that is, institutionalized roles, statuses, and personnel. Both traditions taken together symbolize a world view which represents the unity of civilization.

These traditions, however, are not impervious to changes originating from within and without. Each tradition develops, first, in terms of its own internal creative urge, an orthogenetic process. But simultaneously, traditions also come under external impact, of traditions outside their own civilizational matrix. This may happen through historical contact, war and political domination or migration or communication. Civilizations and their social structures also change through these external contacts or heterogenetic processes. It is assumed by Redfield that all civilizations begin with orthogenetic or primary process of growth and keep on transforming themselves through heterogenetic contact. Presumably, at some point of time the heterogenetic contacts among civilizations might lead to a universal form of civilization.

Redfield's frame of analysis has been applied to study the Indian reality of social change by Milton Singer, McKim Marriott and their associates (Singer 1959; Marriott 1955). Singer (1955-6) formulates a series of statements about cultural change in India. He writes:

(1) that because India had a 'primary' or 'indigenous' civilization which had been fashioned out of pre-existing folk and regional cultures, its 'Great tradition' was continuous with the 'Little tradition' to be found in its diverse regions, villages, castes and tribes. (2) That this cultural continuity was the product as well as the cause of a common cultural consciousness shared by most Indians and expressed in essential similarities of mental outlook and ethos. (3) That this common cultural conscious-ness has been formed in India with the help of certain processes and factors..., i.e. sacred books and sacred objects ... a special class of literati (Brahman) and other agents of cultural transmission ... (4) That in a primary civilization like India's cultural continuity with the past is so great that even the acceptance of 'modernizing' and 'process' ideologies does not result in linear form of social and cultural change but may result in the 'traditionalizing' of apparently 'modern' innovations.

Singer concludes that the resilience of the Indian tradition is such that changes take place in it through selective adaptation rather than basic transformation.

McKim Marriott supports this view. He characterizes the mode of interaction between the 'Little' and 'Great' traditions in the Indian village as 'parochialization' and 'universaliza- tion'. The first is when elements of the 'Great' tradition percolate downward and become organic part of the 'Little' tradition losing thereby their original form. The second process operates when elements of the 'Little' tradition (deities, customs, rites, etc.) circulate upward to the level of the 'Great' tradition and are 'identified' with its legitimate form. Marriott gives many examples of such circular pro- cesses of change from his observations in India. Sanskritiza- tion, according to him, does not proceed as an independent process, it is superimposed on non-Sanskritic cultural forms through accretion rather than simple replacement (Marriott 1955).

Multiple Traditions

The dichotomization of traditions ('Little' and 'Great') as formulated by Singer has been criticized by many sociologists. S.C. Dube (1965) holds the view that analysis of cultural changes with the help of the 'Little' and 'Great' traditions framework would be insufficient because traditions in India are organized not in a bipolar but multi-polar system. He writes:

As far as 'Little' and 'Great' traditions are concerned, there is apparently no precise definition.... Where there are more than one Great or near-Great Traditions, each with its canonical texts and ethical codes, the situation becomes all the more confusing.... It may also be added that the Great Tradition-Little Tradition frame of reference does not allow proper scope for the consideration of the role and significance of regional, Western and emergent national traditions, each of which is powerful in its own way (ibid.: 421-3)

Dube alternatively postulates a classification of traditions which, according to him, are more representative of the Indian cultural realities and offer a better framework for analysis. These are: the classical tradition, the emergent national tradition, the regional tradition, the Western tradition and the local subcultural traditions of social groups.

This classification, however, does not eliminate the basic limitations of the traditions approach to the study of social change. Firstly, it does not formulate explicitly the definitive criteria of traditions that may be logically consistent, exhaustive and exclusive. For instance, the classical tradition is not a singularity but consists of many traditions. Secondly, Dube's approach too does not go beyond a nominalistic or schematic formulation of categories to understand change. Finally, this alternative is mainly helpful in analysing cultural and not structural changes in Indian society, a weakness this approach shares with those of Srinivas, Singer and others. Dube's suggestion is in fact 'theoretically' homologous to the approaches of Srinivas and Singer.

Another attempt to rationalize the classification of the substantive areas for the analysis of change in India seeks to formulate three ramifications of social realities: the elite culture and structure, the folk cultural forms and social structure and the tribal culture and society. At these three levels it is suggested that a comprehensive analysis of social change should be undertaken (see, Unnithan, Deva and Y. Singh 1965). This approach is intended to be a modification over Singer's categories which particularly overlook the tribe, social and cultural organizations in India. But from a theoretical point of view this trichotomous classification too does not offer a theoretically viable alternative. The fact that elite structure may also separately exist in the tribal segment of culture has been overlooked in this classification.

Theoretically, however, most conceptual formulations discussed so far are inadequate to explain social change. If we define social change not merely as new cultural adaptations or positional changes in the status of groups and categories but as structural changes or changes in the principles of social stratification as such, we would find that all the above conceptual formulations on social change tend to be partial. The dependent (where change takes place) and independent (why change takes place) variables used through these concepts do not reach the point of critical mimima to be considered adequate for theoretical generalization. The dependent variables are in most cases culturological, they deal with changes in ideologies, outlooks, traditions and their social organization rather than in the social system or structure as such. Even when the conceptual framework is more sensitizing, as for example, the Sanskritization-Westernization scheme of Srinivas, it focuses upon a limited segment of the social reality. The treatment of the structural processes of social change is by and large neglected.

STRUCTURAL APPROACHES

Although the dominant concern in most analyses of social change in India has been culturological, the structural aspects have not been altogether neglected. A structural focus in the study of change not only implies a variation in the dependent variables through which changes are being identified but also establishing relationship with independent causal variables. This enhances the power of the social change theory. First, the units of observation in a structural study are not ideas, sentiments, and values but the order of roles and statuses which form the basis of social relationships and are schematized into groups or categories. A major principle which governs the form of ordering of social structure is asymmetry of power in relation to command over resources or values. Structural changes may primarily be located by identifying the emerging principles that lay down new rules about this asymmetry and consequent differentiation and transformation in the institutionalized forms of social relationships and their ordering in society. For instance, the abolition of zamindari and intermediary rights in land was intended to alter the pre-existing modes of power asymmetry in Indian society; the extent to which this asymmetry has been removed may be an instance of structural change in the social system, a transition from the feudal-patrimonial to egalitarian liberal social order. The principles through which this transformation is measured are abstractions over the raw social data or the actual social ethnographic portraits of social life. These abstractions forming a set of logically interrelated hypotheses constitute the explanatory systems of the process of social change. The structural approach thus seeks to explain and not merely describe social change.

As Bailey (1959) writes, in structural analysis we ought not to confine ourselves to the raw material provided by the 'principles that people themselves give'; our only task is not to make sense of the 'flagrant contradictions in popular thought' by abstracting out consistent elements which a culturological study attempts. A valid sociological understanding can be achieved, given certain problems, by making abstractions immediately from behaviour or from other non-verbal information, and by using our own concepts and evading the ideas of the people (pp. 88-101). The words written in response to Louis Dumont's treatment of Indian sociology and social change (to which we shall refer later) throw light, not only on the distinction between the structural and the culturological approaches, but also bear out the relevance of role analysis in the structural study of social change.

Consequently, the second major characteristic of the structural study of social change is the observation of the magni-tude and incidence of role differentiation in the social structure resulting from social pressures such as increase in population, diversification and growth of industries, rise of new cities or urban centres and rise in the economic and technological bases of society, which necessitate the creation of more complex organization and new role and status types. In this process the fused structures performing multiple roles, such as the traditional family (which was not only a unit for biological reproduction but also earning of livelihood, recreation as well as education of children, etc.), become differentiated as other specialized groups come into being to take care of many of the functions of its traditional structures. Theoretical formulations about how these

processes come to fruition are many. Some studies suggest
that the breakthrough is achieved when the traditional fusion
of the family system with the economic system breaks down
through new technological impacts that revolutionize the
mode of production (see Smelser, 1959 and 1968; Hagen
1962; Levy 1949; etc.).

In most Indian studies of social change a systematic
structural differentiation model has not been used, but it is
implicit in their analytical framework. We shall briefly analyse
some of them below:

Structural Differentiation of Social Mobility

Social change studies focusing upon the processes of
structural differentiation have covered many areas. Family
organization, caste and community structure, factory system,
leadership and elite categories have been analysed for their
changing role implications to the social system as a whole.
These studies are conducted sometimes independently and
sometimes as a part of the study of social mobility of
occupations, groups or categories. We have treated both these
analytical approaches together in our reporting of the
conceptual trends of such social change studies. Mobility
studies have mainly drawn their data from the studies on
caste, class and occupation; leadership and elite structure are
also covered. The structural differentiation framework is
found, however, in studies on family, community (specially
through study of factional groupings and regroupings), political parties and industrial and factory social structures. There
is also a third group of studies which uses the framework of
tradition-modernity in analysing attitudes and values pertaining to social structures, roles and status constellations.

As we said earlier, the studies focusing upon structural
differentiation have not used a systematic theoretical model.
There is no direct concern to formulate general statements or
a logical sequence of this process (as, for instance, we find in
Smelser's study of the industrial revolution; see Smelser
1968: 79-80) in most such studies. But a continuum or ideal
type classification of states of social phenomena in the process
of change is generally implicit in the treatment of data. We
may find a good example of this in the study of five factories

in Poona by Lambert (1963). Formulating his conceptual scheme he writes:

Throughout this literature, however, a relatively simple polarity occurs ... a set of ideal types whose component parts appear again and again in discussion about changes from peasant to industrialized societies. For our purpose, we will select five changes which are presumed to accompany that process of social change called modernization: status is superseded by contract as the predominant basis of interpersonal economic relations; primary group organized production processes are supplanted by a more complex division of labour, finer job specifications, and the interdependence of separate economic roles; ascribed status gives way to achieved status as the legitimizer of social gradation; status immobility surrenders to rapid vertical and horizontal mobility; and belief in the durability, inevitability and propriety of one's status is replaced by aspirations for improving one's lot.... It is assumed that the introduction of the factory system has certain institutional imperatives that follow from this form of work organization, imperatives which are instrumental in moving a society from one end of the polarity to another, from a static, acquired-status ridden, tradition-bound, primary group oriented, particularistic, fatalistic society into one that is rapidly changing, achieved-status-dominated, progressive secondary-group-oriented, universalistic and aspirin. (pp. 16-17)

Substantively, however, Lambert's findings do not confirm many assumptions with which he started. A more important one was that in the process of modernization traditional structures must give way to new forms. The traditional structures like caste and family, he finds, have undergone only adaptive changes under the impact of the factory system. The differentiating structures such as labour force, unions, and other industrial work groups maintain many particularistic and ascriptive ties and yet participate as effectively in the industrial role structure. Many other studies in the industrial sociology of India also confirm this finding (see Berna, 1960; Hazlehurst 1966).

This is further confirmed by most studies on the changing family structure. The tendency towards conceptual dichotomization, however, has also persisted in this field. Earlier, a stereotyped view prevailed that under the impact of industrialization and urbanization· the structure of joint family would change and be transformed into the nuclear or 'natural family' (Mukherjee and Singh 1961: 37). This was because the Western societies where industrialization was far advanced had a very high incidence of nuclear families. Simplistically, the same model was extended to explain the Indian phenomenon. The European evidence of structural changes in family due to industrialization was then mistakenly built into a thesis of general social disorganization of joint families in less industrialized countries following industrialization.

Many other studies of social changes in family structure have, however, corrected this error of perspective. The focus in change studies has shifted now towards analysing the adaptive capacity in joint or semi-joint family structures in India in relation to the forces of industrialization and modernization. Long-term genealogical studies of family structure have brought out the evidence that joint families pass through circular stages from jointness to nuclear family structure and again to family jointness; also the very concept of jointness has been found to consist of a series of levels or degrees rather than forming a clear-cut dichotomy (see I.P. Desai 1964; Kapadia 1958; Cohn 1962; Nicholas 1961; Orenstein 1961; Madan 1962a and b; Gould 1968; etc.). It is said that:

we cannot speak meaningfully of structural change in the Indian family until we first establish some basis for differentiating such processes from the merely normal arrangements through time which the Indian family, like the human family everywhere, undergoes as a result of the vicissitudes of demography, economy, mobility, etc. One consequence of these *normal arrangements* will be the inevitable emergence of a certain quantum of nuclear families whose existence will in no sense demonstrate that the presence of nuclear families is automatic evidence of disintegrating extended families. (Gould 1968: 414)

Milton Singer (1968) gives three reasons why sociologists made a departure from the dichotomous view on changes in the family structure (that joint family would necessarily be transformed into nuclear in the process of increased industrialization):

(a) the documentation by social anthropologists of the variety of family systems in different parts of the world; (b) the discovery by social historians that the nuclear family may have been prevalent as a cultural norm in Europe and the United States even before industrialization; and (c) the finding by sociologists and social anthropologists that many families in American and European cities maintain widespread kin ties. (p. 423)

The nuclear or conjugal family that comes into being following modernization of economy and technology is of a multilineal type (Levy 1966: 74), and many studies of kinship structure and family in the Western countries have demonstrated the persistence of widespread kinship ties despite industrialization (Levy and Fallers 1959; Firth, 1964; etc.).

The pattern of change observed in the Indian family structure among the business classes in Madras tends to show, according to Singer, elements of compartmentalization, that is, separation in spheres of conduct norms (home becomes sphere of religion and traditional values, office that of business), vicarious ritualization, a symbolic if not real observance of the traditional familial ritual and other sacred obligations, separation of ownership and control, household management of industry and finally also a cycle of authority whereby the older generation on the one hand reconciles itself to the entrepreneurial authority of the younger generation if the latter is more creative and specialized and on the other also maintains its leadership quality by having loyal support from the younger generation (Singer 1968: 438-43). According to Singer, all these are adaptive processes which among the business class families not only reinforce industrial entrepreneurship but also tend to perpetuate many aspects of the traditional family structure. The question, however, is the extent to which such changes in the Indian family do really offer evidence of structural change, and how far these contribute to a theory of social change.

Very few studies of family in India have analysed structural changes from a theoretical perspective, especially if one compares them with Radcliffe Brown's distinction between social physiology and structural change or Murdock's formulation of the set of sequences from which structural changes in the family take place (Murdock 1949). Singer says that 'we may charcterize the recent discussion among social anthropologists and sociologists of the Indian family as moving from morphology to social physiology but not quite yet arrived at structural changes' (Singer 1968: 426-7). The evidence of empirical studies bearing upon social structure of the Indian family does suggest that changes are more adaptive than structural. But the question of adaptive change is complex. It does not preclude extensions, additions and elimination of traditional family roles and its system of authority that may have structural consequences. The seeds of structural changes are embedded in the adaptive pattern of family transformation. Hence the contention that there are no structural changes in the family seems to be overstated. The argument does, however, belie the validity of formulating neat dichotomies in conceptual formulations for the study of change.

Factional segmentation in the structure of caste, community and political parties is yet another phenomenon of change related to the process of differentiation. This process relates to the distribution of relative power, a phenomenon germane to the theory of social structure. Nadel (1957) wrote that 'social structure coincides with power and authority structure' (p. 154). The emergence of factions in the village communities is also treated as a structural prerequisite (Murdock 1949). As a social change process, however, factional subdivision articulates the tensions arising out of the vertical and horizontal cleavages in social stratification especially under the impact of the measures of social and economic reforms. How this process really begins, functions and affects the structural form of community life has been studied by many sociologists and social anthropologists (see Bailey 1963; Barth 1960; McCormack 1959; Mayer 1965; Nicholas 1963, 1965 and 1968; Orenstein, 1965; Y. Singh 1971). Srinivas (1955 and 1959) has analysed this process in a Mysore village. He used the term 'dominant caste' to interpret the new mode of power relationship that emerges when new forces of social change begin to operate in the social system of the village. In a comparative analysis of factional segmentation and its relationship with structural forces of changes as revealed by studies in nineteen villages of South Asia, Ralph Nicholas is able to formulate some structural propositions about the causes and consequences of formation of factions in the rural social system. He also integrates his theory of factional segmentation with the concept of dominant caste. He concludes:

(1) There are two factors found repeatedly in Indian villages, which are conducive to the development of vertical political cleavages: (a) considerable dispersal of agricultural lands among cultivating

families as is found, ideally, under ryotwari and tenure, and (b) a dominant caste group that is a majority of a village population. A combination of these two factors is ordinarily associated with political conflict between factions. (2) A second set of factors often closely associated with one another, also frequently leads to vertical political cleavages; these are joint, or *mahalvari*, land tenure, by a dominant caste group organized on segmentary lineage principles. Each of the vertically divided political groups in this case is generally composed of a partrilineal segment of the dominant caste group, often localized in a 'quarter' of a village, and its servants and dependents among the subordinate caste. (3) Political conflict between stratified groups, horizontally divided from one another, is the least frequent form in contemporary South Asian villages. Such conflict is more often associated with concentration of agricultural lands in the hands of one or a few individuals as is found, ideally, under zamindari land tenure, and/or dominance of a village by a minority caste.

In most villages there is combination of horizontal and vertical forms of political cleavages at work at the same time. The combination of cleavages is an expression of two facts: (a) In addition to the frequently recurring structural features which permit vertical cleavages, even a small local caste group can have a significant political influence, promoting horizontal cleavage. (b) There are economic class differences, not directly dependent upon caste, which also favour the development of horizontal cleavages. Furthermore, the variables considered under the three propositions listed above are not always interdependent, so that, for example, dispersed landholdings and relatively small 'dominant' caste may be associated in one village, while concentrated landholding and a large dominant caste may be found in another. (Nicholas 1968: 279-80)

For Nicholas an essential element in factional division is not merely competition for access to resources and power but also a set of structural conditions under which competition or even conflict for power becomes or appears to be a credible instrument for the realization of the goal. These structural conditions might differ between arenas of factional politics but their general properties remain the same. At the political party level factional segmentation broadly conforms with the above analysis (see Brass 1965; Kothari 1970; Weiner and Kothari 1965). Most studies report mobilization of caste group or community for realization of economic or other social objectives through political participation. Often a caste group or community is internally divided into factions or sub-interest groups for similar reasons. It is a complex process. In the mobilization of such interests the leadership has to play a new role, more so when the scope of competing interests gets enlarged. This throws up new types of leadership. Clear differentiation (as different from systematic changes) in the leadership structure in India has been found in many studies (see Park and Tinker 1959; A.R. Desai 1959). Differentiatibn operates through the emergence of new (formal) leadership and adaptive changes in the traditional leadership institutions. Studies of leadership trends suggest that whereas new cadres have come from traditionally weaker sections of society, the dominant social groups continue to provide the bulk of leadership at various levels.

A similar trend operates at the elite level. During the past few decades and specially after independence a significant diversification has taken place in the recruitment of the elite cadres; especially in politics the predominance of the urban elite has weakened (see Rosen 1966) as more and more rural elite are coming forward to replace them. Another significant structural trend is that of segmentation within the elite structure. Before independence, the Indian elite whether in the field of administration, business, army or politics were recruited from the same class or status groups. So the relative difference in their cultural background and social origin was minimal. This has widened much since ndependence, specially between the political elite and the rest of the elite subgroups. This difference has been noted by social scientists (see Beteille 1969; Broomfield 1968; Bottomore 1967; Rosenthal 1970; Y. Singh 1971) although there is a divergence of opinion about whether this cultural lag in the internal composition of the elite at various levels would be dysfunctional to modernization. Bottomore (1967) holds that despite cultural and social differences between the political and non-political elite in India their integrated role in the modernization of Indian society should not be adversely affected. Others accept this conclusion with qualifications.

The important point for analysis of social change in the studies of elite structure is the extent to which we get evidence of the process of structural differentiation at this level, and the extent to which changes here suggest emergence of adaptive processes rather than transformation of the social structure. D.B. Rosenthal after studying the political elite in Agra and Poona concludes that:

the diminution of some aspects of traditional group authority over the individual does not imply the total disintegration of such groups as meaningful units for social or political action. In India as in the United States, ascriptive ties are likely to maintain their salience for some members of the society so long as democratic structures persist. Thus collectivities such as jatis ('castes' or 'sub-castes' depending on the particular context), continue to function in a transmuted form to the extent that they are able to adapt their traditional function in a society to the 'System rules' of the new order—an order which they have participated in moulding to their own political needs. At the same time, the hold of traditional primordial groups and of the status system with which they were associated have appeared to loosen under the pressure of general social and economic change; the political and social relevance of the group depends increasingly upon voluntary identifications rather than on legally or ritually enforced distinctions. (Rosenthal 1970: 223)

This suggests that adaptive changes far surpass the extent of structural changes in the elite substructure. This process of change too conforms to the overall pattern of social change in India.

Social Mobility and Social Change

Social mobility is directly linked with the system of social stratification. It is, like change in family, community structure and leadership, a process that directly reflects the direction which the structural changes in society may be taking. The goals of Indian nationhood being the establishment of a democratic and socialist society, changes in the system of social stratification assume added significance. There are a few studies in India which throw light on this aspect of social change, besides offering important contextual insights for the study of social change. Although we shall concern ourselves mainly with the conceptual formulations of social change, a discussion of some substantive issues will be unavoidable.

The tradition-modernity dichotomy in the studies of social mobility has often led to a confusion of perspective. It led to the contention that mobility was absent in the social system of traditional India, which was said to have a closed system of social stratification. This misconception was based upon classical literature and its ideology which overemphasize the element of continuity. Also, for the Western scholars, the most striking feature in the Indian system has been the contrast it offered to their own society. Moreover, the historical literature on social mobility not being well-developed sociologists have been handicapped in making objective generalizations. Above all has probably been the ideological bias, a moral sense of superiority felt by most Western scholars over the Indian society and culture which were considered to have fallen under their colonial rule because of their own limitations (see Barber 1968: 27).

Srinivas (1968) corrects this perspective saying that, 'while traditional, that is pre-British, Indian society, was stationary in character, it did not preclude the mobility, upward as well as downward, of individual castes in the local hierarchy' (p. 169). Much evidence has been adduced in this direction recently by both historians and sociologists (see Barber 1968: 18-35: Stein 1968: 78-94; Cohn 1962; Habib 1963; Panikkar 1955; Shah 1964; Damle 1968; etc.). Burton Stein distinguishes between familial mobility, which he says was most common in medieval India, and corporate mobility (of entire castes or *jatis*) which followed later in history. Older aristocratic families used to decay and new aristocracies emerged by conquest or by amassing wealth. Panikkar states that most Kshatriya royal houses after the time of Mahapadma Nand were established by non-Kshatriya castes. Many tribals also ascended to the position of royalty in India by establishing claim to Kshatriyahood by conquest and accumulation of power (see Orans 1959; Sinha 1957). Both Stein and Irfan Habib have stated that during the medieval period vast tracts of land were available for settlement, and enterprising families could move from one region to another and settle down as rajas or feudal lords and establish peasant settlements. Mobility of this kind was caused by 'outside' forces like military invasion or war which led to the establishment of new rulerships. These rulers encouraged promotion of their supporters to higher positions of office or patronage (this was done both by the Mughals and the British in India). Mobility was also possible through accidental factors, such as a good harvest or famine, which respectively contributed to upward or downward mobility of families. Among the internal structural factors were fluctuations in population, accumulation of property and technological changes leading to emergence of new occupational groups (see Barber 1968).

Traditionally, another form of social mobility was available to members of Indian society—mobility through renunciation or by becoming *sanyasins*. In the traditional scheme of the *ashramas* the stage of renunciation was institutionalized. It was meant mainly for the twice-born castes. In practice, however, members of the lower castes also became sadhus or *sanyasins* from time to time, often to escape the deprivations of their own place in the social hierarchy. Some sociologists, who consider that the Indian tradition did not allow for the concept of the individual, find in the idea of renunciation its sociological equivalent (see Dumont 1970). Silverberg writes: 'For individuals in India there have always been means of escaping the stratification system, e.g. as sanyasis or family ascetics.' But he rightly criticizes the inference that this process accounted for a significant degree of social mobility. According to him 'if such individual escaperoutes have functioned as a pressure valve, as some suggest, their significance might be principally that of facilitating the perpetuation of an otherwise rigid system of stratification in which there was little mobility' (Silverberg 1968: 128).

Social mobility as a process has become more active in recent times. It has resulted from sets of endogenous and exogenous factors that have loosened the summation of status principles which the traditional caste stratification represented. The congruence of ritual status, economic status and power status as in the traditional caste stratification is withering away under the impact of social legislation, education, democratization, industrialization and urbanization. These processes have created many alternative resources for supplementing one's social status and have broken the exclusiveness of the traditional principles of social status determination as a consequence of increased social mobility. Many studies in India which have analysed this process have shown the divergent functioning of caste, power and economic factors in the determination of social status. Mobility thus causes status incongruence or inconsistency (see Bailey 1957, 1960, 1963; Leach 1960; Beteille 1965; Barber 1968; etc.). This growth of autonomy or divergence among the determinants of traditional system of caste hierarchy has also led to much speculation about the transformation of the caste system into class system of social stratification (see Davis 1957; Bose 1968; Desai 1966; Berreman 1967; etc.). The terms 'caste' and 'class' are used as conceptual dichotomies for the analysis of change.

Caste is getting more rationally organized into caste associations and federations and assuming to itself the functions of rational corporate groups. In this sprocess both fusion and fission are taking place in the structure of caste organization in different parts of the country (see. Hardgrave 1968; Kothari 1970; Rudolph and Rudolph 1969; Gould 1968). Srinivas (1968) confirms the new role of castes in India by concluding that the contemporary process in the structure of castes is that of fusion in contrast to the past trends which were in the direction of continued fission.

An essential analytical element in studying these processes of change relates to the formulation of referents or units at the level of which mobility in the system of stratification may be analysed. One might also distinguish between one unit and another for their sociological relevance. For instance, Stein (1968) holds that in traditional India social mobility used to operate more often at the level of family whereas in contemporary India it has assumed a corporate unit character. Here a distinction has been made on the basis of group context in mobility. Many other distinctions, however, may be necessary to make for an objective study of the social mobility pattern.

Marriott (1968), reviewing a number of studies on social mobility, finds relevant distinctions at three levels in the ranking system related to the Indian mobility pattern. These are based on distinctions between: (1) rural from metropolitan types of ranking systems, (2) individuals or groups from corporate units in ranking, and (3) a series of successively wider zones of reference for the units in any local system, the several zones being characterized by distinctive values. The zones according to him are the village, the linguistic region and the whole civilization.

A question may now be posed: how far do the studies of mobility and social differentiation contribute to the growth of relevant conceptual schemes or systems for the analysis of social change in India? And in what form do these conceptual frames offer a possibility of theoretical integration for adequacy of social change explanation?

One broad conclusion that emerges from most analyses of structural differentiation and social mobility in India is that the processes of change defy being comprehended through neatly formulated continua or conceptual dichotomies. Whether it is the family, polity, caste, or occupational mobility, there is one constant factor observed in their process towards change, that of structural adaptation. The failure of conceptual continua and dichotomies in comprehending social change reflects the need for formulating a *dialectical* rather than *dichotomous* approach for the study of change. It also warrants that change may be analysed through native conceptual categories rather than borrowed conceptual models.

We find some realization of this theoretical need in contemporary sociological analyses. Rajni Kothari (1970) refers to it saying:

The prevailing dichotomy between tradition and modernity has created a curious cognitive hiatus—in ideological thinking as well as in much of social science theorizing—between society on the one hand and polity on the other. The former is conceived as if by definition, as 'traditional', the latter as 'modern' and 'developmental'. In reality, however, this is a false approach to the phenomenon of modernization. (p. 3)

In the same vein Rudolph and Rudolph write:

the difficulties that can arise from the use of ideal-typical concepts in empirical investigation have often been recited. They can screen out perceptions of the particular and the exceptional that contradict dominant trends and motifs. Such theoretical screening is especially inimical to the analysis of social change because it eliminates from consideration latent, deviant, and minority alternatives. With some alteration in historical circumstances, such alternatives may become the source of new or transformed identities, structures, and norms. Social change and new realities it creates arise not only from the impact of objective, exogenous, or revolutionary forces on established systems but also from alternative potentialities within such systems. Marxist theory brilliantly stresses this insight when it emphasizes the creative possibilities of historical contradictions. Ideal-typical or heuristic analysis of modernity and tradition in particular historical and national settings are likely to miss these creative possibilities in so far as they assume that the characterological, structural, and ideological components of each are absent in the other and thereby place modernity and tradition in a dichotomous rather than dialectical relationship. (Rudolph and Rudolph 1969: 7-8)

In the analysis of 'social change, the concept of dialectical 'levels' should introduce a dynamic-historical element. This approach is adapted to the explanation of social change in its historical individuality as well as cumulative propensity. Continuum models, on the other hand, are less viable as explanatory systems; itself their significance as diachronic models is doubtful. Most continuum models take a consensual view of society and place undue emphasis on the process of acculturative diffusion. Elements of conflict and intergroup contradictions of material and existential interests—in other words, structural dilemmas of change—are not taken into consideration (Y. Singh 1970: 269-70). Evidently these conceptual formulations cannot do without a sound historical perspective.

We have noted earlierhow studies in structural differentiation of family, caste and community have been theoretically misdirected because the Western-derived continuum type concepts were used to analyse social change. What matters most in formulating conceptual categories for the study of changes is that native 'initial conditions' or historicity of social processes must not be overlooked, and the researcher should try to observe the dialectical relationship between the system interactions and social change. How uniquely the historicity of the Indian social reality has impinged upon the nature of social change has been objectively analysed by a number of sociologists (see Eisenstadt 1970 and 1965; Beteille 1969; Y. Singh 1970; Bendix 1964; Iswaran 1970) recently in India and abroad.

Most of these studies bring out that social change processes, even though structurally similar—being generated by universal forces such as population growth, diversification of occupational structures, industrialization and growth of technology and science—assume historically different shapes and propositions in each society due to its pre-existing systems of social institutions and ideologies. An important historical element in traditional Indian social structure was that of inter-substructural autonomy, such as the autonomy between polity and stratification, stratification and culture, and culture and polity, etc. (see Eisenstadt 1970; Y. Singh

1970). This structural autonomy between social subsystems helped in the acceptance of many social and cultural innovations at one level of the system without affecting the other systems. The nature of this process was segmental. Changes of great significance could thus take place without evoking resistance from other social segments (see Karve 1961). The contemporary process of social change, however, is basically different from the traditional form (up to the early phase of the British rule in India). Most changes have now ceased to be segmental; they have become organic. This is because the structural autonomy of the social subsystems is slowly breaking down with the erosion of traditional structural insularity. This takes place following various institutional changes in society which affect all other systems and activate most of its segments for participation in a wider national scene. The mechanisms for such mobilization are economic or existential, the urge for equality, mobility and economic security. As noted earlier, these urges in social segments do continue to operate through the traditional social media of caste, kinship groups and factions, perhaps because these are the natural structural entities through which the social systems could be mobilized. No wonder that mobili-zations for equality, mobility and security also inadvertently reinforce the caste, class and communal identities. But the quality of the consciousness in these identities is not the same as existed in traditional society with its autonomy of sub-systems. Now all social segments tend to be activated because of the constraint towards organic social growth. This growth is symbolized by the emergence of Indian nationhood. The caste associations, factions, fissions and fusions and structural entities manifest the diverse ramifications of this process.

DIALECTICAL-HISTORICAL APPROACH*

The use of the dialectical-historical model for the study of social change has not been as common in India as the other approaches discussed above. Probably the explanation lies in

---

*We have not used the simple term 'Marxist approach' mainly for two reasons: (1) the Marxist contribution consists of not one but a series of models of which social change theory is one part; and (2) some authors whose studies we may review may not be followers of the orthodox Marxist

the colonial linkages of the Indian social sciences and social scientists, which were historically conditioned. Nevertheless, some important studies of social change have been made using a dialectical-historical framework.

Paradoxically, Marx's own writings on India, though underlining the need for revolutionary changes, focus more prominently upon the static and the primeval character of Indian society. Of course, he constantly changed his opinion as new facts came to his knowledge. Daniel Thorner (1968) notes this paradox in Marx's views about social change in India. He writes:

There is an element of paradox in Marx's emphasis (in his writings up through *Capital*) on the primacy of India as the point of departure of European development. On the one had Marx insists that the ancient Indian form of common property as embodied in joint ownership and joint cultivation of land by the entire village is the original form from which all others evolved. On the other hand he holds that these characteristic features of the ancient Indian village plus the tight union of agriculture and handicrafts provide the basis for the static, unchanging nature of Asiatic society. The self-same ancient Indian community to which all the subsequent European societies owe their origin provides, by its very nature, the explanation of why these later forms had failed to emerge in Asia. (p. 66)

Marx tried to resolve this paradox in his later writings. In his early writings around 1853 Marx was deeply impressed by the static, ahistorical and primeval nature of Indian society. Partly, his views were also influenced by British despatches of that period which painted Indian villages in a highly exaggerated static colour (see Dumont, 1966: 67-89). Also Hegel's view probably influenced him when the former wrote: 'India, like China, is a phenomenon antique as well as modern; one which has remained stationary and fixed...' (quoted in Thorner 1966). Marx also thought that Indian

---

view. For instance, D.P. Mukerji, one of India's most eloquent sociologists, who applied many elements of the Marxist theory in his interpretations and analyses of social change preferred to call himself a 'Marxologist' as distinguished from orthodox Marxist. Moreover, in a number of new analyses of social processes where the dialectical-historical approach has been applied significant departures have been made from the tenets of classical Marxism. Finally, most theoreticians of Marxism now treat it as a growing or self-correcting system of scientific theory than a specific or everlasting dogma.

society consisted of a series of autonomous communal bodies, and there was no concept of individuality in this society.

Although he characterized the British rule in India as 'swinish', he did feel that it would bring new enlightenment and technological revolution in the society.

In 1857-8, we find Marx further elaborating upon this thesis. He distinguishes between the primary and secondary forms of societies. Among the primary forms he included community settlements where both working and property owning members lived. Community authority here merged into a hierarchical series with the despot at the top. The secondary form emerges due to war, serfdom and slavery. In the primary form there is generalized slavery and in the secondary form institutionalized. The first type Marx compared with the Asiatic and Slavonic societal forms and the second with the German and Roman ones. Differentiating the primeval social form into these two types Marx propounded his evolutionary and dialectical thesis of social change the mechanisms of which were the four types of modes of production. These, he said, 'in broad outline we can designate the Asiatic, the ancient, the feudal, and the modern bourgeoisie modes of production as so many epochs in the process of economic formation of society' (Marx 1904).

Important for us to note in this sequential arrangement of modes of production is that for Marx India still presents an archaic social form. This view, however, changed when Marx came into contact with the Russian scholars during 1870-80 (see Thorner 1966). Kovalevsky' work, *Communal Land-holding: the Causes, Character and Outcome of its Disintegration* (1879) impressed him deeply and as a consequence Marx prepared a note on the sequences of structural differentiation and change in the Indian social system which completely alters his earlier views on this theme. He noted five stages in social differentiation: (1) tribal community with undivided property in land and agriculture in common; (2) disintegration of tribal community and its transformation into family communities with loosening of common property; (3) land shares being fixed by inheritance rights or the degree of kinship thus creating inequality. Tribal wars further increase this inequality; (4) passing of inequality-based kinship to that of possession as expressed by actual cultivation; (5) system of periodic redistribution of communal land; and its gradual shrinking, first this redistribution included house land, arable land and pasture but gradually the sphere of communal property shrank and was limited only to the community woodland and waste. Such progressive differentiation of property in ancient and medieval India also logically inheres for Marx the unfolding of the rest of the historical forces of change and its march to subsequent stages of social transformation.

At this stage Marx also radically revised his evaluation of the role of British colonialism for Indian society.

In 1850 Marx had welcomed the British introduction of 'private property' in India, as a necessary precondition for Indian development. In 1881 he condemns the suppression of communal ownership of land as an act of English vandalism. It had brought not an advance, but a setback to the native peoples. (Thorner 1966)

The Marxist sociology of change that grew in India was not based on the earlier pessimistic picture of the staticness of the Indian society which Marx was tempted to draw because of partiality of social and historical accounts that were available to him. Studies conducted with the help of the Marxist model have covered many areas of Indian social life, e.g. caste and social polity, stages of social evolution corresponding to modes of production (Dange 1949), nationalism (Desai 1966), historical developments (Kosambi 1956), social stratification and social institutions (Pavlov 1964; Mukerji 1958). We shall refer to some of these studies, particularly those which have a theoretical orientation.

In D.P. Mukerji's writings we witness an illuminating example of historical-dialectical perspective for the analysis of social change. Mukerji's main focus is on the emergence of a new class structure, especially that of the middle class under the impact of British colonial rule; the structural forces behind this class differentiation which led to the growth of the nationalist awakening in India were, according to Mukerji, governed by the Indian tradition. Tradition in India, according to him, offers the resilient yet adaptive social and cultural force which must be kept in the framework of sociological analysis, even if the change generating capacity of economic forces (modes of production and its relationships) and institutions is accepted. He writes:

The value of Indian traditions lies in the ability of their conserving forces to put a brake on hasty passage. Adjustment is the end-product to the dialectical connection between the two. Meanwhile is tension. And tension is not merely interesting as a subject of research. It leads upto a higher stage, it is desirable. That higher stage is where personality is integrated through a planned and a socially directed, collective endeavour for historically understood end, which means, as the author understands it, a socialist order. Tension will not cease there. It is not the peace of the grave. Only alienation from nature, man and work will stop the arduous course of such high and strenuous endeavour. (Mukerji 1958: 76)

We find Mukerji's views conforming closest to the dialectical-historical approach to social change. According to him social change is a process of movements through conflicts and contradictions; the contradiction in the Indian case is between its tradition, culture and value systems which are holistic or devoid of the atomistic principle and the ramifications of class interests that have successively emerged through the changing material conditions and modes of production. For understanding this the social scientists will have to devise their own conceptual categories and tools. The process of change would contribute to the growth of a socialist society, but not one that would be a historical repetition of others. Mukerji believed in Dilthey as much as in Marx. For him history matters, but it does not repeat itself.

We have another exposition of the dialectical-historical approach in A.R. Desai's writings. He analyses the processes of change in India in the context of the history of nationalism. This according to him emerged due to the special historical conditions, created in India by British colonialism. Nationalism, according to Desai, did not exist in pre-British India. British rule led to India's economic breakdown and simultaneously also to the rise of nationalistic consciousness. The urge for political freedom grew as the urge for economic freedom became acute. This urge among the Indian business classes was manifested by their demand for protection of native industry. The educated classes wanted Indianization of the services and the agriculturists reduction in land taxes. The nation as a whole wanted freedom for association, expression and political articulation. Thus, the catalytic factors in the entire process of nationalistic movement were the new economic interests and their institutionalization through various class interests. In his analysis of change in the rural and urban societies Desai has extended his dialectical methodological frame. The changes generated by the Community Development Project, the educational, political and other developmental measures have, according to Desai, succeeded or failed to the extent that the pre-existing material conditions, especially the class contradictions were mature or not (see Desai 1959).

Ramakrishna Mukherjee has used the dialectical-historical concepts for the study of change. In his study of *The Rise and Fall of the East India Company* (1958) one may find use of Marxist categories to interpret the forces that led to British colonial expansion in India. Mukherjee refutes the theory popular with some historians that British rule was beneficial for Indian society rather than pre-colonial regimes. He undertakes a thorough examination of the material forces which led to the emergence of the merchant bourgeoisie in Britain, their expansion in India which was itself undergoing a process of internal class disintegration (the disintegration of feudalism and aristocratic despotism), and subsequently the fall of the East India Company due to the rise of a new class of exploitors in Britain, the industrial bourgeoisie. The emergence of the latter class was conditioned by the industrial revolution and the material forces that it had released in society; ultimately these forces also rendered the merchant bourgeoisie obsolete as a class. Mukherjee writes:

... after 1813, the final limit was placed on the scope of British merchant capital in India and the path was cleared and new avenues were opened for the successful penetration of British industrial capital in the colony. Merchant capital could no more keep pace with the march of time; so it was laid aside. Its monopoly was abolished and thus it was devoid of its real vigour.

In a later work (1965) Mukherjee extends the dialectical model of social change analyses to the rural society. He attempts to analyse the village social structure in a historical setting, in terms of its dynamic class structure and the processes of inherent contradictions. He lays emphasis on the systematic and organic character of Indian society for under-standing its processes of change. He refutes the thesis that the factors generating social change could be delimited to any singie set of variables. For instance, he offers proof to falsify the view prevailing in some quarters that urbanization necessarily contributes to social change. After a painstaking analysis of facts he concludes that:

(1) there is not, yet any evidence of significant rural-urban difference with reference to the basic problems of *social* development, (2) a causal or concomitant relation between cultural changes due to urban living or urbanization and 'social' development cannot be legitimately deduced, and so (3) the concept of rural-urban dichotomy or rural-urban continuum need not be meaningful in the context of urbanization and social transformation of India at the moment. (p. 48)

While the debate on the value of the rural-urban continuum still continues (see Rao 1970), serious note needs to be taken of a point that emerges from Mukherjee's analysis of social change. It is that most studies of change are poor at the level of causal analysis. There is absence of multifactoral analysis of change. commensurate with the structural properties of the Indian social system. A paradigmatic statement of this position has been attempted by Mukherjee in some of his essays (see Mukherjee 1969, 1970). Here one may witness a subtle change in his position as he moves towards a near formal theoretical construction of change corresponding to a *probabilistic nomological approach*. This approach in essence is a meeting point between the Marxist and the positivistic nomological theories in contemporary sociology (see Gouldner 1970). Mukherjee writes:

If we look into the social history of India we find that it is characterised by an assortment of different behaviour patterns, by their accumulation, adjustment and compromise, and not always by their successive replacement. Changes are, no doubt, taking place in society, but they do not necessarily destroy the existing social system, at any rate the governing ones.... A simple *sequential model of social change,* therefore, is inadequate for these societies when the phenomenon is studied in contemporary perspective.

The model may be found ineffective in the contemporary analysis of social change in the 'developed' societies also; while, for all kinds of society, it may be appropriate for the study of social change in a historical perspective. In that case, change is *a matter of deduction* after it has taken place and new social formations have replaced the corresponding previous formations.

If, however, social change is invariably regarded as a matter of deduction and any alteration in any behaviour pattern (as the consequence of any alteration in any societal arrangement) is considered as an evidence of 'social change', then the concept loses its analytical relevance for diagnostic investigation in the contemporary perspective. It will merely substantiate the obvious fact that any society, at any given point of time, is in a state of *dynamic equilibrium* and alterations are inevitably effected in a social organism. It is necessary, therefore, to distinguish between studies of social change from the *historical or the contemporary perspective and as an explanatory or diagnostic proposition*. (R. Mukherjee 1970: 1160-1)

Mukherjee is of the view that a proper theory of social change can be formulated by testing a set of hypotheses that may be based on any type of theoretical system (he mentions Marxian and Weberian types), and then generalizations can be obtained after these hypotheses have been tested through a research design 'which is based on the concept of statistical probability and which is conducive to multivariate analysis of the quantitative and/or qualitative data, as found appropriate and available' (1970: 1163). The hypotheses may, however, be formulated in terms of a hierarchy of unit-concepts that are mutually subsuming. He suggests concepts of social action, behaviour pattern, social relationships, institutions and social groups as determinant of the mechanics of the social system in a taxonomic order. These social system units may be used for generation of hypotheses in consonance with any ideological preferences of the researchers (1970: 1163), but the 'tier' of these conceptual units should offer a uniform and relevant social framework for the analysis of change. To render these hypotheses derived from conceptual units diachronic, these may be tested with reference to place, time and object.

The element of ideological neutrality that Mukherjee introduces in his suggested method for the analysis of social change along with his continuing emphasis on discovering the broad historical principles of social change generalization brings his theory closer to the nomological rather than 'dialectical' approach. But as we said earlier, nomology of a certain variety is built into the dialectical-historical model of social change theory.

A neo-Marxist model for the analysis of social change in India and other developing societies is offered by Andre Gunder Frank (1970). He formulates a new hypothesis on the nature of social change and the poverty of new nations in Asia, Africa and Latin America. He prefers a systematic and dialectical approach to other approaches, especially Myrdal's institutional theory and Rostow's theory of universal stages of economic growth. He also rejects the cultural institutional hypotheses for the lack of development in the Asian and other underdeveloped countries, which assumed that if these countries are not developing it is due to their socio-cultural systems. He also rejects the theory of Westernization for economic and social development of the less developed nations. All this he postulates on the basis of his own causal interpretation of the nature and function of Western colonialism in the new nations.

Frank develops a systematic theory of colonial relationship between what he calls the 'metropolis' or the developed capitalist countries of the world and the 'colonial or neo-colonial' nations of Asia, Africa and Latin America. Tracing the history of this type of relationship he writes:

Throughout this history we can see three major elements. One is a colonial or new neo-colonial relationship between the metropolis and its colonies or neo-colonies in Asia, and Africa and Latin America. Second, this colonial relationship forms and transforms the whole domestic economic, political, social, cultural, even psychological structure of Asia, Africa and Latin America. And, third, this new economic and class structure creates the economic and class interests of a bourgeoisie which is tied to the metropolis as a colonialised junior partner of the metropolis. The colonial relationship or structure as well as the economic and class structure at home give this dependent bourgeoisie a natural interest in pursuing policies in the colonial countries that do not generate economic development but rather generate ever more economic, social and cultural underdevelopment. From these three conclusions it becomes apparent that it is not possible to achieve economic development in Asia, Africa and Latin America without destroying both the (neo) colonial dependence on the metropolis and the resulting internal economic and class structure. (Frank 1970: 1179)

Frank's thesis is that wherever Western colonization took place the motivation was to exploit the natural, human or mineral resources of those nations for the colonizer's own markets. The colonial nations, according to him, did not deplete the economy of the colonies as much through capital drain as by completely subjugating the production structure of these nations to their own metropolitan ends. This is exactly what the British did in India. This was done not because of any personality or cultural characteristic of the metropolitan bourgeoisie but because of the structural com- pulsiveness of their system in which they could not do any- thing else. He adds:

so it is not that the bourgeoisie in Britain was smarter or more entrepreneurial than was its counterpart in the colonies, but simply that the structure and functioning of this world-wide system, that Adam Smith had already talked about, necessarily induced interests and possibilities among the metropolitan bourgeoisie that generated very different results from the quite different economic interests that the bourgeoisie in the colonial countries had. (ibid.: 1183)

Even after independence most of these nations including India are bound by new ties of foreign investment and there is dependence of their industries on the multinational corporate system led by the United States of America. The national industrial bourgeoisie of India, Latin America and Africa to this extent, according to Frank, are transformed into 'dependent-colonial or neo-colonial bourgeoisie'.

Frank concludes his arguments with a definite suggestion for developing a new social science theory. The theory

must be historical, structural and dialectic. Most important of all, it must embrace the really determinant social system—world capitalism—whose historical development, complex structure and dialectical conflict relations have created both the wealth of the new and the poverty of the vast majority of the world's people. (ibid.: 1184)

What is of importance in Frank's propositions relates to his emphasis on two aspects of social science theorization: First, that social change processes in India (he mainly focuses upon economic development) should be seen as part of a larger systematic network of relationships. The minimal unit for this would be the arena of world capitalism. Secondly, the approach should be structural and dialectical; in other words, processes of development should be seen as a resultant of the contradictions of economic interest between rich and poor nations or colonial and colonized nations and between different classes in an international setting.

COGNITIVE HISTORICAL APPROACH

Another systematic approach to the study of social change is that of Louis Dumont. The theory of social change is not his primary concern as he is interested in analysing the cognitive or ideational structural nature of the Indian social system. But in this context he also makes comparisons of the Indian social system with that of the West. It is here that some relevant social change propositions emerge. Dumont conceives of the Indian social system not as a system of social relationships but as systems of ideational and value configurations or patterns. Social change study, according to him, should be focused on analysing the 'reaction of Indian minds to the revelation of Western culture' (Dumont 1964: 66). This reaction would lie in the cognitive transformation from the principle of hierarchy to equality. Essentially, change consists in the adaptive or transformative processes within the traditional Indian cognitive system. Thus cultural change is the precursor of individuality and of social change (see Dumont 1964, 1965).

Dumont's model seeks mainly to compare the diversities of the ideo-structures in different traditions or civilizations. Distinguishing between synchronic and diachronic studies, Dumont is critical of studies of social morphology at two points of time which are taken for proper studies of change. At best such studies can be called double-synchronic. For a diachronic study 'time' would have to be built into the paradigm of the study, and the comparison in historical contexts may be essential.

Despite the emphasis on history and ideology, Dumont's main interest, as mentioned above, does not lie in the analysis of social change. He contends that 'study of social change answers a strong public demand, and for a part corresponds more to the subjective needs of the student as a member of modern society, than to properly sociological issues' (Dumont 1964: 12). For structural studies of the type he is interested in, time may be devoid of meaning. Hence the basic locus for the analysis of change, according to Dumont, is comparison and abstraction in which emphasis on change is implicit rather than explicitly formulated as a theoretical system.

INSTITUTIONAL APPROACH

Myrdal has studied social change in a systematic framework based on institutional models. In his three-volume *Asian Drama: An Inquiry into the Poverty of Nations,* which incorporates the labour of a team of workers, a comparative evaluation of the nature and possibility of economic growth and development is undertaken. Myrdal says:

> our approach is broadly 'institutional', and we plead for greatly intensified research efforts along these lines. We should remember that to be really fruitful this new approach cannot be restricted to the insertion of qualifications and reservations meant to take into account the things left out by the conventional economic analysis along Western lines. As the very theories and concepts utilised in the analysis guide it away from those 'non-economic' factors, what is needed is a different framework of theories and concepts that is more realistic for those societies. (Myrdal 1968: 27)

As part of this institutional approach Myrdal redevelops his theory of circular or cumulative causation which he had earlier used in his study of the race problem in the USA (Myrdal 1944). For interpreting this process he formulates a set of *conditions* which operate in the South Asian nations, particularly India. These conditions in sets of combination form *social systems.* The conditions are: output and incomes, conditions of production, levels of living, attitude towards life and work, institutions and policies. The first three are primarily economic conditions, the fourth and fifth are non-economic, and the sixth is a mixed condition.

Myrdal postulates an upward growth in the system if any one of these conditions moves in a *desirable* direction and sets similar momentum in the other conditions; a downward movement takes place if one or a set of these conditions begins to operate in an undesirable direction. Value premises are thus built into the processes of development in the social systems. These value premises also relate to each of the conditions which may be having either an independent or instrumental value significance. Independent values constitute an end by themselves; instrumental those which are desirable as a means. Conditions may vary on account of their being valued for independent on instrumental reasons. Each nation, however, formulates its own value priorities for development on the basis of which values are associated with conditions.

For India, Myrdal is of the view that the chosen value premises were incorporated in a 'modernization ideal' whose ingredients were 'rationality, development, and planning for development, rise of productivity, rise of levels of living, social and economic equalization, improved institutions and attitudes and national consolidation' (see Myrdal 1968: 39-69). The other South Asian nations too have accepted the same modernization ideal but in each of them the process operates differently due to differences in the 'initial conditions' or their history and culture.

Regarding India, Myrdal's prognosis is qualified, mainly because of the lack of emphasis on institutional changes. The odds against successful development commensurate with the modernization ideal are population growth, international tangles (against China and Pakistan), fragmented domestic politics, problem of 'emotional integration' of the nation and finally India's more wilful emphasis on a sort of moral conversion rather than on institutional changes. He writes: 'In India an intellectual and moral conversion tends to be advanced as panacea for all kinds of ills. But to change attitudes without changing social institutions is a rather hopeless quest. This remains the basic dilemma and challenge of Indian politics' (Myrdal 1968: 303).

The roots of Myrdal's theory on social economic development go back to Max Weber and Max Scheler. It is a viewpoint that has been repeatedly refuted by many researches done on the process of Indian development. Myrdal's entire approach suffers from a curious ambivalence. At the same time that he articulates the need for the South Asian countries to evaluate their processes of social change and its various facets with the help of their own conceptual categories and in the light of their own initial conditions, he blames the same 'initial conditions' for their poor development. There is much merit in his emphasis on institutional and systematic reasoning, but the greatest weakness of his evaluation is that he is unable to look at the South Asian social reality except from the Western socio-cultural perspective.

Yet another formulation of social change concept is that by

Narmadeshwara Prasad (1970). He postulates a model of social change based on a social, psychological and cultural framework. He categorizes the factors of social change into external or objective and internal or subjective levels. Objective levels are: material and behavioural. The subjective level consists of values, motives, needs, perception and belief. Each can influence the process of change in terms of its quality, quantity, and function. Changes may begin at either level but their success depends upon the mode of fit between the two levels of categories and their interaction.

One major limitation in Prasad's formulation is that he does not seem to have applied the model that he formulates to actual assessment of the processes of social change. Consequently, his approach tends to become eclectic and is devoid of analytical coherence, especially when he discusses the substantive issues of social change.

Social change study from an institutional and systematic conceptual frame has also been made by M.C. Shekhar. He formulates a

theoretical model with fourfold constituent structures. These structures are related to the value-orientation, social structure, polity and economy. With the help of the theoretical model the interaction of these structures has been analysed. The process of social change is referred to here as institutional change which is directed by the Government (Shekhar 1968: 339).

Shekhar adopts the Parsonian framework for his formulation of the concepts of structure and system; he also uses Parsons' concept of pattern variables. But he holds that Parsonian formulations of systems may not be adequate for analysing the Indian situation of social change, and suggests introduction of the concept of 'super-system' which includes the entire nation (p. 342) as an analytical category. He reviews the role of charismatic movements in the emergence of new structures in addition to other processes of social change. He concludes: 'Due to certain looseness of the structure and multiplicity of action-orientation, the Hindu social structure is amenable to change on certain lines. It has the capacity to absorb the changes on a telltale level without undergoing structural differentiation' (p. 347).

AN OVERVIEW

The formulation of a theory of social change is one of the most involved issues in contemporary sociology. Even those sociologists who profess nomological and systematic theoretical concerns are sceptical about an easy solution to the theoretical tangles related to social change. The conceptual formulations about social change in India thus present heterogeneous and heteronomous theoretical standards. This is not unique. In most other countries too (with the probable exception of the socialist countries) the theoretical issues about social change remain unresolved. The problems of social change theory not specific to Indian sociology but to sociology in general. It becomes an Indian problem to the extent that our sociologists develop a keen awareness about the historicity of our socio-cultural conditions in formulating conceptual schemes or theories of social change. There is evidence to suggest that such awareness has existed among scoiologists and social scientists in our country. The need is to push it further into action.

There are many 'conceptual schemes' about social change but no 'theories'. Among the conceptual schemes we may notice an emerging polarization between two types: those that postulate continuum models and others that are oriented to the dialectical model for the study of social change. Whether it is a study of caste, social stratification, social mobility, family and kinship or modernization one comes across similar divergence in the conceptual formulation of change. There are social scientists who think that the two approaches are reconcilable (see, Steward 1955; Berghe 1958). But considering the theoretical issues involved it is difficult to assume that the basic presuppositions in the two approaches could be easily reconciled. The continuum approach takes an ideological position where the process of change is assumed to be accretive, integrative and is seen moving from one position of equilibrium to another until the other end of the continuum has been reached. Conflict is characterized as mere deviation. It postulates two distinctive ideal-typical forms of social phenomena which set the limit to the transition from one form to another. Such ideal-typical formulations are often levoid of systematic concerns. Social change is analysed in narrow contextual framework without studying how other components of the social subsystems impinge upon the system as a whole. The tradition-modernity dichotomy is a result of such reasoning.

The dialectical model of social change focuses upon the latent and manifest areas of social conflict, their aggregate articulation and relationship with specific structures in the social system as whole. It postulates change as a process of transformation through reconciliation (resolution) of a series of conflicts. Ideologically, conflict is treated as the basic process of social change. The nominalism of the continuum models is avoided and social phenomena are seen to be endowed with an imminent quality of self-transformation. The systemic concern is logically related in this model to the element of historicity. It treats social history as an essential component for the analysis of social change. The sources of change in this model are assumed to be both endogenous and exogenous, but these operate only through the immanent internal social forces. Thus, it avoids the pitfall of misplaced polarity in the formulation of the stages of social change as implied in the continuum models.

The theoretical and conceptual schemes of social change in India have so far remained limited to formulation of ideal types and continua. Consequently, most analyses of change are deficient in theoretical power and explanatory sophistication. There is urgent need, therefore, to study social change from a systemic and dialectical-historical frame of reference so that a truly diachronic study may be possible. Continuum models have essentially a synchronic character and their maximum theoretical relevance for the study of change is limited to comparison or at best the taxonomy of social phenomena. A truly viable theory of change needs to go beyond comparison to the level of formulating general propositions based on time-bound logical set of variations in social phenomena. This is possible only when the concept of time—both 'reversible' (mechanical) and 'irreversible' (evolutionary), to use Levi-Strauss's phrase—is built into the theory of social change. The dialectical-historical approach partially answers this need, since depending upon the extent of methodological sophistication it offers scope for incorporating time into the theoretical analysis of change.

RESEARCH GAPS AND PRIORITY AREAS

The gaps in social change studies in India are both methodological and theoretical. The difficulty in making suggestions to cover the gap arises from the fact that the value-frames or preferences of individual social scientists may differ and avoid being forged into some predictable schedule. The preferences for theoretical approaches and their relevance to substantive areas of interest might also differ between social scientists.

This does not, however, negate the need for formulating priorities for social research. Each academic discipline, on the basis of the problems that it encounters, formulates research priorities. The process operates through a consensus among the scientists and the rest of the national elite. Within a discipline, however, consensus on priorities also emerges on collective realization of theoretical and methodological lags. These factors together provide the *raison d'etre* for formulating social change research priorities.

Let us first take the salient theoretical and methodological gaps that seem to emerge from the above review of literature on social change. We find that, so far, the most popular model for the study of social change has been the continuum model; the dialectical and historical methods have been neglected by and large: with the exception of some studies mentioned in this report, rich historical data are not used for sociological analysis of change. Another gap in most studies of social change is the absence of the systematic frame. Specific social isolates like caste, family, occupation, etc., have been studied in a local or at most in a regional setting, but analysis of the interaction among these isolates in the light of changes in the social system as a whole has not been attempted. How changes in one aspect of the social system impinge upon changes in others does not find meaningful coverage in most Indian studies of social change. Obviously, in future studies, care may have to be taken to introduce a methodological and theoretical perspective commensurate with these requirements.

The priorities of social change studies may next be defined in the context of the substantive areas or issues that need urgent professional attention. Here, the most reliable criterion could be the consensus of the social scientists. The majority of sociologists seem to prefer studies on urbanization, industrialization and the impact of education, technology and economic factors, etc., on social change in India. The next in order of priority is the preference for the analysis of political processes that lead to social change. One could not say, however, that a professional consensus in Indian Sociology exists for laying down the priorities for studies on social change.

To obtain some idea of what the sociologists and social anthropologists in the country feel about the priority areas in social change we sought the opinion of sixty scholars. Thirty of them responded. The areas suggested by them for study of change on a priority basis are given in the table which follows:

Area	No. of times mentioned
Industrialization and Urbanization	15
Study of Factors (educational, economic, cultural, technological, etc.) in Social Change	15
Social Mobility	6
Political Process and Change	9
Family Structure and Change	6
Law and Social Change	5
Study of Movements	4
Agrarian Conflict and Change	4
Tribes and Castes: Their Relationships of Conflicts and Integration	4
Emergence of Formal Organizations and Social Change	4
Youth and Social Change	4
Social Stratification and Inequality	4

The maximum score that a problem area has obtained is 15, which is an indication of the lack of strong consensus on selection of the study themes. The figures give us only an impression of relative choice of the areas of research, and not a consensus. This will have to be obtained through other means.

4

Country-Town Nexus:
Social Transformation in
Contemporary Indian Society

The process of social transformation today generates many serious contradictions. The emerging pattern of country-town relationship constitutes one such aspect. It is, therefore, timely that this problemis analysed from perspectives that are both theoretical and substantive. One is particularly impressed by theoretical sensitivity in Indian sociology to recognize the relevance of this problem for understanding the processes of social change. There have existed two kinds of theoretical and methodological impulses in Indian sociology and social anthropology: one is indigenous and the other Western-inspired. The theoretical and methodological advances that Indian sociologists and social anthropologists have made so far have been a result of interaction between these two historical conditions. Broadly, one could hypothesize that the centrality of focus on macro-sociology, or on studying linkages among structures and institutions that constitute the reality of Indian society, its culture and civilization as a holistic entity has fluctuated depending upon either of the two frames of reference in theory and methodology. The focus upon nexus or on binding relationship between country-town, or other levels of interrelationships was wanting in the works of British administrators-cum-sociologists or social anthropologists. We find that during the early 1920s

many British and European writings on Indian society and culture used conceptual categories which were Eurocentric in cognitive and value terms; some of these also tended to distort history and imputed meanings to Indian reality in the abstract.... Concepts such as 'caste' 'tribe', 'village', 'community', 'family and kinship' were defined as segmentary entities, often analogous to their socio-historical equivalents in European society. The emphasis was on showing how each of these social entities affirmed the principles of segmentation of autonomy rather than being parts of an organic whole. The element of discreteness was over-emphasized and the linkages, both social and cultural, which bound these entities into an organic system of social structure and civilization were neglected. (Y. Singh 1986)

In contradistinction to this, we witness a macro-sociological perspective in the study of Indian social structure and culture in the writings of G.S. Ghurye, Radha Kamal Mukherjee, D.P. Mukerji, N.K. Bose and other founders of sociology. The basic categories of sociology that we find in the analytical scheme of their writings are those of region, civilization, cultural area and rural-urban interactions. Individual forms of social structure are no doubt the focus of observation but from the perspective of social and cultural linkages.

This theoretical and methodological tradition of indigenous sociology was weakened during the decade of the 1950s, when the era of single-village studies began in India largely under the inspiration of American social anthropology. The village studies generated useful data on the functioning of individual social institutions; they even focused upon the inter-institutional relationships or linkages but within the boundary of the village as an autonomous system. Erroneously, the autonomy of tribal or rural settlements found in other societies was taken in such studies to be equally applicable to Indian society, without recognizing its civilizational base and institutional linkages developed over several millennia. This period also saw the growth of urban studies based largely on the methodology of social surveys. These generated some useful empirical statistical data but without much sensitivity to organic linkages among social systems within the city or between country-city inter-relationships. The studies both of the village and towns during the decade of the 1950s shared a feature in common: both were grounded in the theoretical presuppositions of functional-structural sociology and both were devoid of macro-sociological orientation.

By the middle 1960s new developments in the global shape of sociology and social anthropology took place which contributed to disenchantment both with functional-structural theory and the tendency to treat micro-structures such as village, town, tribe, caste, class, etc., as autonomous entities. Several historical factors were responsible for this development in sociology. First, the tensions of social and cultural alienation that swept most countries of Europe and North-America during the mid 1960s culminating in a series of strifes of youth, students and working classes rendered the basic postulates of functionalism, such as consensus, integration, voluntarism and autonomy of structures or cultural systems obsolescent. Not consensus but conflict or contradictions both at the levels of social interaction and ideology seemed to govern the processes of society. Hence, Marxism and conflict theory in different modes of their manifestation began to emerge as dominant theoretical traditions in sociology and social sciences. This tendency also coincided with new traditions of research in history, political science, economics and social psychology where analysis of social institutions and structures was conducted in holistic and comparative historical settings. The contributions of Indian historians, economists and political scientists during this period offered sociologists rich material for their more meaningful treatment of social institutions and their linkages from a macro-sociological point of view.

Sociological and social anthropological research from the middle 1960s increasingly demonstrated the concern for explorations of nexuses among institutions and subsystems of society. Even the writings of European and American sociologists on India can be observed to have shown this orientation. Louis Dumont, Milton Singer, Bernard Cohn, among many others, recognized the need for a historical, comparative and systemic approach for understanding of specific institutions such as caste and kinship, town and country and economy and culture in India. These studies reinforced the work of Indian sociologists and social anthropologists who had already been using macro-sociological and comparative theoretical perspective in their studies. In most of these studies, not only was the assumption of autonomy of the village or city as a social unit challenged but doubts were also expressed on the validity of these as sociological categories. Momentum was thus created for adopting a macro-sociological and comparative historical perspective in the studies of social structures and cultural elements of the Indian social system. In the early 1970s, the Indian Institute for Advanced Study, Simla organized a national seminar of sociologists and social anthropologists, with the theme 'The Macrosociology of India' and its proceedings were appropriately titled 'Beyond the Village: Sociological Explorations'. This seminar made concrete methodological contributions as each member participant had to report from an empirical study of his own. Though it did not directly deal with country-town nexus, it made contributions to some aspects of methodology and theory of macro-sociology. Later, more systematic studies followed using the conceptual frameworks of macro-sociology. These demonstrated the linkages between micro- and macro-structures and Little and Great Traditions of Indian society. Similarly, many studies on folk-urban cultural continuum were conducted from a cross-regional and comparative theoretical point of view. These clearly demonstrated the deeper cultural interdependence and linkages between country and town and between one linguistic region and another. Moreover, the folk culture perspective on the study of Indian society also enriched the theoretical and methodological dimensions of Indian sociology.

The direction of these theoretical and methodological developments in macro-sociology of India constitutes one area of relevance for the study of country-town nexus. Another important dimension of this relationship belongs to the emerging processes of social transformation that Indian society is going through. The concrete direction of this change gives urgency to undertaking a thorough and systematic analysis of this problem. Historically, country-town relationship had a pattern of interdependence in India that was governed by tradition and economy. Traditional Indian cities throughout history had a near symbiotic relationship with the countryside. Their economic relationship was complementary, the occupational specializations and division of labour offered opportunities for continuities as well as change and mobility. Folk-elite cultural tradition and its role structures established meaningful nexuses between country, town and capital cities. Commerce, political administration, ritual and religious practices and art and aesthetics constituted nodal principles around which this country-town relationship was maintained. Commensurate with the level of technology and modes of production and distribution a near equilibrium between country-town relationships had traditionally evolved.

Colonialism disrupted this pattern of interdependent relationship. The fiscal, industrial and political policies pursued by the British regime of India contributed to the decline of both country and town through increasing deindustrialization. Large-scale pauperization of artisans and peasantry took place as a result of massive disruption of traditional Indian economy and its social base. The pattern of country-town relationship that emerged during the colonial and post-colonial periods of Indian history, despite the release of new forces of modernization, could not restore the balance in country-town relationship. The pre-eminent place that village-oriented ideology was accorded in Gandhiji's social and economic agenda for reconstruction of Indian society was probably in recognition of this historical distortion in country-town relationship. Ironically, the process of modernization in India took a highly segmentary form as a result of colonial distortion. The pace of modernization grew mainly from urban metropolitan centres, and had a narrow base in class and caste structure in specific areas of the economy. It was only after independence that an attempt was made to broad-base the process of development. Successive plans endeavoured to implement a development policy which aimed at a balanced growth of social strata but its ideological framework made it difficult to achieve quick results.

The policy of industrialization encouraged a form of urbanization which only contributed to the enlargement of social contradictions. It led to massive migration of rural poor to cities without their integration in the urban-industrial economy. The result is the growth of slums and street corner population in cities which is rapidly outnumbering the rest of the urban population. Industrialization has not been without its successes, but its social base remains narrow, grooved in a class character which increases the hiatus between country and town and rich and poor sections of society. While the rapid pace of industrialization has given strength to the Indian economy, the unintended consequences of urbanizaion and industrialization have led to social alienation and encourage exploitation. The technological and economic growth has introduced new forces of social stratification and social mobility. A substantial urban middle class has emerged in cities; new entrepreneurial and professional groups have rapidly enlarged their numbers, but the social character of these classes does not promote a balanced relationship between country and town. The ideological orientation of these middle classes alienates them from establishing fruitful linkages with the countryside. Rather, the institutional set-up in the rise of these classes is such that it promotes and strengthens the dependency of village upon the city. We witness the paradox of industrial and professional growth without social justice.

Industrialization, technological advancement and processes of reform in the rural agrarian structures have contributed to development in agriculture in various parts of the country, popularly known as the 'green revolution'. The leaders of the green revolution in most cases come from the traditional peasant castes, the former tenants of village landlords or feudal nobility. The emergence of this group in villages has had a dual consequence for country-town relationships. On the one hand, the dependence of modern agriculture on urban industrial inputs, banks, market and pricing mechanisms, etc., has enlarged the nexus between city and country, but on the other, this relationship itself has precipitated a crisis in country-town relationship in general. The spurt in political, cultural and physical levels of communication and contact between the two social entities has intensified the self-consciousness and identity of the new rural middle classes. Their relative economic strength has given them access to some opportunities in education, political power and political participation. It has strengthened their voice in the developmental processes of rural society. This awareness is often compounded by the solidary character of these middle classes in villages on caste and kinship lines. Most of them come from similar caste background and enjoy numerical advantages in the rural population. They dominate over village panchayats and their block and district level representations. They constitute a powerful political resource on which the professional politicians must depend for electoral successes in state legislatures, and often in parliamentary elections. In some states, such as Maharashtra, Gujarat, Punjab and Andhra Pradesh, where such agricultural development is linked also with the production of cash crops, their political and economic clout has been further enlarged.

There are many levels of relationship that these rural middle classes tend to establish within and outside the village scene. Within the village their relationship with the weaker sections and landless labourers ranges from outright indifference to pugnacity. This increasingly alienates the working classes who resort to urbanward migration, not in all cases due to attraction for city life, but to escape from rural exploitation. The rural middle classes have ideological affinity at one level with the urban middle classes as both these groups share conservative and narrow utilitarian ethos. But for peasant middle classes, anchorage in this ideology also generates at another level a feeling of intense conflict with the urban middle classes, entrepreneurs and professional groups. There is historical basis for this contradiction. The process of development in agriculture has slowed down due to structural and technological stagnation. Even the so-called rich peasants have over the past few years confronted the prospect of downward mobility in terms of social and economic status due to unfavourable price policy, stagnation in productivity of agriculture, fragmentation of landholding due to population pressure in the family and non-availability of other avenues of employment for their youth. This post-green revolution underdevelopment in agriculture further reinforces the alienation of middle class peasantry from the urban and industrial middle classes as it constitutes a setback to their level of aspiration, having already reached a high peak during the early periods of the green revolution. The existing policies of communication and media exposure further aggravate their sense of relative deprivation. This has resulted in a series of farmers' protest movements in most parts of the country, which views country-town nexus from a highly negative ideological perspective. This perspective is based on facts about highly uneven levels of rural-urban development and inequitous availability of resources, fiscal and market opportunities.

The ideological stance of the middle class peasant

movements is to draw support from the starkness of the unequal development between country and town in India. Indeed it is held that cities and industries have grown in India at the cost of villages and agriculture. This is supported by developmental statistics as well. Of the total energy generated in the country the share of villages is only slightly above 9 per cent where more than 70 per cent of the population resides. It is said,

that most villagers being illiterate are voiceless. Taking advantage of these circumstances, the new (urban-based) rulers of India have succeeded in imposing a system, in which the rural masses have been reduced to the status of 'captive-producers and captive consumers'. They are left with no choice but to sell their produce at the cheapest, and buy their requirements at the highest prices. Besides exploitation through price twists, the rural masses have also been denied their due share in plan expenditure, supplies of power and credit, and facilities for proper education and medicare. Agriculture has been contributing from one half to one third to the national income, yet combined allocation for all the rural programes from III to VI plan has never exceeded 23% of the total public sector plan expenditure. Allocation for education was brought down from 7.7% of the total to 2.7%, and for medical services from 2.6% to 1.8% during the same period. And these reductions have been made at the cost of the rural population, because no one can see any reduction of these facilities in cities.

If one were to draw a statistical profile of the country-town differentials in levels and quality of development and allocation of developmental resources, the unequal pattern in favour of cities and discriminatory of villages can be clearly outlined. These indicators of unequal development are increasingly being converted into an ideology of rural-urban opposition, which despite being relevant, is being made use of from a class point of view. This results in farmers movements and protests, which sometimes take violent forms. These get entwined with political processes and party ideologies, as we witness.

Where does this leave us in terms of the country-town nexus? Obviously, there is need for a systemic perspective which could diagnose the nature of these problems more objectively and introduce corrections in ideological uses of indicators of development and underdevelopment. A simple correction would be to replace the categories rural and urban with sociological categories of rich and poor, privileged and under-privileged or propertied and propertyless groups or classes in analysis. One could not deny that the model of economic and social development that the country has adopted during the past decades has contributed to an elitist pattern of development, encouraged consumerism in a small section of about 10 per cent, mostly urban population. It has not created effective institutions for equitable distribution of resources to different sectors and sections of society. From another point of view, one could not be oblivious of the fact that the massive investments made in infrastructure, for example, power, irrigation, fertilizers, transport and capital goods industries, have contributed to the growth in agriculture and these benefits were made available more to rich farmers than smaller ones or landless workers. The policy of industrial development could not, therefore, be considered discriminatory in terms of country-town divide. It could, however, be treated as discriminatory from the normative perspective if we introduce the categories of rich and poor in India. It cannot be denied that the development model within the framework of a mixed economy contained built-in contradictions, but most of these contradictions were envisaged as resolvable by suitable orchestration of policies.

These policies have not worked as effectively as anticipated. Development activities in villages reinforced the better-off classes, and activated caste and kinship solidarities along new cultural and political alignments. They affected the legitimacy both of the democratic institutions and principles of social justice in society. The skewed economic development both in villages and cities led to distortion of the political and cultural ideologies. Uneven development of groups and classes both in cities and villages has hindered the effectiveness of democratic institutions in socially purposeful implementation of social and economic reform policies. It has contributed to a political culture in the country which is losing its ability to be responsive to the genuine needs of the people. Instead, it relies increasingly on political manipulation of sectional interests, generally through the dominant classes both in cities and village. The political nexus between country and town clearly articulates this hegemonic relationship.

The country-town nexus as it has emerged in the process

of social transformation in India during the past four decades tends to intensify the alienative rather than integrative forces in the Indian polity, economy, culture and social system. Segmentary identities based on social and cultural cleavages have increased their hold on the institutional apparatuses of society. Communalism, regionalism and casteism, the forces that pose the greatest challenge to the national ideology, can be seen establishing new alliances across country and town. The momentum for it is being provided by the emerging new middle classes in our society. No doubt, these classes have demonstrated their entrepreneurial and economic dynamism by selective adoption of utilitarian rationality. But they are devoid of a social ethic commensurate with national ideology, the ethic of democracy, socialism and secularism. The country-town category as a sociological phenomenon suffers from this uneven and negatively ideological process of development. The problem is deeply structural and ideological.

India is at a crucial stage of its development. It is timely, therefore, to examine the roots of our structural and cultural contradictions, distortions and errors in our development policies or strategies. From this possibly we might gain insights about how to mend our approach and move towards a balanced social and economic development in our society. First, we might examine the approach to development itself, more particularly the nature of linkages between decision-making and implementation of policies. These linkages have their weaker points in our social setting, administration and political initiatives at the grassroot levels of society. Secondly, we might also analyse how decentralization in decision-making, specially through local elected bodies both in cities and villages, could be strengthened in order to effectively implement policies of development and to suggest corrections to these policies wherever necessary. It may be well to undertake intensive study of the ideology of the emerging middle classes to diagnose the cultural crisis that we encounter through the rise of communalism, casteism, genderism and superstition. We are in a phase of development that poses major ideological challenges. The impact of our cosmopolitan nationalist ideology has weakened over the past few decades due to the ascendancy of a narrow utilitarian culture, in politics, professions, business, administration and agriculture. The new middle classes are products of this culture and serve as its carriers. They do demonstrate entrepreneurial ability and skill in manipulative operations but there is a certain short-sightedness to their cultural ethos. It tends to be non-emphatic and non-cosmopolitan in nature.

Such ideology can prove dangerous in a country where a large majority of people are poor, without shelter or availability of basic necessities of life. We need to combat this ideology through suitable responses from our education, communication and media policies. We might like to examine the contribution that education and media are making to give direction and balance to the country-town relationships in our society. A closer examination of this aspect might bring to light many anomalies. Finally, we may also examine the ecological, demographic and physical side of the problems of country-town nexus. At present we prepare master plans for cities, without considering planned development of villages. We might consider how far an integrated physical, ecological and institutional planning process could be evolved which is anchored in the perspective of a country-town nexus, in their mutual binding relationships, and not in opposition.

5

Some Emerging Issues in the Indian Sociology of Social Stratification

During the past four decades, the sociology of stratification has made rapid strides in India. No other area of concern has perhaps occupied the attention of sociologists as much as this problem. Its orientation has been shaped by our social and historical legacy, ideology of the nation-state and the quest to establish a socialist society based on the principles of equality, justice, secularism and democracy. It has also been influenced by the continuing historical interest in the study of caste, tribe and oppressed communities initiated by the British administrator-cum-social anthropologists and its continuity and change in the studies by Indian sociologists and social anthropologists. The focus upon establishing a casteless and classless society in the national movement led by Gandhiji and his emphasis upon the liberation of the 'Harijans' and socially oppressed communities in India, added momentum to the wider interest in the sociology of stratification. Most scholars during the 1930s to 1950s in these areas, however, studied caste, tribe and communities as individual subsystems, postulating a degree of social and economic autonomy for them which indeed they did not enjoy. The structure and function of systems and subsystems of caste and tribe were profiled in detail but the linkages of these systems with other institutions in the wider Indian society, such as its political economy and administration, etc., were either neglected or were treated marginally. Nevertheless, these studies made substantial contributions in establishing a scientific foundation for Indian social stratification studies later in terms of methodology, conceptual schemes and generation of data for comparison and analysis.

After India gained independence, studies in social stratification formed part of most empirical studies of villages, towns and urban centres, the areas in which most sociologists engaged themselves during the period. The relationship between caste and tribe and caste and community was explored by a few sociologists mostly in search of conceptual clarification. Among the important features of these studies were: focus upon ritual bases of caste stratification, structural-functional perspective in analysis, collection of data through fieldwork observation and a limited space-time boundary in delineation of the system of caste stratification. With few exceptions, studies of social stratification neglected the use of historical sources of data, did not go into the questions of origin or evolution and did not attempt to view the caste system in the macro-structural perspective of social transformation. Most studies tended to be diagnostic or descriptive with a microcosmic view of social reality. The emphasis was on mapping out the social terrain in India, rather than raise issues of concept, ideology or method. Class analysis as a frame of reference was either absent or negligible. Most studies at this stage of Indian sociology focused upon caste, tribe and village community from a descriptive perspective. The analytical notion of social stratification was present in these studies only as an inferential aspect of empirical observation.

By the 1960s, however, the conceptual and methodological issues became basic in studies of social stratification. An important development in this direction was the shift in emphasis from observation of empirical entities of social stratification (pre-eminent in most studies of the 1950s), to the *principles* of relationship among these entities of stratification. In the study of caste stratification, Louis Dumont's contribution would stand out. He raised the level of studies of social stratification much above the substantial plane to that of questions of theory and ideology. In his sociology, both tend to be integral parts of one another. This trend was supplemented, though from a different direction, by the increasing number of studies of social stratification using Marxist theory and method. Here the class frame of historical materialist analysis was applied. These studies, though still fewer in sociology, came largely from economists studying the agrarian social structure of India. Moreover, many systemic studies of social stratification using analytical conceptual frame were conducted. André Beteille's use of the conceptual categories of 'caste', 'class' and 'power' for the analysis of social stratification in a south Indian village illustrates the shift towards 'principles' and theory. F.G. Bailey in his theoretical essays and empirical studies of the tribe-caste-nation linkages in Orissa also exemplifies this trend. Both Beteille and Bailey have used the notions of 'open and closed' social stratification in their treatment of this process.

These developments in the social stratification studies had several general consequences for sociology in India. First, sociological studies entered a new level of maturity in respect of theory. The debates now ranged about choices among conceptual typologies *versus* continua, historical specificity *versus* comparison, structure-function *versus* conflict and dialectic *versus* ideology in the analytical propositions of social stratification. Secondly, social stratification studies now increasingly tended to be problem-oriented both conceptually and substantively. This is reflected in two directions: first, more and more studies began to focus upon problems of caste and class exploitation, economic, political and cultural domination and the relationship between poverty, social and cultural alienation and distributive justice. The studies of the Scheduled castes and tribes, of backward classes and the dominant castes or communities formed a large proportion where the analytical approach was that of social stratification. Secondly, studies of social stratification developed an independent theoretical focus instead of being marginal elements in the study of a village, township or community. In such studies several theoretical tendencies emerged, such as structuralism, structural-functionalism, systemic theory, structural historicism and Marxism. Most of these theoretical tendencies, however, have a degree of overlap or paradigm mixes. This accorded with the universal tendency in sociological theory of the time, as also with the proposition that a general theory in sociology remains problematic. It is probably with this view in mind that one talks of 'quasi' or 'a-theoretic theory' in social sciences and sociology. This indicates the ambiguous and complex position of theory in the sociology of social stratification.

The difficulties of theorizing in the domain of social strati-fication are linked with the fundamental philosophical issues that are involved. Sociologists have raised these issues in the context of the nature of equality and inequality among men.

Others have linked it with the problem of social order. The notion of social order offers a meeting point both for dealing with the problems of so-called 'natural inequality' and its social expression either in the principles of moral voluntarism or social contact. The theory of social stratification is thus organically linked with the theory of social order. The questions related to these issues have been recurrently raised in Indian sociology. The discussions on the nature of caste and class in Indian society had led sociologists to the perspective on Indian tradition, its moral order and its functional or utilitarian significance. Curiously, whenever the focus on the study of caste in India has shifted on tradition, the historical or even speculative questions of its origins and comparison with similar institutions elsewhere have also arisen, but, whenever the functionalist orientation has dominated, the question of history and origin of caste-class receded into the background. The theoretical questions related to the principles of social stratification in Indian society have vacillated in accordance with the relative role and influence of either tendency.

The emerging conceptual and theoretical concerns in studies of social stratification culminated in several new orientations during the 1970s and 1980s. Some of the more significant among these are: (1) debate on the role of ideology in the paradigms of social stratification studies, (2) revival of historical and evolutionary perspectives, (3) emergence of dialectical paradigm as a new theoretical orientation in social stratification studies, and (4) increasing concern about issues of relevance both from social and conceptual points of view. These developments have resulted from the changing theoretical and methodological orientations of sociology at the global level, and also from changes within the cognitive structure of Indian sociology. Its inner dialectic, its changing professional character and social concerns have also contributed to these developments.

IDEOLOGY AND SOCIAL STRATIFICATION

The question of ideology in studies of social stratification has emerged during this period in two main contexts: first, as a general theoretical problem of sociological method, and secondly, as a problem of social determination of concepts and themes of studies of social stratification. In the first context both structuralism and Marxism as theoretical paradigms for social stratification studies in India have incorporated the notion of ideology. It forms an organic element of theorizing on social stratification. Louis Dumont in his well-known study of caste system as 'hierarchy' assigns an important place to ideology as a component of the structuralist paradigm. The term ideology in his analysis connotes ideas and norms derived from the Hindu civilization of which the caste system is an archetypical manifestation. The dominant principle in its normative structure is that of 'hierarchy' contained in the dialectical relationship between the principles of purity and pollution in the ritual and behavioural domains of the system. The central issues in the study of social stratification, according to Louis Dumont, are thus the ideology of the caste system and its significance to the comparative study of social structure.

The notion of ideology, despite having a key role in the Marxist theory of social structure and stratification, has been unevenly emphasized in the Indian studies of social stratification. In Karl Marx's own writings, ideology is treated as an organic element in all cognitive processes. It is reflected in the mystification between 'form' and 'substance'. Marx's notions of 'fetishism of commodities', 'alienation of labour' and his distinction between 'infrastructure and super-structure' are examples of the significance of ideology in the formation of concepts and propositions in sociological studies. The task of social scientists, according to Marx, is to demystify the fallacies in the choice of sociological categories and methods and to establish their proper relationship with social praxis and relevance. Marx's own formulation refers to the dual level of ideological mooring of knowledge; first, in the mystification of sociological categories for the study of social reality, and secondly, obfuscation of social praxis due to a specific class character of the production of knowledge.

Marxist studies of Indian social stratification raise these ideological issues but not comprehensively. Most studies focus upon the class background of sociologists as being the key determinant of the place of ideology in their work. A distinction is often made between the 'bourgeoisie' and the 'Marxist' sociologists for ideological debunking of the non-

Marxist studies of social stratification without, however, seriously questioning the cognitive or theoretical framework of such studies, especially with regard to the choice, definition and operationalization of categories as Marx envisaged. In the process, pertinent gaps are often identified but the paradigm as a whole is not successfully refuted. A more creative aspect of the Marxist studies of social stratification is the 'mode of production' approach on which much empirical data have recently been generated. The manner of its operationalization, largely by the economists and historians is such that the notion of ideology plays a relatively marginal role in its formulation. The focus is more upon empirical indicators than upon the normative presuppositions behind those indicators as such, except in a more generalized form. The pre-eminent role of ideology as reflected in the Marxist studies of social stratification is to establish its class character as such. It deals with ideology only at the social level of its manifestation and leaves out of purview the deeper aspect of its existence in the cognitive structure of sociological categories.

A related development in the assessment of the role of ideology in the studies of social stratification, which in some cases bears relationship also with the Marxist tradition, is the emergence of 'counter-Brahmanical ideology' of the caste system in India. This ideology, largely reinforced by the increasing mobilization of the protest movements and the rise in the social consciousness of the educated classes among the deprived communities, tribes, Scheduled castes and backward classes, questions the validity of the ritual model of the Hindu caste system based as it is on the world-view of pollution and purity. It attempts to reinterpret several myths and legends of the Hindu and Buddhistic traditions to explain how the class and power domination of the 'twice-born' castes established the Brahmanical ideology of caste to a position of un-challenged supremacy. The competition was between two competing ideologies of social structure, one based on the Brahmanical model of caste, and the other on a casteless model of groups and communities based on occupational specialization. The latter is reflected, though in a subdued form, in the Buddhist literature and tradition. The success of Brahmanical model in the competition for power is symbolized, according to proponents of the counter-

Brahmanical ideology, in the myth of King Bali who was exiled to the nether-world for challenging the supremacy of the Brahmanical world-view as it was.

This counter-Brahmanical ideology of caste finds reinforcement through the conversion of a large number of the 'Harijans' and other Scheduled castes to Buddhism in several parts of the country. It forms an important part of the ideology of the Dalit movement and its agenda for social reform and protest. There are a few examples also in the mainstream of sociological writings where ideological interpretation of the contributions of fellow sociologists has been given on the basis of their caste origin. A perspective in sociology has grown according to which the social and class origin of sociologists is held accountable for a good deal of biases in the choice of themes, concepts, methods and generalizations on social problems. Specially while studying the problems of the exploited and weaker sections of society, several sociologists, both Indian and Western, have held that a more objective perspective would emerge if the reality is observed empathically, through the eyes of the victims themselves. This involves beyond empathy greater involvement of sociologists coming from the weaker sections themselves in such studies to correct the imbalance.

This consciousness, emerging in the 1960s, gained further impetus in the ensuing decades. The process of educational and social mobility among the weaker sections and the implementation of State policy have brought forth an articulate intelligentsia among these groups who can correct the perspective. The ideological debate relates to the significance of caste in the Indian social structure and tradition and the choice of relevant social policies to bring about social transformation in Indian society in accordance with the objectives of social justice, freedom and equality as laid down in the Constitution. As ideologies often constitute the axiomatic domain of the normative structure, it is difficult to enter into questions of their objectivity or otherwise. Nevertheless, the emergence of this counter-Brahmanical ideology of caste and social stratification itself marks a new phase of development in the conceptual and methodological perspective on studies of this problem in sociology.

EVOLUTIONARY PERSPECTIVE

Another noteworthy trend from the 1970s onwards is revival of the themes of origin or evolution of the institutions of caste, occupational groups and classes. An associated new phenomenon is the increasing use of history and historiography in the analysis of social institutions. The three factors that seem to explain this trend are: (1) the decline in functional paradigm of social stratification, which took a completely ahistorical view of institutions and structures of society, (2) the rise in the dialectical and historical materialist paraigm of social analysis with the revival of Marxism in social sciences after the mid-1960s, and (3) the greater ideologization of the sociology of social stratification through the emerging new consciousness of the mobile classes from among the weaker sections of society. All these factors have largely converged in India in the realm of social sciences in general and in sociology in particular during the 1970-80 period.

One set of studies have reopened the question of origin of caste in India by attempting to explain it in ecological and occupational differentiation of groups into hereditary entities over a period of time. Other attempts seek its genesis in the structure of domination, especially cultural domination of a set of communities over others on the basis of exploitation of wealth and power. The studies using Marxist methods, which increased substantially during the 1970s and 1980s, have brought historical depth to bear upon the studies of caste-class relationship by attempting to sketch out its evolutionary path through changing modes of production and production relationships. Very recently, a debate on the specific pattern of the caste mode of production has been postulated by some scholars. The significance of these new orientations is not that a scientific thesis on the origin of caste stratification in India has been established but they reflect the ideological tensions in the sociology of stratification, its theory and methods.

The predominance of the functional method in the studies of caste and class relations and its patterns in India during the 1950s and 1960s contributed to a rich harvest of field data, indepth observation of the structure and values of these institutions, and their interlinkages with other social, economic and political institutions. But a major limitation of these studies was their static portrayal of institutions, particularly the caste and occupational structure of rural and urban societies. The functional postulates being also founded upon a consensus ideology of normative voluntarism, the reality of social stratification was viewed in most such studies from the perspective of social stability and continuity rather than conflict and change. The notion of change of necessity brings in the idea of time, history and dialectics. These elements of sociological analysis were missing from most early studies of social stratification. Also most such studies were based mainly upon empirical observations of social stratification in the setting of a village or town; these did not make use of historical records nor did they use a comparative macro-social perspective.

The limitations of the functionalist model became increasingly obvious to sociologists in India during the 1970s and 1980s as elements of social conflict and dissension arising from social inequalities of wealth and power began to surface as the results of planned development and social transformation began to show results. The new developments in social sciences, particularly history, economics, political science, psychology and behavioural sciences reinforced this process. Historians increasingly looked at social structure and its formations in India in a broad historical time-frame; some schools in historiography, particularly the subaltern approach to history even undertook explorations of substructures and sub-cultures of society in depth ,both in terms of time and space. The influence of Marxist orientation in the formulation of conceptual schemes and methods of social analysis among economists, particularly agricultural economists threw up new insights into the process of social stratification in rural India. Their findings influenced the sociological paradigms of stratification studies. Similar trends were also visible in other social sciences. All this added up to the emergence of a historical and evolutionary framework in the studies of social stratification.

DIALECTICAL ORIENTATION

The emphasis on history and questions of origin led social stratification studies in the direction of new methodological awareness. An important development in this regard is the emergence of the dialectical orientation. This took two main operational forms: first, an emphasis on the observation of social processes of social stratification and its emergent properties rather than substance or form. Secondly, the focus shifted from the consensus ideology of social stratification to the study of social dialectics, conflict and designation. In studies using Marxist theory these became the basic parameters of observation and analysis. The focus on social processes arises from a debate on the methodology of operationalizing the notion of social stratification. Should the reality of caste or class be sought in the substantive properties of these social entities or in their processes of formation? It is argued that emphasis on substantive properties of the parameters of stratification, such as caste and class, has contributed to a static and ahistorical perspective in studies. Assuming social entities to exist in a state of 'being' and not of 'becoming' has some logical consequences for interpretation of data and uses of the notions of social transformation.

These consequences are manifest both in Marxist and non-Marxist studies. We have already mentioned the partially in comprehension of the processes of social stratification in studies using the functional frame of reference. The focus on consensual aspect, so predominant in this method, portrayed the reality of social stratification as a question of maintaining social order rather than its transformation. Many studies which have looked at the phenomenon of caste and class in villages and townships have recognized how the significance of these entities rests today on the extent to which these contribute to or hinder the processes of social mobility and restructuring of positions in terms of wealth, status and power. Over-emphasis on their 'being', as evident not only in the functionalist but also structuralist studies, results in the abstraction of social reality from its historical dialectics. In empirical sense, questions related to these issues have arisen in the analysis of caste and class in India. Traditionally, these institutions were studied either through a set of attributes (indicators) or through a set of interactional patterns related to social, economic and cultural dealings. In both these approaches emphasis has rested upon the facticity of caste-class phenomenon, its *structure* or set of relationships and their quality. In Marxist studies the structural reality of caste and class is seen through modes of production defined in terms of system-states such as 'feudalism' or 'capitalism'. Intensive studies have revealed, however, that both caste and class situations and their patterns of relationship not only converge but these also operate in transient or even interchanging forms of relationships which are not easy to dichotomize as social processes. Although caste does offer a more enduring set of relationships that constitute its social structure, it also responds to dialectics of situations under the pressure of social, economic, political and cultural forces generated in the larger society. Hence, what is of interest in the studies of caste or class in India today is not only their form as social institutions *per se*, but the nature of their dynamics, the degree of 'caste-ness' in caste or 'class-ness' in the class structure. This has been widely identified by several sociologists studying caste and class relationships and the changes in these in contemporary Indian society. The novelty of this approach has contributed to a debate in the Marxist, structuralist as well as the functionalist circles of sociology and social sciences. Among the historians, the subaltern approach to historiography has contributed to this awareness. It not only links the social processes of the macro-structures with micro-structures but also the notion of social order with social processes as such.

While these developments have led, on the one hand, to further intensification of cognitive and methodological contexts of sociological paradigms such as structuralism, ethnomethodology, ethnosociology, Marxism, functionalism, etc., there has also been an increasing theoretical convergence in the analysis and understanding of social reality in general and the process of social stratification in particular. The widening social science approach to the studies of social stratification during the 1970s and 80s goes beyond the disciplinary confines of sociology or social anthropology. The historians, economists, political scientists and psychologists are making contributions which have significant relevance for the understanding of social stratification. Also, with this interdisciplinary orientation, there are indications that theoretical convergence is taking place. The subaltern historians show increasing evidence of a synthesis between the Marxist and structuralist paradigms for the analysis of class and social movements. Most recent studies of social stratification conducted from the Marxist theoretical framework show increasing concern with notions of tradition, structure and function along with those of dialectics and transformation. The functionalist studies have shown acute concern with issues of conflict, contradiction and historical processes. The increasing interest in study of social movements and their linkages with caste and class relationships, the study of agrarian, demographic and urban structures, the processes of political and economic formation and the study of ideology behind social stratification reflects these tendencies. The over-arching orientation in these studies is to focus upon social dialectic rather than social order.

ISSUES OF RELEVANCE

Social relevance has been a criterion in studies of social stratification in India since early times. The context of the debate on relevance, however, has been changing. In the 1950s most studies were oriented to processes of social, economic, political and cultural developments under the inspiration of the national effort for planned social transformation. They focused on community development, panchayat processes, role of caste, class and elite formations in the development of rural, urban and industrial sectors of society. Some studies were mainly sociographic but most were concerned with social developments and with identifying institutions and practices which aided or inhibited such processes. Relevance was identified largely with planned development. In the 1960s, there was a major change in the ideological outlook and the debate was directed towards the epistemological and social contexts of relevance. The first direction led to debate on the cognitive and theoretical nature of Indian sociology, in which the debate on social stratification figured as a question of comparison of caste and class. As Dumont argued, the distinction between the hierarchical principle of caste organization in India from the equalitarian principle of class organization in European society evoked much interest in sociology. Similarly, the debate on the appropriateness or relevance of paradigms for the study of Indian social reality including social stratification emerged in this context. The second context of relevance was related to the contribution that social stratification studies could make in accelerating social praxis and social change in India.

The concern with social praxis and change in the study of social stratification has diversified its conceptual and operational orientations. Thus, in the process of social development, the significance of the principles of social stratification, such as caste and class inequalities, have been viewed more and in terms of conflict and contradictions. Non-critical acceptance of the policies of change has given way to critical analysis of both the processes and policies of change and development to ensure social equality and justice. This has made theoretical approaches to the study of social stratification more relevant from the perspectives of critical theory and Marxism. The quest for understanding the basic principles and processes of structure and change in social stratification of Indian society has also diversified during the 1970s and 80s. Consequently, the studies are not confined merely to the study of caste and class. The processes of modernization and restructuration taking place in Indian society have brought up many new issues of social stratification, such as the professions, elite, categories of weaker sections of society, women, children, tribes and Scheduled castes, etc., which constitute new domains of inequalities and equalities. As study of these social entities and their role in the process of social stratification in the context of modernization and development is the new direction of relevance. Sociology has yet to fully recognize the significance of these emergent social formations and structural entities influencing the principles and processes of social stratification in India. But awareness in this direction has begun. This, together with other new orientations in the study of social stratification, offers new fruitful dimensions of growth in Indian sociology.

6

Sociology of the Integration of Marginalized Groups in Indian Society

The contemporary global situation bespeaks an unprece-
dented rise in the level of self-consciousness among the ethnic
groups, minorities and other socially and culturally localized
groups, both in developed and developing societies. This
has triggered ideologies of sub-nationalism and contra-
nationalism, and posed challenges to the notion of
sovereignty. Ironically, these processes coincide with increased
levels of development in the social, political, economic and
cultural life of people. The eclipse of colonialism and
imperialism in Asia and Africa brought resurgent nationalism
to the forefront, but it has also kindled in these societies
ethnic, factional and cultural conflicts. All this puts into new
perspective the received notions of modernization, development and nation-state. The dialectic of this tension varies with
the historicity and complexity of social structure, cultural
systems, the nature of polity and the level, direction and
ideology of development to which a country shows
commitment.

The term 'integration' into a society, in these circumstances
evokes suspicion among groups where ethnic, tribal and
localized social identities are intensely subliminal or sharp.
Even otherwise, integration is a value-loaded term, as most
concepts in social sciences are. It is essentially a normative or
ideological notion. In India particularly, the ideological nature
of this concept has evoked sharp responses over centuries
from caste and tribal leaders, social reformers, religious
prophets and saints. Challenges to the ideology of caste and
its corresponding customs or rituals came from many
quarters in the past, but these assumed a new social dimension during the British rule. Colonialism gave rise to a two-

pronged movement in India: among the traditional upper caste elite, who got access to Western education and had a cultural encounter it kindled nationalistic values along with soul-searching as to the need for basic social, cultural and economic reforms. Among the depressed classes or castes such as the Shudras, Adivasis, Panchamas (Dalits) and the minority communities of the artisans and craftsmen it exemplified intensity of exploitation. Ambedkar identified 'Dalit peasants' as the most exploited group under colonialism and made this group the anchorage of his Independent Labour Party. Control over natural resources and their exploitation, fiscal and economic policies destructive of the traditional rural and urban economy, and the systematic policy of the British to extract surpluses, the poorest and the weakest section of pauperized Indian society, such as the depressed castes, peasants, labourers and tribal groups.

This set in motion the depressed caste (Dalit) social movements, tribal movements and peasant movements on the one hand, and on the other, it contributed to resurgence in the national awakening against colonialism. The British were the targets for both these types of movements, but there was a great deal of ambiguity in their interrelationship or its definition. Nevertheless, these developments brought into focus the issue of 'integration' into the Indian society of the categories of the Dalits, the tribes, the Shudra-peasants and religious minorities, etc. Externally, these movements reacted to the alien British rule and played demand politics; internally, these reacted to one another, particularly between the national and the caste-tribe-minority movements, for settling the terms of integration. It was in course of the evolution of this relationship that the early paradigms of integration of these marginalized groups with Indian society emerged.

EARLY PARADIGMS OF INTEGRATION

The early paradigms of integration of the Dalits and Shudra-peasants—who later came to be known as the Scheduled Castes and Backward Classes—into Indian society emerged with the rise of their protest and reform movements. The main centres of these movements were Nagpur-Vidarbha region of Maharashtra, coastal Krishna-Godavari region of Andhra (Madras Presidency), Mysore and Hyderabad. Between 1903 and 1920 these regions saw the beginning of the debate on integration. The movement did have a relationship with the economic condition of the depressed or marginalized groups. It grew in regions where the initial economic condition of these groups was relatively better, such as among the Mahars, Holeyas and Dheds in Maharashtra (Bombay Presidency) 43.50 per cent of whom were cultivators in 1921, but less so among the Mang and Madiga amongst whom only 6.33 per cent were cultivators and 66.79 per cent were field labourers. There were variations in other regions too. The data from the 1921 Census show that

while the Dalits tended to be agricultural labourers, there were significant qualifications to this with regional variations. The Holeyas (and even more the Madigas) in Mysore state, and the Mahars and Mang-Madigas in Bombay Presidency and the Central Provinces-Berar were economically in a somewhat better position in the sense that a respectable proportion of them were 'cultivators'. Mahars in Bombay Presidency even came close to competing with Kunbis in this respect. (see Omvedt 1994: 75-8)

The lack of similar advantages in the initial economic condition perhaps explains why in other regions, such as northern and central India, the growth in the Dalit movements had to wait for the emergence of new processes of development.

The perspective on integration began to emerge in course of the rise of these movements. Its frame of reference, however, remained the Brahmanical caste-Hindu society. Kisan Faguji Bansode (1870-1946), Vithoba Ravji Moonpandit (1860-1924) and Ganesh Akkaji Gavai (1888-1974) were the early leaders of these movements. Bansode started educational reforms in 1903, and edited several papers. Moonpandit concentrated on internal Mahar reforms through the Mahar Sudhark Mandal. Gavai together with Kalicharan Nanda-gawali (1886-1962), a wealthy *malguzar,* founded the first girls' school. Bansode and Gavai, though extremely critical of the caste-Hindu Brahmanism and its rejection of the Dalits and Shudras, gravitated towards Tilak's ideology of nationalism (pro-Hindu orientation); others moved closer to Ambedkar's movements and organizations for Dalit autonomy. Crystallization of this process is reflected in the 1913 Mahar Conference, the 1920 Akhil Bharatiya Bahishkrit Parishad, and in the 1930 Depressed Classes Conference. The Mahar Conference of 1913 with Moonpandit as leader was sponsored by the Mahar elite. It focused upon internal reforms in Mahar society. Gavai and Bansode, who organized the Depressed Class Association in 1915, joined Vitthal Ramji Shinde—a nationalist Maratha leader—and associated with him in the activities of the Prarthana Samaj, a Hindu reform movement. Despite Hindu nationalist orientation or affiliation either with the Congress or the Hindu Mahasabha, these leaders, particularly Bansode voiced militant non-Aryan themes in their perception of the Dalit-Shudra segment of the caste society. Brahmanism was identified with Aryan domination over non-Aryan Dalits. However, one finds some ambiguity in the articulation of this ideology; the dichotomy between the Aryan-non-Aryan theme of separation and exploitation subsists along with pulls towards integrative and reformist Hindu nationalism.

A much sharper and systematic formulation of the autonomy of the Dalit-Shudra segment of the Hindu caste society can be found in the writings of Jotiba Phule (1826-90). According to him, 'Shudras and Ati-Shudras', the original inhabitants of India, were dominated by the Brahman-Aryans who imposed upon them caste-based Hinduism with its ritualistic and exploitative economic-cultural systems. Phule's was an early enunciation of the unity between the Dalits and the backward castes (classes) to forge an alliance both against the Brahmanic system of caste exploitation and the exploitative colonial State. The Shudras in Phule's scheme included the Kunbis and Malis (he himself belonged to the Mali caste) and the Ati-Shudras comprised the depressed castes such as the Kolis, Mahars and Mangs. He wanted unity of the Shudra-Ati-Shudras to fight Brahmanism and colonialism through the acquisition of knowledge. Not ritualism but education was his means to bring about a cultural revolution. He postulated a new religion and prescribed marriage rituals without Brahman priests. He called it Sarvajanik Satya Dharma. Obviously, on the question of integration of the Dalits, Shudras and other Hindu marginalized communities Phule took a position of cultural autonomy. But he did not, unlike Ambedkar, exhort them to renounce Hinduism. He felt that a true nation in India could be created when 'all the people of the land of King Bali', which included the Ati-Shudra, Shudra and the tribes, could be truly educated, so that they could think for themselves and could establish social unity and emotional integration (see Phule 1991).

The ideology of the Dalits and the depressed classes during this period oscillated between exhortation for cultural and social autonomy and a pull towards integration with a reformed Hindu society. Over-arching most of these movements was the emphasis on the historical argument that these marginalized groups indeed were the original or Adi settlers of India upon whom later the Aryan Brahmans established their domination. The statements of Bansode and Phule in Maharashtra, Guduru Ramachandra Rao and Bhagyareddy Varma in Andhra, Murugesh Pillai in Mysore and Periyar's movement in Madras emphatically convey this understanding. Interestingly, quite a few leaders who sponsored this ideology of the origin of the marginalized groups belonged to the upper castes. For instance, Gopalaswamy Aiyar, a Brahman, led the Adi-Dravida and Adi-Karnataka organizations in Mysore. The mainstream leaders, however, belonged either to the Dalit or the backward caste groups in the region. Adi-Hindu, Adi-Dravida, Adi-Karnataka or similar such movements during 1910-20 represented, on the one hand, rare cases of patronage by the upper castes of the autonomy-seeking ideology of the Dalit-Shudra and, on the other, the manifestation of a truly autonomous ideology of cultural and social consolidation of the Dalits and Shudras in opposition to Brahmanical Hinduism. However, the nature of the alliance with the Hindu mainstream society was mostly left undefined.

AMBEDKAR AND THE NEW IDEOLOGY
OF INTEGRATION

A totally new perspective on autonomous social and cultural space for the Dalits (markedly different from the one they had in Brahmanical Hindu society) was given by Ambedkar. A rationalist, liberal and humanist in ideological leaning Ambedkar led the Dalit movement through a complex set of strategic and tactical changes in policy. A prolific writer, journalist, political leader, activist, administrator and constitutionalist, Ambedkar made an immense contribution to the theory and practice of Dalit ideology. Being a humanist, he did not se merit in 'mechanical Marxism'. He abhorred the inequalitarian and exploitative Brahmanical caste order in which he did not see any future for the Dalits. Indeed, he believed in the total abolition of the Brahmanical social order. Gore in his study of the ideology of Ambedkar between 1920 and 1930 summarizes it thus:

(1) The untouchables might belong to the same religion, but they are not a part of the same society as the caste Hindus. They constitute a separate interest group. (2) Untouchables had historically been an exploited group; untouchability was the culmination of a religious philosophy based on inequality. (3) The philosophy of Brahmanism was a philosophy of graded inequality and Hinduism was the same as Brahmanism. It was inflexible and had frustrated till then all previous efforts at reform in this basic structure. (4) The untouchables sought equality and justice, not favours. Social graces were unimportant. (5) Justice demanded not just proportional representation, but protective discrimination for the untouchables. (6) The untouchables would seek to attain legitimate equalitarian goals and special protection, in political and economic spheres, within the fold of Hinduism as far as possible, but would reject Hinduism if necessary. (Gore 1994: 120-1)

The reflection of this ideology in action could be seen from Ambedkar's social, political and economic agenda for the Dalits both during the 1920-30 period and in the second phase of its evolution between 1930 and 1956. In the second phase, political orientation takes the central place in his action plan and ideology. The establishment of the Independent Labour Party in 1936 articulates it. It also indicates how he had visualized the unity between the non-Brahmans (read the backward classes or castes) and untouchables to fight against the traditional social system. His emphasis for reform in the *watan* system was a link between peasant caste and the untouchables in Maharashtra. In 1933 when he met Gandhi, Ambedkar's attitude towards Hinduism was transparent; not reforms in the caste system through *varna* or occupational division but equal political rights for the untouchables had priority for him. He said, 'Let me say this unambiguously that we do not wish to live as "Shudra" in the four fold *varna* structure.' He did not accept Gandhi's view that *chaturvarna* (four *varnas)* could exist without untouchability or that it defined status without inequality. The supremacy of political rights for the untouchables led Ambedkar to make his policies towards the national movement, the British reforms and the strategy of alliances and protests. He demanded separate electorate for the untouchables which led Gandhi to undergo fast, and later (1932) to the Poona Pact in which Ambedkar compromised for reserved constituencies for the Dalits. Two trends during 1930-56 seem to be contending in Ambedkar's ideology on Dalit integration with Indian society: first, his emphasis on political rights guaranteed equally to all Indians irrespective of their birth or social status. This was deeply influenced by the republican revolution in Europe, particularly France and Britain; secondly, his increasing disillusionment with caste-Hinduism and Brahmanism.

The first pull led him to make a leading contribution in the framing of the Constitution of India, his participation in the government after independence and his political participation through party activism. He outlined his political approach in the manifesto of his party, the All India Scheduled Caste Federation in 1951 (the party was founded in 1945). The manifesto regarded every Indian 'as an end in himself with a right to his own development'; it would insist on the maintenance of liberty, equality and fraternity and affirmed that it would stand for the parliamentary system of government. It also said that these principles, though adopted by the Scheduled Caste Federation, would apply to all downtrodden humanity in India. The manifesto, thus included in its ambit for support both the tribal and the backward classes in addition to the Dalits. It also abjured all forms of 'isms' or dogma in its philosophy of development.

The second direction in Ambedkar's ideology (after independence) was towards disillusionment with Hindu-Brahmanism, culminating in his conversion to Buddhism and call for all Dalits to convert to Buddhism. Two factors which worked in favour of Buddhism were: appeal to rationality and value of equalitarianism. Probably, the indigenousness of the Buddhist tradition and its long root in the history of Dalit emancipation, its fight against obscurantism, etc., weighed with him in his choice, as indicated in his writings on Buddhism and Hinduism.

CONSTITUTIONAL PARADIGM OF
SOCIAL INTEGRATION

The constitutional paradigm of social integration and nation-state slowly evolved through the contending forces of the national movement. It included the National Congress, the Dalits, the minorities and the left movements. Towards the last phase of his life, Ambedkar had lost faith in the effectiveness of party politics or electoral politics in emancipating the Dalits and other marginalized groups from their social, cultural and economic bondage. He had lost faith not in the Constitution, but in its working. This sets the background for our evaluation of the contemporary paradigm of integration of the marginalized groups in India into the fold of a democratic Indian society. The Constitution recognizes 'the people of India' as the unit for operation in the civic life. It gives equal status to all communities; it annuls untouchabilities and their consequent disabilities; it ensures to all citizens basic human rights irrespective of birth, creed or colour. It has the features of a secular, democratic, welfare-oriented republican constitution. It, however, also insures protective discrimination in favour of the Scheduled castes (SC) and Scheduled tribes (ST) through ensuring access to political offices, employment in government jobs, access to educational facilities and to many other opportunities related to their social and economic development. Special protective provi-sions have been made for the religious minorities. The Constitution also envisages protective discrimination in favour of the socially and educationally backward classes (OBC) as a part of the Directive Principles of State Policy.

The Constitution embodies the dominant normative goals of the national movement, but it also articulated most of the values that Ambedkar cherished. This is how it should be. Even though the Constitution recognizes reservation for the SC and ST and provides eventually for identification of the OBC for protective discrimination, these are not visualized as a permanent feature but as a time-bound policy. In this respect, enough flexibility has been provided. The core values of the Constitution remain enshrined in the civic culture of a rational, universalistic, humanistic and liberal republicanism. Even though most normative elements of the Constitution are thus historically related to the national movement and Dalit-depressed caste-class movements, the Constitution ushers in a totally liberal-democratic paradigm of integration of the marginalized groups in society. It rejects caste and religion as the basic principles for such integration although in a limited sense it does use the categories of SC, ST, OBC and minorities for protective discrimination or access to privileges. This would be clear from the pronouncements of the various courts, even at the highest level (see Galanter 1984) where issues in this regard have been raised. In other words, it brings into operation a democratic developmental paradigm of integration of the marginalised groups in Indian society.

THE PROCESS OF INTEGRATION: SCHEDULED CASTES

To what extent has this paradigm been effective in bringing about integration? To answer, we would have to review the extent to which the processes of social mobility, economic and educational advancement and political empowerment has taken place among the marginalized groups. The impact particularly in the light of the constitutional privileges and planning for development may have to be reviewed. On these counts, the empirical studies and reports indicate a mixed picture. The marginalized groups have significant achievements to their credit in educational and cultural areas but in the economic and social mobility there is cause for concern. The nature of even this impact is dissimilar with differential quality among the SCs, STs and the OBCs. Within each category of these groups (castes, subcastes) there is uneven impact of the protective discrimination and development policies.

Take the SCs; political empowerment through reservation of constituencies, removal of social and cultural disabilities through legislation and protective discrimination for education, employment in state services, and their overall economic, educational and social development have contributed to their status mobility in significant measure. SCs have indeed gained

more and wider political influence (though one is not sure
about their power) in state- and centre-level politics. The SC
members of Parliament and assemblies coming from the
reserved constituencies and a few elected outside of it,
however (see Dushkin 1972; Galanter 1972), have more
effective power or influence only under varying alliances and
cooptations (Omvedt 1994). The massive occupational mobility
in general taking place since independence has had some
significant bearing upon the status of the SCs as well. It is
reflected in their growth in education and employment in
state and other services.

The literacy rate of SCs increased from 10.27 per cent in
1961 to 21.38 per cent in 1981; the growth rate of literacy in
their case has been higher than that of 'general India'. There
has been growth in female literacy as well but it remains
lower than the general average. Their employment in
educational institutions in India in 1987 shows that they
occupy 10.53 per cent of research associate posts, 3.16 per
cent lecturer positions but only 0.61 per cent and 1.04 per
cent posts respectively of professors and readers. Their
representation in ministerial posts (in 41 universities) for
groups A, B, C and D jobs is 3.33 per cent, 4.57 per cent,
8.51 per cent and 14.93 per cent respectively (*Report of the
Commissioner of SC/ST, 1987-88*). In the Government of India,
public sector undertakings and in public sector and nationa-
lized banks, the representation of SCs in Group A, B, C and
D level jobs is relatively much better; in C and D category
jobs it is proportionate to their population or exceeds it, for
instance in the public sector undertakings (*Report of the
Commissioner of SC/ST, 1987-88*). In the reduction of poverty
or access to property, however, the status of the SCs remains
backward. Their occupational mobility is relatively lower than
that of the other communities. This is because majority of
them (above 72 per cent) are marginal farmers; about 12 per
cent are landless and only 0.28 per cent can be categorized as
'large farmers' (see NSS Round 37, 1982). The percentage of
SCs below the poverty line was estimated at 64.0 per cent in
rural India in 1977-8 which declined to 53.1 per cent in
1983-4. In urban India, the decline during this period has
been from 54.3 per cent to 40.4 per cent (see Rao 1986). At
this rate about one third of their population should be below

the poverty line. Qualitatively, the transformation in the cultural style and consciousness of the SCs has been much more widespread and effective than meaningful structural changes in their economic and social conditions.

An elite class has now emerged in their midst whose social base and numerical strength is larger than ever before. It commands very substantial influence though it may have limited power. Hence, it is also called a 'limited elite' (see Ram 1993). The more important point, however, is the emergence of such elite and educated sections of men and women among the SCs, especially as they are incorporated in systems and institutions like schools, colleges, universities, banks, corporate industries, assemblies and Parliament, etc., which are organized on cosmopolitan principles and not those of caste or religion (despite reservations for recruitment). This puts pressure for conformity to the integrative principles of a new Indian society. This society is a product of the norms and values envisaged by the Constitution following independence.

THE BACKWARD CLASSES

Historically, the SCs and the OBCs have been partners in movements against Brahmanism and caste society. Existentially, however, the OBCs have had a much better social and economic position. A very large section among them were substantial peasants having middle or large size landholdings. Under the joint zamindari system in northern India, quite a few of them were landlords, and in southern and western India under the ryotwari land settlement they held important positions in the agrarian revenue system. Gail Omvedt writes: 'These peasant *jatis* provided most of the "state overlords", variously known as deshmukhs, zamindars, *nayak*, and these families holding power and land differentiated themselves from the common peasantry' (Omvedt 1994: 67). The common peasantry among these castes was, however, impoverished by the exploitation of the upper caste landlords. The Dalit-Shudra alliance before independence was led, as we have seen, by upper sections of the backward classes. After independence, with the abolition of landlordism, intermediary rights in land, imposition of ceiling on landholding and investment in agriculture, a very large section of this peasantry, possibly about 5-10 per cent of the 27 per cent of the OBC population estimated by the Mandal Commission, participated in the 'green revolution' in Indian agriculture. Former tenants of landlords, these castes historically have had a strong agricultural tradition.

In the Constitution, the Directive Principles exhort the State to provide reservation to the 'socially and educationally backward classes'. Many states of the Union have been implementing this policy. The first Report of the Backward Classes Commission in 1956 for reservation in the central services (chairman Kaka Kalelkar) could not arrive at definitive conclusions. In 1977 a new Commission headed by B.P. Mandal in its report (1981) made definitive recommendations for reservation of 27 per cent jobs in the central services. The debate on the reservation policy for the Backward Classes has generated divergent views primarily because of its peculiar and uneven social and economic character in the caste society of India. In most regions of India, the dominant peasant castes such as the Yadav, Kurmi, Kapu (Reddy), Kamma, Vokkaliga, Kunbi, Maratha, etc., have agitated and obtained backward class status. While a large section of marginal farmers and the poorer sections among them do deserve benefits of protective discrimination, a substantial minority among them have accumulated considerable economic and political power and have emerged as leaders in their own right.

This phenomenon has contributed to the rapid integration of the backward classes in Indian society. In the states, political power has already shifted in their favour despite their varied party affiliations. Economically, in peninsular and western India these castes are gaining control over trade, professions, and corporate industries, in addition to their control over the agricultural economy. With their dominance over political power and nascent growth in their social and economic status, the process of their integration takes a new meaning. They no longer constitute the periphery which has to be integrated with the centre, that is, Indian society. Rather due to their numerical, economic and political power they constitute the new centre of Indian society in the making. The Mandal Commission estimated the population of backward classes in India to be about 56 per cent, which is revealing in this context. As the backward classes move up as a whole in the social, economic and cultural scale of Indian society, they would increasingly determine its dialectic and dynamics instead of being governed by it.

THE SCHEDULED TRIBES

The place that the tribes occupy in Indian society has been a matter of research and speculation from the beginning of British rule in India. The views have oscillated between those who have viewed tribes as being ethno-structurally separate from the caste Hindu society and those who have emphasized the elements of continuity and linkages between the tribes and the caste system in India. The debate between Verrier Elwin and G.S. Ghurye on this theme is revelatory of this problem (see Elwin 1943; Ghurye 1943). The tribes inhabiting the border or less accessible regions of India with high degree of racial or ethnic individuality, remained outside the pale of the caste system and its hierarchy. But those inhabiting regions in contiguous contact with the caste society, established both social structural and cultural linkages. In the middle regions of the country and the peninsula, there are instances of feudal or semi-feudal linkages and reciprocities between tribe and caste (see Y. Singh 1986). Despite these linkages, the tribes always have enjoyed a distinctive life style, culture and features of social organization. And, with very few exceptions indeed, their social and economic position in Indian society has been of extreme marginalization and deprivation.

Like the SCs, tribes were enlisted for protective discrimination by the Constitution of India. The policy was subject to review continually in a ten-year time-frame as in the case of the SCs.

According to the Census of 1981, STs constituted 7.76 per cent of the total population. Out of this 93.80 per cent are in rural areas and only 6.20 per cent are in urban areas. Studies made by the Anthropological Survey of India have revealed that the tribe generally remained outside the *varna* system. Therefore, only 11.8 per cent of them recognize their place in it. Another 31.6 per cent are only aware of the *varna* system. Among those who recognize their place in it nearly 8.3 per cent claim to be Kshatriya, 7.5 per cent Shudra and 0.9 per cent Brahman (see K.S. Singh 1994: 4). There is a notion of hierarchy among the tribes based on economy, descent, ranking, status etc. Tribal women have much larger work participation than women from non-tribal groups. The Survey reports,

the tribes do not suffer from any social stigma. They have remained beyond the pale of caste society except for those who have interacted closely with peasant castes in few regions.... The impact of development processes, particularly education, has created a new stratum of entrepreneur/businessmen (256 tribes), teachers (380 tribes), administrators (156 tribes), engineers/doctors (150 tribes) and members of defence services (178 tribes). There has also been a rise in the political leadership, at the village panchayat (362 tribes), regional (185 tribes), and national level (45 tribes).

There is widespread evidence of shift from traditional to new occupation among the tribes although about 80 per cent of them are engaged in the primary sector of economy (see K.S. Singh 1992).

As among the SCs, social and political movements have had a long history among the tribes. They have continually fought for their rights and against their natural, social, economic and cultural resources being appropriated increasingly by outsiders and the State. Messianism has been a widespread strategy. Later with its intermingling with search for political autonomy it has assumed rebellious and militant forms in various regions, particularly in the north-east. Demands range from creation of separate states, e.g. Jharkhand, Bodoland, etc., to outright separation such as in Nagaland, Mizoram, etc. Constitutional flexibility and democratic processes have helped in accommodating such demands in most cases, but it has not been achieved without misery and bloodshed in extreme cases. These processes have not yet ended, but even in the most difficult phases of such movements it has been found that restoration of democratic rights and acceleration of economic and social developments increase the constructive linkages of tribes or other marginalized groups with the larger society. Education and access to modern occupations and jobs not only restore political self-assurance but also increase people's incorporation into structures and roles in the larger Indian society. Access to business, professions, administration, media, management and polity widens the world-view of tribal citizens and strengthens their linkages with Indian society. The transition from tribe to nation is full of difficulties and yet is assured of success if the strategy of development maintains its transparency, empathy and welfare commitment.

TOWARDS A PARADIGM FOR SOCIETAL INTEGRATION

The resurgent movements of tribes, Dalits and backward classes, all historical legacies of the initial conditions of social, cultural and economic development in India, provide a context to the suitable paradigm for integration of the marginalized groups in Indian society. Even though the principles of primordiality on which all these groups have sought to mobilize their movement offer effective anchorage to their ideology, these cannot serve as stable bases of their integration into the larger Indian society. Both social structurally and culturally, tribe and caste cannot provide enduring principles of such integration. There are at least more than a thousand castes which could be identified as other backward classes, and most of them are divided into subcastes. Castes do not have a sociological meaning outside a small regional boundary, either linguistically, or techno-ecologically, or in matters of kinship, marriage and ritual practices. Caste is a self-fragmenting, regional or local institution. That is why caste associations formed to enlarge the scope of caste-integration since the late 1950s have undergone the process of continual fusion and fission.

The ethnographic surveys reveal that SCs have a total of 751 communities or castes; 374 are reported as main, 71 as segments, and they are scattered over 306 territorial units. STs have a total of 635 communities, 278 reported as main and 178 as subsidiary. They have 179 territorial units. The OBCs are divided into 1,045 communities (castes), 607 of them main and 159 as subsidiary. They are spread over 280 territorial units (see K.S. Singh 1992: 208). No wonder, we have continually faced both intra-caste and intra-tribal conflicts along with inter-caste and inter-tribal ones. Moreover, in situations where castes or tribes are mobilized ideologically into a larger formation for demand politics or protest, the goals are mostly economic, political and social, usually defined in the larger societal frame of reference. Primordiality is used in such movements as an instrument of mobilization for functional convenience, but the issues at stake transcend primordiality. This is also a result of the limitations that the initial social structural conditions of Indian society impose upon such mobilization.

Integration does not imply assimilation but functional linkages and reciprocities based on relative autonomy of specific segments that constitute the system. Caste society had such a system through the *jajmani* relations in the traditional past; but it legitimized inequalities. The republic and the nation have emerged after independence as the alternative principles of integration of communities and groups in India into a plural societal framework. This is ensured by the Constitution and legislative evolution in India. Not caste or tribe but association of interest groups offers the new paradigm of societal integration.

India is a society of unique complexities. Castes, tribes and religious groups in ever varying segments and as totalities have given it a historical depth rare in character. But to assume that other societies which have today evolved a democratic republican national tradition did not experience pressures of primordiality in the nation-building process would be erroneous. The long and painful history of the European nation-building process bears testimony to this fact. The debate on this process in India, however, has suffered from two fallacies: that of historicism and of reification. The historicist fallacy leads us to evaluate nation-building experiences or its paradigm in India entirely in the context of the concrete manifestations of institutions and ideologies in other societies (largely Europe and North America) where the paradigm has been relatively successful. The fallacy of reification on the other hand misconstrues the idea of nation into a set of concrete attributes (again largely borrowed from Western society) rather than postulating the notion of nation as a process (see Y. Singh 1993). The processes of nation-building include a range of institutions, activities and ideas related to development, political mobilization, participation (parties, centralization-decentralization of power and decision-making) and economic, industrial and urban growth, etc. As the scale of these processes and their outcome increases, the utility or rather the indispensability of working through interest-group associations voluntarily organized on civic principles rather than primordial gathers momentum. The functional utility of associations based on birth or locality correspondingly declines. The evolution of this process of replacement of local-primordial paradigm of societal integration may be less or more painful depending upon the historicity of circumstances in a particular society. India cannot but move towards this paradigm of societal integration in the future years. This paradigm alone would ultimately offer maximum space for fullest development of the marginalized groups of today into equal and vigorous partners of nation-building tomorrow. It may also provide a meeting ground for the dreams of Gandhi, Ambedkar and Jawaharlal Nehru about future India.

7

Present Social Situation in India:
A Sociological Analysis

The social situation in India could be analysed in two ways: the conceptual-philosophical and attributional. The philosophical treatment of India, though of ancient origin assumed importance during its encounters with the outside world including its intellectual and cultural traditions and its designs of power. The Western contact looms large in this context. Depending upon the attributional traits of the Indian society under focus and the implicit domains of value loads in the analysis, one might observe a range of perceptions of the Indian phenomena in the Western tradition of scholarship. These include the positive overtones of the 'orientalist' school of the Western philosophy, the negative judgement of the 'evangelists' and the 'reformative' orientation of the English utilitarians, who championed the colonial cause. A common element in all these perceptions is the sense of ambiguous puzzlement—Indian as an enigma.

Cntemporary Western social sciences analysing the Indian social situation have not remained untouched by this heritage. Even in more recent writings about Indian society the focus is exclusively on normative metaphors such as 'hierarchy' or 'imagination' or 'ideas' (see Dumont 1970; Inden 1990) and less on ethnography or social attributes and their inter-linkages. The Indian reality may, therefore, appear as purely holistic in an ideational sense or purely segmentary and divisive, neither of the contradictory views recognizing the role of interaction or linkages in the functioning and evolution of the Indian social institutions.

In any treatment of the present social situation in India it may, therefore, be useful to proceed from the attributional approach and outline first the basic social profile of India and then to analyse it normatively. Happily, we have today abundant ethnographic and sociological data about India to portray its salient attributes not only in a static structural sense but also in the perspective of social change. The Anthropological Survey of India (ASI) has nearly completed a massive all-India ethnographic survey named People of India project (POI) which outlines the aspects of structure and change in Indian society. It highlights the diversity of the social and cultural institutions and the processes of their interaction.

THE PEOPLE OF INDIA

The social categories such as caste, tribe, class and minority (religious) and linguistic groups through which the Indian social reality has been analysed by social scientists have yielded rich insights into the processes of change in society. The report entitled 'People of India: An Introduction' adds new insights and also reinforces several existing social science perceptions. Its ethnography centres on the concept of 'community' as 'studied in ethnography which is marked by endogamy, occupation and perception' (K.S. Singh 1992: 23). This category has similarities with caste and tribe but is not exclusively bounded by these. It is found that 'the triangle of endogamy, hierarchy and pollution norms is breaking down.... For operational purposes the community, therefore, is considered the appropriate term which could relate to caste, tribal and other non-caste-like categories' (ibid.: 24).

There are 4,635 communities in the states and Union territories of India; religious groups are differentiated on community lines; most communities report they have migrated from other regions; 71.77 per cent of the communities are located within the boundary of state/Union territory showing 'that our states/Union territories are not only linguistic and cultural but also social categories'; there are 111 (3.97 per cent) communities that are distributed across the country. The country is divided into identifiable cultural regions marked by 'a distinct language/dialect, territorial identity and cultural variations and varying levels of economic growth'. There are 91 such cultural regions in India. Some smaller states such as Goa constitute a single cultural region. Communities are also integrated with ecology: although the majority of communities bear their name after the occupation they pursued traditionally, their occupational categories are related to ecological and territorial endowments of the area where they subsist. The nomenclature of most of these communities is derived from the occupations they pursue, and only about 3 per cent communities derive their names from their religious affiliation. The stereotype in the Western mind about India being a land of the ascetics, other-worldly people devoid of materialist orientations in life is found to be a myth. The findings of the 'People of India' survey reveal:

Alcoholic beverages are consumed by men in the communities studied as follows: occasionally in 2,469 and regularly in 1,106. Women occasionally consume alcohol in 1,037 communities. Smoking is very common. Chewing of tobacco and the use of snuff are also widespread. Chewing of betel is used by people in a large number of communities. We are, therefore, largely a·drinking, smoking and meat-eating people. (K.S. Singh 1992: 65)

Indeed, major changes in people's style of life, consumer habits and social aspirations have taken place during the past three decades. Consumption of eggs and poultry, considered taboo among the upper and middle class/caste Hindus has become widespread throughout the country. Even the Hindu peasant castes who carried the tradition of vegetarianism in the past are rapidly taking to non-vegetarianism. There is some evidence, however, that members of the Scheduled castes and tribes, in a few cases, are giving up non-vegetarianism. Production of milk, fruits and vegetables has undergone massive increase, and its consumption, which was earlier confined to the upper and middle rungs of society, has started reaching the lower working class people in India.

Changes are also reflected in many significant social and cultural domains of people's life. Caste or community still remains the dominant social identity through which most Indians articulate their social intercourse and mediate their social, political and cultural goals. But its traditional organizing principle, the caste panchayat has increasingly been transformed into caste associations. The caste association ushers in new principles of mobilization, management and communication for realizing the political, cultural and economic goals of the community. The traditional role of the caste councils of enforcing norms of endogamy, pollution and purity or settlement of caste disputes has given way to an enlarged and modern institutional practice through which caste associations seek their objectives. It extends their functional and federative scope as caste enters into solidarities with several other castes or communities placed in identical social, economic or political space. The caste associations are very active and as many as 2,879 communities or castes have reported their active functioning.

Family system has shown high resilience in India in terms of its role and structure. It has undergone functional changes keeping its structure largely intact. It has adapted constructively to new demands of social and economic changes in society. Nuclear family is the predominant type. It is found among 4,122 communities, with 'vertical extended type' among 2,272 communities and 'horizontal extended type' among 536 communities; the 'mixed extended type' prevails among 1,518 communities. Significant changes have also taken place in marital practices: the age at marriage has gone up; brideprice is giving way to payment of dowry with enhancement in social status; rules of residence are changing (from matrilocal and bilocal to patrilocal) and there is liberalization of rules permitting divorce. In about 596 communities there has been a change in rules of inheritance and in 186 rules of succession have changed. The predominant rule of residence is patrilocal (4,517 communities) and only 42 communities have matrilocal rule of residence.

The social profile of communities is indicative of many dimensions of linkages and interactions among segments of region, culture, social categories and communities. It is reflected in the migration of people between regions which has contributed to increase in bilingualism. The Census of India 1971 (using its own model of estimate) placed bilingualism conservatively at 13.4 per cent; the survey of communities has estimated it to be as high as 64.2 per cent. Interaction and commonality among cultural regions too is reflected in shared cultural traits, which is also true of a large number of communities across regions and territories. Such cultural traits belong not only to rituals and institutional practices but also to technologies of occupation, skills and division of labour. Most communities have also moved away from their traditional occupations and show keen awareness of developmental programmes sponsored by the government. They also have sharp awareness of political issues and policies. This awareness together with high aspirations introduces in the social system a measure of tension and conflict now manifest in various dimensions of our social life.

ACHIEVEMENTS AND CONTRADICTIONS

What has India achieved since independence? In answer there is much to be counted: major changes in the structure of society and its system of authority were introduced by the abolition of the feudal system of zamindari, jagirdari and the princely states. It revolutionized the social and economic base of our rural society, results of which can be seen everywhere in India's villages. The liberated tenantry has now emerged as the powerful rural middle class. It commands a major voice in the political domain. The 'green revolution' in the country has largely been a contribution of this class. The traditions of hard work, social and cultural resilience, tolerant indifference towards Brahmanical tradition, continual involvement in cultural and agrarian movements and a pugnacious utilitarianism endow this class today with a major role in the country's social and economic development. Within the caste hierarchy this group occupies the middle space, and today leads the powerful backward class movement.

Over the past 45 years, the nation has achieved a credible development in establishing a sound foundation of industrial, technological-scientific and managerial growth. A very substantial technological and scientific manpower has been created. A new middle class, quite different in character from the middle classes of the early twentieth century, has emerged; it has a much broader social base, coming as it does from the middle and lower middle caste and social strata of society. The new entrepreneurs and professional classes in the urban areas and the rich peasantry in the villages constitute a middle class estimated to be around one-fourth of the total population. There has been a progressive increase in the percentage of the service sector in the GDP of the country, which indicates the extent of changes in the economc structure and the composition of society. Colonialism had totally emaciated the industrial foundation of Indian society; now the country ranks about thirteenth in industrial advancement. India has reached a high degree of excellence in scientific, managerial and technological education. These achievements have resulted from the planned development of society in basic sectors of its life.

COMMITMENT TO LIBERAL DEMOCRACY

Yet another realm in which success can be attributed to the people of India is that of commitment to a liberal democratic polity. Despite a very short aberration during the 'emergency' the country has been able to maintain a vigorous participatory culture of democracy. This is despite India ranking quite low in terms of many prerequisites of Western democratic culture and polity. Looking back, the historical depth of Indian civilization, to which the people of India are consciously and unconsciously linked, has helped them maintain democratic traditions even though more than 40 per cent of them are illiterate. The traditional institution of 'panchayat' at the levels both of caste and community could also be held responsible for inculcating among the people a native spirit of democratic interaction and participation. There may be problems in Indian democracy in respect of its legitimization norms, such as the use of caste, religion and region or use of money and muscle power to secure votes, but the fact that democracy has been institutionalized can hardly be disputed. From its fragile base, since the early years of independence, democracy should be taken as a major indicator of the development of Indian society.

There are many other indicators of development, such as the progressive rise in life expectancy, growth in literacy rates, decline in the incidence of child mortality and increased media exposure of people. On each of these indicators, for the same duration of time, other developing countries have, however, done far better. On many counts in comparison not only to the Pacific countries such as Korea, Taiwan, Indonesia and Malaysia, but also its immediate neighbours such as Sri Lanka and Pakistan, India ranks lower in economic performance. The contemporary crisis in India, therefore, has its roots both in the nature of its achievements and also in the lack of growth in crucial areas of its social and economic life.

There have certainly been positive developments in India since independence. Yet, 40 per cent of its population is still below the poverty line, and a substantial part of it is destitute. The poor come largely from the Scheduled castes and tribes and are concentrated in villages. Due to the policy of reservation in education, government employment and in political representation, etc., a minor section from among them has risen them to middle class economic status but remains victim of social and cultural discrimination. The pace of development has created both a psychological and social hiatus between these caste groups and other castes in rural society. Traditionally, the relationship between these deprived or Dalit castes and the upper and middle castes was that of exploitation through patronage, but following independence, due to a high degree of politicization, communication, exposure and social awareness the Dalits now not only reject and resent the patronage of the upper-middle castes but also maintain a hostile competitive relationship with them. In rural areas the conflict between the two groups has increased. In the country this conflictual relationship has taken the form of violent movements such as Naxalism, People's War Group, etc. .

The tribal population has also shown similar tensions and has made separatist demands for territorial demarcation for themselves with substantial autonomy. Some demands have already been conceded, such as the accord with the Nagas and the Mizos in the northeast and the establishment of Gorkhaland in West Bengal with regional autonomy.

Talks are on with the tribes of Chotanagpur for a Jharkhand region. The Bodos in Assam are also demanding autonomy for themselves. Such demands are not confined to tribal groups. Punjab witnessed a violent movement for a separate Khalistan for several years. In Assam there is a similar movement employing violence.

In a large measure (with few exceptions) the conflict between the castes and classes, as also the demand for separation or autonomy, are related to structural changes in society caused by the social and economic changes since independence. The rise of a new middle class among these various groups seems to hold the key to such processes. It is in turn related to the character of the social development in which the State has played an instrumental role through planning. Some changes have been in the anticipated direction, but a large part of these changes could not have been anticipated.

ASCENDANT RURAL MIDDLE CLASS

In rural areas planned efforts for development have contributed to the 'green revolution'. It was led by traditional peasant castes throughout the country. In comparison with the upper castes, who used to be their landlords before independence, they still feel culturally and educationally deprived. Hence, their movement for reservation for the socially and educationally backward classes in the central services. They already enjoy reservation in most state government jobs and have reservation in educational institutions in the states. This ascendant rural middle class has today a relationship of competitive rivalry with the upper castes. With the rising Dalit self-awareness there is rising incidence of violence in many parts of the country between these two groups. As the Dalits and other poorer sections of rural society feel more insecure there is a rising incidence of migration to cities in search of jobs. On the one hand this contributes to imbalanced urbanization (increasing ghettoization of cities, particularly the metropolises) and on the other, increases the rural class-caste conflict. The conflict results from the rebound effect of urbanization of the rural poor. In this urban migration linkages of the migrants with the rural economy and society are not broken (unlike in Latin America). Caste and kinship linkages play a crucial role in migrant settlements in urban slums. Not only do they earn better, particularly working in the unorganized sector, but they also undergo a great deal of exposure to political education, habituation to urban-style consumerism and leisure and enhanced aspiration to move upward in life. It is not uncommon for the migrant groups to accumulate enough savings to raise assets in their rural home by building houses or purchasing land. The sale of land (particularly in northern India) is by upper caste pauperized families who have not been able to adjust to the new economic and social changes.

Land is also sold by urban migrants who want to sever their links with the village.

There is thus emerging a new context of relationships among castes and classes in rural India. Traditional feudal style patronage and exploitation relationships of the past are increasingly being replaced with relationships of conflict and competition. The villages have not been able to evolve a new institutional framework for integrating the changing relationships, having ceased to be social communities. They have been transformed into political communities, but without an institutional set-up whose legitimacy all groups could recognize.

There is a widespread and deep sense of delegitimation about State-sponsored institutions reinforcing the people's alienation from the State. This portends a deeper structurally induced crisis which is often used by some sections as ideologies of separatism, terrorism and violence. It contributes to disenchantment among a section of society not only about the institutional structures but also the ideology of a nation-state and the model of development. Why is it so? Which processes of change have brought it about?

CHANGING PERCEPTION OF STATE

The changing perception of the State on the one hand and new structural and ideological changes in society on the other might seem to have induced these contradictions. Both the Constitution and the planning ideology of the State emphasize principles of social justice, egalitarianism or socialistic pattern of society. Universalization of primary education and removal of illiteracy were given a place of prominence in the 'Directive Principles of State Policy' in the Constitution but efforts in these directions of change have at best been half-hearted and halting. Even today about half of the population remains illiterate; among the womenfolk in some states illiteracy is up to 90 per cent. Only in Kerala and a few districts in some states and Union territories has total literacy been achieved. It is found that the benefits of the egalitarian policies of the State reach the target groups more effectively and bring better results if such groups have education. The education of the girl even up to seventh standard renders acceptance of the small family norm most effective, as is evident in Kerala. It improves health and hygiene, contributes to a decline in school dropout rates (endemic among the poor) and to more effective use of the benefits of State resources. It also contributes to enhancement of a family's entrepreneurial ability.

The monumental failure in tackling the problem of illiteracy and universalization of education bears organic relationship to failures in the domains of population and health policies. Control of population holds the key to most problems that have reached the dimension of a crisis in India, such as social structural issues of distributive justice, unemployment, pressure on infrastructure and other related development goals.

The figures of the 1991 Census do not indicate optimism on this count. The rate of population growth is lower in states where the standard of education and organized voluntary efforts in implementing State programmes are higher, but this rate (of population growth) is much higher in Uttar Pradesh, Madhya Pradesh, Rajasthan and Bihar which together account for the bulk of the population. Interestingly, these are also the states which rate poorly on most indicators of development: high degree of poverty, lower productivity in agriculture, high rate of illiteracy, poor indigenous mobilization of voluntary bodies for development, and endemic problems of social unrest and violence. This pattern of what Gunnar Myrdal called 'cumulative causation' in the process of under-development has to be reoriented through planned investment in crucial sectors, such as the economy, education and infrastructure.

The rate of population growth with its numerous implications for the gathering crisis in our society and economy bears closer relationship with inter-class-caste tensions. With the rise of middle (caste) peasantry to power in villages, the conflict between them and the Dalits on the one hand and between the Dalits and the upper caste-class groups on the other has intensified, generally in the same states such as Bihar, U.P. and parts of Madhya Pradesh, etc., where the incidence of poverty and population growth is higher. A similar process could also be observed in other parts of India having similar structural conditions. The push from rural areas due to these structural conditions further aggravates the urban crisis.

Urban growth in India follows a curious pattern. It is the highest in the metropolitan cities and correspondingly declines as we move from the capital towns to smaller cities and towns. This only indicates that employment generating activities in the informal sector are the highest in metropolitan urban centres and capital towns and lower in other urban centres. This is generating a serious structural cleavage since it contributes to increasing ghettoization of these centres. A consequence is increased urban unrest, violence and crime. The political pressure of the slum dwellers comes into direct conflict with the interests of the urban middle classes with increasing and unbearable pressure on infrastructures of city life. Since, in India, urban migrants maintain their links with the village, the inequitous perception of urban life and the discontent that it generates are carried over to the country-side, further reinforcing social conflict and violence there.

From time immemorial, rural and urban social and cultural systems have interacted closely in our country unlike in many other parts of the world. But with increasing population pressure the balance of relationships is breaking down. In structural terms it generates conflict and ideologically it engenders disenchantment with the State. The rural-urban poor show disenchantment with the State, blaming its policies of development as being pro-rich. The middle classes also do not empathize with State policies. The rural middle classes perceive in State welfare policies, e.g. reservation policies, a threat to their well-being.

CASTE SPECIALIZATION OF OCCUPATION

Although there are continuities in cultural and political domains between the rural and urban middle classes, in the economic realm there has existed an awning discontinuity. The urban industrial or business classes, due to caste speciali-zation of occupation have had a separate existence. Jainism, which produced a dominant business leadership, was aliena-ted from taking to agriculture. No doubt, since independence, a substantial section of political elite have emerged from the rural upper and middle castes-classes; the professional elite of rural origin still come primarily from the rural upper castes. The rural middle castes have gained in political power but lag behind the upper castes in technical and professional occupations or in administrative and managerial services. Hence the demand for reservation for the backward classes. In business and industry both the upper and the middle rural castes-classes have lagged behind as they did not have such traditions since these were caste specializations.

The dependence upon land for livelihood and maintenance of a middle class standard of life (which qualitatively keeps* on changing due to overall social and cultural changes) puts enormous pressure upon peasant families. In a generation or two, even a landholding of about 15-18 acres irrigated land, which is within the ceiling limit permitted by the State, gets fragmented. And without avenues for mobility to non-agricultural employment the younger generation of peasants finds itself exposed to unavoidable downward social mobility or even pauperization. This may lead to political radicalism or violence. The instances of farmers accumulating capital and investing their surpluses in business or industry are rare in our country. It has not happened in Punjab where the country's first green revolution took place. It has very partially happened in Maharashtra and Gujarat. Some evidence of such transition (from agriculture to business and industry) may be found in parts of Andhra Pradesh where rich farmers, particularly Kammas and Reddys of the Krishna-Godavari valleys, due mainly to cash-crop cultivation, have slowly moved out towards industrial production graduating through commercial and real estate enterprises. Such mobility is, however, rare. Avenues of employment outside agriculture, especially in agro-industries, services, industrial production and professions, etc., are important for a healthy development of the agrarian economy and society even though the green revolution might offer us a succour for a while. Already in our villages, especially among the youth, there is total disenchantment with rural life. Its community life is broken due to over-politicization on the basis of caste-class tensions, and its economy burdened by over-population and structural precariousness. To overcome this problem an integrated plan of rural-urban and agro-industrial development would be required. In its absence, even our green revolution (its shine is already growing dim due to capital and technology lag) may offer us only momentary relief from the impending social structural crisis.

URBAN CRISIS

The cleavages between the class-caste groups in rural society have their parallels in the urban-industrial sector as well. We have already drawn attention to urbanward migration from villages which has serious consequences. The estimates of the National Commission on Urbanization are disquieting indeed. By the second quarter of the twenty-first century India's population is likely to cross the one billion mark (outstripping that of China) and its pressure on the urban centres, (metropolitan ones particularly) would be unbearable. Our rural crisis is most likely to be compounded with a major urban crisis in the making.

The cultural consequences of these changes too are not system-integrative. The new rural middle classes and urban professionals and entrepreneurial groups have shown a capacity for initiative and innovation. It has, however, been accompanied by a sharp decline in values of social responsibility, social welfarism and personal asceticism (values which inspired our freedom movement led by Gandhiji). Unlike in Europe the new entrepreneurial and professional classes are not inspired by values of puritan ethics or by consumer-nationalism as in Japan.

The utilization of connections, of family and kinship, of regions and language and of political leaders and bureaucracy had been central to the Indian entrepreneur's success in business and industry. Structurally it has often foreclosed the entry of new entrepreneurs to business but it has also maintained a continuity of tradition in the process of economic modernization of society. Its most vitiating consequence, however, has been the misuse of 'political' connections which, under a controlled economy regime, did build up a large number of business families but at the same time delegitimized ethical norms. The State being the sponsor of most such opportunities, helped in the creation of a cultural disorientation, has bred an unprincipled go-getter utilitarianism which today pervades through business, profession, politics, education and governs the value system of the new rural and urban middle classes. Corruption in public life and cynicism in the ideology are its logical results.

This has deeply affected the work ethic in our society. The State, which was rightly brought into the role of establishing welfare through its active initiative in economic and social interventions, has been misperceived as an institution that rewards manipulators, is permissive and offers enormous scope for quick upward mobility through corrupt appropriation of public resources and wealth. It has reinforced 'jobism' and not a work ethic. The demand for government jobs as distinct from opportunity to work is a result of this process. Reservation of jobs for the socially and economically deprived sections of our society has been a correct policy intended to restore the balance of forces that handicapped them for centuries. But it has been, or is most likely to be, converted into a hereditary privilege.

COMMUNALISM AS DEPRIVATION-ANXIETY

Such developments have brought an ideological chaos in India without the end of ideology. Ideologies still survive and are competing for domination. Mention may be made of two crucial ideologies which also reflect the crisis facing India. These are ideologies of nationalism and communalism. Both have a long historical past in our freedom movement. The ideology of nationalism got flawed by the trauma of partition but it survived. But communalism poses a serious threat to this ideology. Communalism, in its narrow sense of conflict and intolerance among religious groups, particularly the Hindus and the Muslims, is often orchestrated by social forces and groups (new rural-urban middle classes) whose rise in society we have examined. Communal violence erupts recurrently as an apotheosis of ethically rootless economism here or political opportunism there. It is anchored not in commitment to religious values, which have maintained a tradition of pluralism and tolerance in India through ages, a spirit which has not yet fully declined. Communalism thrives on the exploitation of deprivation anxiety. As such, it could possibly be contained through judicious administration of policies of egalitarianism and social welfare in favour of the deprived groups among the religious minorities.

Communalism poses a threat to India in an even more vital sense in that it counterposes itself against nationalism. Being a plural society with its divisions based on caste, religion, language, ethnicity and region, etc., bonds of unity in India have always been provided by a diffuse and flexible sharing of certain common values, occupational skill, technologies and artefacts and market relationships despite differences of religion, language or region. This we could characterize as the 'civilizational' unity of India as different from a nation-state. That is why through millennia India has remained a land where people of all faiths and cultural and linguistic diversities could live together in harmony. The rulers of India, coming from different religious backgrounds, respec-ted and fostered this tradition. It provided for enormous regional autonomy with varying degrees of central control. Some historical and anthropological evidence suggests that the degree of centralization increased with the coming of Mughal rule and went on increasing during the British regime. The British colonial regime and its institutional innovations had an effect that spurred the ideology of a nation-state deriving substantial inspiration from the West. Despite this the Constitution of India is a unique document, tilting more towards centralization though with enough flexibility for decentralization of power.

The normative structure of nationalism that the Consti-tution projects is of a State that is secular, socialist democratic and protective of all basic human rights irrespective of birth, religion and gender. But the character of social and economic development since independence has been such that a consensus on its operational strategies and premises has today declined. The processes of social mobility have sharpened the conflicts but the cleavages are not yet crystallized on class lines. These cut across divisions on the basis of caste, class and religion.

FOR PLURALISM

Under these milieux the growth of the middle classes in both the Hindu and Muslim communities has created an articulate support base for the propagation of communal ideology. In recent times this development has given a fillip to political parties and caucuses openly legitimizing communalism. The erosion in the influence of the Congress party, the rising wave of Islamic fundamentalism in the Muslim countries, interpreted by Hindu and Muslim communalists out of context, sharpen communal prejudices. This face of communalism has, structurally speaking, more enduring and fearsome implications. It is not based on short-run passions which erupt into communal violence orchestrated by vested interests, it has deeper and wider implications. It poses a threat to the notion of civilization which Indian tradition has fostered since millennia—one of pluralism and heteronomy, that is tolerance for all religious faiths and styles of living. Partly, religious fundamentalism manifests oriental disillusionment with the Western model of modernization.

This religious orientation takes a communal form when it is politicized and starts setting down rules for nationalism and economic and social development. Without offering clarity on how such an ideology would cope with issues of a modern secular democratic State, its response is only hazy. Communalism of this variety could be most threatening for India which is still in the process of making itself into a nation-state. A nation is not a state of being like a completed architecture but a process of becoming. Religious fundamentalism, in its communal manifestation, can be disruptive for this process of becoming a secular nation-state.

One may be tempted to attribute much of this crisis to our chosen path of development since independence. To us this appears to be flawed if not fallacious. Development is not a linear but a retroactive process; and considering our options and limitations of social structure and its historicity, the planning model with State initiative has been the best choice. Sustainability is an issue which emerges historically; it is so in the West and we should look at it with a sense of history. Some lessons from the history of planning are already evident, such as: relevance of decentralization, involvement of the people and the voluntary groups in the development process, crucial role of education in development (especially of women and the removal of illiteracy), need for integrated rural-urban planning, improvement of infrastructures and ecofriendly industrialization. The need to create job opportunities in villages and small towns and the urgency to improve their quality of life is now widely recognized too. But most of these innovations are organic to the planning process as envisaged.

CHANGE, CONFLICT AND SOCIETAL RESILIENCE

The present social situation in India throws up two rather contradictory processes. First it generates tensions through a broad set of patterned social relationships based on caste, class, ethnicity, religion, etc. Recently, ecological concerns with implications of class and gender have also emerged in the process of development and assumed added significance. On the other hand, the processes of change also contribute to strengthening of a series of traditional social bonds affirming the intrinsic resilience within society to reconcile with contradictions. This ability of reconciliation and societal resilience is probably rooted in the civilizational depth of Indian society and the collective consciousness of the Indian people (see Y. Singh 1993: 128-48). Among the social institutions which have shown adaptive resilience to forces of change and modernization are caste, family, religion and democracy. These institutions, which in Western social science paradigm were treated as embodiment of traditionalism and, therefore, hindrances to modernization, have indeed adapted to the process of modern social change in India. Castes have changed into caste associations; family system has played a pivotal role both in the 'green revolution' in the countryside and in the rise of corporate capitalism. Religion, both Hinduism and Islam (the two major religions of India), has not come in the way of industrial and entrepreneurial growth. Jainism and Sikhism are already well known for their dynamic contribution to economic modernization of our society. Democracy, considered to be a system impossible to implant in a tradition-bound Indian society, has established its deep roots. Electoral processes have indeed brought about a salient revolution in people's consciousness.

The forces of change which India encounters have a continuity but in some areas there are qualitative innovations. The cultural, social and political tensions based on caste, ethnicity and demand politics of the interest groups rampant today have been a part of this process ever since independence. But today the cultural dimension of change has assumed a new significance. It is reflected not only in the search for new identities by the Dalits, minorities and women but more importantly the information revolution and the electronic and print media are adding a new sharpness to this process. As the process of economic development gains momentum the social inequalities are bound to sharpen further, but with the added media exposure the perception of inequalities undergoes a dangerous metamorphosis resulting in extremisms of various sorts. Will the societal capacity of resilience withstand this new tension of social change?

To the extent that these processes of tension and conflict manifest themselves through the established institutional system endowed with resilience they may be moderated or even adaptively contained through reconciliation. Reconciliation and institutional innovation are the two most effective strategies for tension management in a democratic society. In the past, India has reasonably succeeded in implementing reconciliation but a new momentum of institutional innovation is required today to cope with conflicts. The strategy of decentralization and mobilization of non-governmental organization might be steps in this direction. During the past decades there has been some movement on both these policy issues. The new Panchayati Raj may prove an effective instrument when fully introduced. The increasing role of the voluntary groups and non-governmental organizations in mobilizing people for change is gaining momentum which needs to be continued. These may prove more effective tools to bring about social change with social justice in India.

Bibliography

Agarwal, P.C., 1971. *Caste, Religion and Power: An Indian Case Study* (Delhi: Shri Ram Centre for Industrial Relations).

————, 1977. 'Pariahs in Non-Hindu Villages' in Harjinder Singh (ed.). *Caste among Non-Hindus of India* (Delhi: National Publishing House).

Ahmad, Imitiaz, 1965. 'Social Stratification Among Muslims', *Economic and Political Weekly*, 10.

————, 1966. 'The Ashraf-Ajlaf Dichotomy in Muslim Social Structure in India', *The Indian Economic and Social History Review*, 3(3).

————, 1972. 'For a Sociology of India', *Contributions to Indian Sociology* (N.S.), 6.

————, 1973. *Caste and Social Stratification among the Muslims in India* (Delhi: Manohar).

Ahmad, Zeyauddin, 1977. *Caste among the Muslims of Bihar* (Delhi: National Publishing House).

Alavi, Hamza, 1975. 'India and the Colonial Model of Production', *Economic and Political Weekly* (Special Number), 10(33-35), 1235-62.

Allardt, Eric, 1968. 'Theories about Social Stratification' in J.A. Jackson (ed.), *Social Stratification* (Cambridge: Cambridge University Press).

Aron, Raymond, 1969. 'Two Definitions of Caste' in Andre Beteille (ed.), *Social Inequality* (Harmondsworth: Pengiun Books).

Atal, Yogesh, 1968. *The Changing Frontiers of Caste* (Delhi: National Publishing House).

————, 1971. *Local Communities and National Politics* (Delhi: National Publishing House).

————, 1972. *Changing Pattern of Caste*, Indian Sociological Society.

Aurora, G.S., 1972. *Tribe Caste Class Encounters: Some Aspects of Folk Urban Relations in Aligarh Tehsil* (Hyderabad: Administrative Staff College of India).

Baden-Powell, B.H., 1892. *Land Systems of British India*, Oxford: Clarendon Press (3 vols.).

————, 1908. *The Origin and Growth of Village Communities in India* (London: S. Sornonschein).

Baeber, B., 1968. 'Social Mobility in Hindu India' in James Silverberg (ed.), *Social Mobility in the Caste System in India, Comparative Study in*

Society and History, Supplement III (The Hague: Mouton).

Bagchi, Amiya Kumar, 1970. 'European and Indian Entrepreneurship in India' in E.R. Leach and S.N. Mukherjee (eds.), *Elite in South Asia* (Cambridge: Cambridge University Press).

———, 1972. *Changing Patterns of Caste,* Indian Sociological Society.

Bailey, F.G., 1957. *Caste and the Economic Frontier* (Manchester: Manchester University Press).

———, 1959. 'For a Sociology of India', *Contributions to Indian Sociology,* No. III, 88-101.

———, 1960. *Tribe, Caste and Nation: A Study of Political Activity and Political Changes in Highland Orissa* (Manchester: Manchester University Press).

———, 1963. 'Closed Social Stratification in India,' *European Journal of Sociology,* 4(1).

———, 1963. *Politics and Social Change: Orissa in 1959* (Berkeley: University of California Press).

Banaji, J., 1972. 'For a Theory of Colonial Modes of Production', *Economic and Political Weekly,* 7(52), 2498-2505.

Bandopadhyaya, N., 1977. 'Causes of Sharp Increase in Agricultural Labourers 1961-71: A Case Study of Social Forms of Labour in North Bengal', *Economic and Political Weekly* (Supplement), *12*(53), A111-A125.

Bandopadhyaya, Swaraj *et al.,* 1975. 'Entrepreneurship in West Bengal, 1959-1970', *Economic and Political Weekly,* *10*(9), M25-M27.

Barber, Bernard, 1968. 'Social Mobility in Hindu India' in James Silverberg (ed.), *Social Mobility in the Caste System in India* (The Hague: Mouton).

Bardhan, Pranab, 1970a. 'Green Revolution and Agricultural Labourers', *Economic and Political Weekly* (Special Number) 5(29-31), 1239-46.

———, 1970b. 'Green Revolution and Agricultural Labourers: A Correction', *Economic and Political Weekly,* 5(46), 1861.

Bardhan, Pranab and Ashok Rudra, 1978. 'Interlinkage of Land, Labour and Credit Relations: An Analysis of Village Survey Data in East India', *Economic and Political Weekly* (Annual Number), *13*(6-7), 367-84.

Barth, F., 1960. 'The System of Social Stratification in Swat, North Pakistan' E.R. Leach (ed.), *Aspects of Caste in South India, Ceylon and North West Pakistan,* Cambridge.

Bendix, R., 1964. *Nation-Building and Citizenship: Studies of Our Changing Social Order* (New York, John Wiley and Sons).

Berghe, P.V., 1958. 'A Theory of Synthesis', *American Sociological Review,* 28.

Berna, James, 1960. *Industrial Entrepreneurship in Madras State* (New York: Asia Publishing House).

Berreman, G., 1967. 'Stratification, Pluralism and Interaction: A Cooperative Analysis of Caste' in A.D. Roucek & J. Knight (eds.), *Caste and Race*, (London: CIBA Foundation).

Beteille, Andre, 1965. *Caste, Class and Power* (Berkeley: University of California Press).

———, 1966. 'Closed and Open Social Stratification in India', *European Journal of Sociology*, 7.

———, 1967. 'Elites, Status Groups and Caste in Modern India' in Philip Mason (ed.), *India and Ceylon: Unity and Diversity*, Oxford University Press.

———, 1969. 'Ideas and Interests: Some Conceptual Problems in the Study of Social Stratification in Rural India', *International Social Science Journal*, 21(2).

———, 1969a. *Caste: Old and New* (Bombay: Asia Publishing House).

———, (ed.), 1969b. *Social Inequality* (Harmondsworth: Penguin Books).

———, 1969c. 'Ideas and Interests: Some Conceptional Problems in the Study of Social Stratification in Rural India', *International Social Science Journal*, 21(2).

———, 1970. 'Peasant Associations and the Agrarian Class Structure', *Contributions to Indian Sociology* (N.S.), 4, 126-39.

———, 1971. *Harmonic and Disharmonic Social Systems* (Sydney: University Press).

———, 1974. *Studies in Agrarian Social Structure* (Delhi: Oxford University Press).

———, 1977. *Inequality Among Men* (Delhi: Oxford University Press).

Bhalla, Sheila, 1976. 'New Relations of Production in Haryana Agriculture', *Economic and Political Weekly* (Supplement), 11(13), A23-A30.

———, 1977a. 'Agricultural Growth: Role of Institutional and Infrastructural Factors', *Economic and Political Weekly*, 12(45-46), 1898-1905.

———, 1977b. 'Changes in Acreage and Tenure Structure of Landholdings in Haryana, 1962-72', *Economic and Political Weekly* (Supplement), 12(13), A2-A15.

Bhargava, S., 1935. *Indigenous Banking in Ancient and Mediaeval India*, Bombay.

Bhatt, Anil, 1975. *Caste, Class and Politics: An Empirical Profile of Social Stratification in Modern India* (Delhi: Manohar).

Bhattacharya, Pranab, 1976. 'Impact of Green Revolution on Output, Cost and Income of Small and Big Farmers', *Economic and Political Weekly* (Supplement), II (52), A147- A150.

Blackenburg, Peter Von, 1972. 'Who Leads Agricultural Modernization: A Study of Some Progressive Farmers in Mysore and

Punjab', *Economic and Political Weekly* (Supplement), 7(40), A94-A150.

Bose, N.K., 1968. *Calcutta: A Social Survey* (Bombay: Lalvani Publishing House).

Bose, Pradip Kumar, 1979. 'Agrarian Structure, Peasant Society and Social Change: A Study of Selected Regions in West Bengal', unpublished Ph.D. Thesis (Delhi: Jawaharlal Nehru University).

———, 1981. 'Social Mobility and Caste Violence: A Study of the Gujarat Riots', *Economic and Political Weekly, 16*(16), 713-16.

Bottomore, T. B., 1967. 'Cohesion and Division in Indian Elites' in Philip Mason (ed.), *India and Ceylon: Unity and Diversity* (Oxford University Press).

Bougle, C., 1958. 'The Essence and Reality of Caste System', *Contributions to Indian Sociology*, No. 2, April.

Brass, Paul, 1965. *Factional Politics in an Indian State: The Congress Party in Uttar Pradesh* (Berkeley: University of California Press).

Braudel, F., 1980. 'Daniel Thorner' in E.J. Hobsbawn *et al.* (eds.), *Peasants in History* (Delhi: Oxford University Press).

Breman, Jan, 1976a. 'A Dualistic Labour System: A Critique of the Informal Sector Concept-II: A Fragmented Labour Market', *Economic and Political Weekly, 11*(49), 1905-8.

———, 1976b. 'Dualistic Labour System: A Critique of the Informal Sector Concept-III: Labour Force and Class Formation', *Economic and Political Weekly, 11*(50), 1969-44.

Broomfield, J.H., 1968. *Elite Conflict in a Plural Society: Twentieth Century Bengal* (Bombay: Oxford University Press).

Buckley, William, 1959. 'Social Stratification and the Functional Theory of Social Differentiation', *American Sociological Review, 23*(3).

Carter, Anthony, 1975. 'Caste Boundaries and the Principle of Kinship Amity: A Maratha Caste Purana', *Contributions to Indian Sociology* (N.S.) *9*(1), 123-37.

Chanana, Dev Raj, 1961, 'Sanskritization, Westernization and India's North-West', *Economic Weekly, 13*(9).

Chandidas, R., 1969 'How Close to Equality Are Scheduled Castes?' *Economic and Political Weekly, 4*(24), 975-9.

Chandra, B., 1966. *The Rise and Growth of Economic Nationalism in India* (Delhi: People's Publishing House).

Chandra, Bipin, 1970. Indian History Congress: *Presidential Address to the Thirty-second Session*, Jabalpur, December.

Chaturvedi, H.R. and Ghanshyam Shah, 1970. 'Fusion and Fission of Castes in Elections: A Case Study of Chhata, U.P.', *Economic and Political Weekly, 5*(35), 1642-8.

Chaudhuri, Nirad C., 1967. *The Intellectual in India* (Delhi, Vir Publishers).

Chauhan, B.R., 1967. *A Rajasthan Village*, (Delhi: Vir Publishers).

Chauhan, S.K., 1980. *Caste, Status and Power: Social Stratification in Assam*, (Delhi: Classical Publishing Co.).

Chitnis, Suma, 1972. 'Education for Equality: Case of Scheduled Castes in Higher Education', *Economic and Political Weekly* (Special Number), 7(31-33), 1675-81.

Cohn, Bernard S., 1955. 'The Changing Status of Depressed Caste' in McKim Marriott (ed.), *Village India: Studies in the Village Community*, Chicago.

————, 1959. 'Changing Traditions of a Low Caste' in Milton Singer (ed.), *Traditional India: Structure and Change* (Philadelphia: American Folklore Society).

————, 1961a. 'From India Status to British Contract', *Journal of Economic History*, 21.

————, 1961b. 'The Past of an Indian Village', *Comparative Studies in Society and History*, 3.

————, 1962. 'Political System in Eighteenth Century India: The Banaras Region', *Journal of American Oriental Society*, 82.

————, 1968. 'Notes on the History of the Study of Indian Society and Culture, in Milton Singer and Bernard S. Cohn (eds.), *Structure and Change in Indian Society*, (Chicago: Aldine Publishing Co.), 3-28.

Crooke, W., 1896. *The Tribes and Castes of the North Western Provinces and Oudh* (Calcutta: Supdt. of Govt. Ptg.).

Dahrendorf, Ralph, 1958, 1966. *Class and Class Conflict in Industrial Society* (Stanford: Stanford University Press).

Dalton, D.G., 1970. 'M.N. Roy and Radical Humanism: The Ideology of an Indian Intellectual Elite' in E.R. Leach and S.N. Mukherjee (ed.), *Elites in South Asia*, Cambridge.

Damle, Y.B., 1968. 'Reference Group Theory and Mobility in the Caste System' in James Silverberg (ed.), *Social Mobility in the Caste System in India* (The Hague: Mouton).

Dandekar, V.M. and G.J. Khudanpour, 1957. *Working of Bombay Tenancy Act, 1948*, Report of Investigation.

Dange, S.A., 1949. *India from Primitive Communism to Slavery* (Bombay: People's Publishing House).

Das, Veena and J.P.S. Uberoi, 1971. 'The Elementary Structure of Caste', *Contributions to Indian Sociology* (N.S.), 5, 1-81.

————, 1977. *Structure and Cognition: Aspects of Hindu Caste and Ritual* (Delhi: Oxford University Press).

Davids, C.A.F. Rhys, 1923. 'Economic Conditions According to Early Buddhist Literature' in E.J. Rapson (ed.), *Cambridge Ancient History of India*, New York.

Davis, Kingsley, 1951, 1957. *The Population of India and Pakistan* (Princeton: Princeton University Press).

Davis, Kingsley and Wilbert Moore, 1945. 'Some Principles of Stratification', *American Sociological Review*, 10 April.

———, 1966. *Social Background of Indian Nationalism* (Bombay: Popular Prakashan).

Den, Ouden, J.H.B., 1979.'Social Stratification as Expressed through Language: A Case Study of a South Indian Village', *Contributions to Indian Sociology* (N.S.), 1979, *13*(1), 33-57.

Desai, A.R. (ed.), 1959. *Rural Sociology in India*, Bombay.

———, 1966. *Social Background of Indian Nationalism* (Bombay: Popular Prakashan).

———, 1969. *Rural Sociology in India* (Bombay: Popular Prakashan).

Desai, I.P., 1964. *Some Aspects of Family in Mahuva* (Bombay: Asia Publishing House).

———, 1965. 'The New Elite' in T.K.N. Unnithan, Indra Deva and Y. Singh (eds.), *Towards a Sociology of Culture in India* (Delhi: Prentice Hall).

———, 1971. 'Understanding Occupational Change in India', *Economic and Political Weekly*, *6*(22), 1094-8.

———, 1975. 'The Politics of Survival: Peasant Organisation and the Left Wing in India', *Sociological Bulletin*, 24(1).

———, 1976, 'Peasant Protest and Politics—the Tebhaga Movement in Bengal (India) 1946-47', *The Journal of Peasant Studies*, *3*(3).

———, 1976. *Untouchability in Rural Gujarat* (Bombay: Popular Prakashan).

Dhanagare, D.N., 1974. 'Social Origins of the Peasant Insurrection in Telangana, 1946-51', *Contributions to Indian Sociology* (N.S.), 8, 109-34.

———, 1977. 'Past and Present', *Journal of Historical Studies*, 74.

Djurfeldt, G., and S. Lindberg, 1975. *Behind Poverty: The Social Formation in a Tamil Village*, Scandinavian Institute of Asian Studies, Monograph Series No. 22 (Delhi: Oxford University Press).

D'Souza, Victor S., 1969. 'Measurement of Rigidity-Fluidity Dimension of Social Stratification in Six Indian Villages', *Sociological Bulletin*, March *18*(1).

———, 1972. 'Caste Structure in India in the Light of Set Theories, *Current Anthropology*.

———, 1975. 'Social Inequalities and Development in India', *Economic and Political Weekly*, *10*(19), 770-3.

Dube, Leela, 1973. 'Caste Analogues Among the Lacadive Muslims' in Imitiaz Ahmad (ed.), *Caste and Social Stratification Among the Muslims* (Delhi: Manohar).

Dube, S.C. (ed.), 1965. 'The Study of Complex Cultures' in T.K.N. Unnithan, *et al.* (eds.) *Towards a Sociology of Culture in India* (Delhi: Prentice Hall), 423.

———, 1976. *Social Sciences and Social Realities: Role of the Social*

Sciences in Contemporary India (Simla: Indian Institute of Advanced Study).

Dubois, Abbe J.A., 1906. *Manners, Customs and Ceremonies of the Hindus,* Oxford.

Dumont, Louis, 1961. 'Caste, Racism and Stratification: Reflections of a Social Anthropologist', *Contributions to Indian Sociology,* No. 5, October.

———, 1964 'Change, Interaction and Comparison', *Contributions to Indian Sociology,* No. VII, 10.

———, 1965. 'The Modern Conception of Individual, Notes on its Genesis', *Contributions to Indian Sociology,* No. VIII.

———, 1966. 'A Fundamental Problem in the Sociology of Caste', *Contributions to Indian Sociology,* No. 9, December.

———, 1966. 'The "Village Community" from Munro to Maine', *Contributions to Indian Sociology,* No. IX.

———, 1970. *Homo-Hierarchicus* (Delhi: Vikas Publications).

———, 1970. *Homo Hierarchicus: The Caste System and Its Implications,* (London: Weidenfeld and Nicolson).

———, 1971. 'On Putative Hierarchy and Some Allegies to It', *Contributions to Indian Sociology,* N.S. (November-December).

Dushkin, L., 1961. *Economic and Political Weekly,* October-November.

———, 1972. 'Scheduled Caste Politics', in J. Michael Mahar (ed.), *The Untouchables in Contemporary India* (The University of Arisona Press).

Dutta, N.K., 1931. *Origin and Growth of Caste in India,* Calcutta.

Dutta, Ratna, 1969. 'The Party Perspective in Fourth Lok Sabha', *Economic and Political Weekly* (Annual No.), January.

Eisenstadt, S.N., 1965. 'Social Transformation in Modernization', *American Sociological Review, 30.*

———, 1970. 'Prologue: Some Remarks on Patterns of Change in Traditional and Modern India' in K. Ishwaran (ed.), *Change and Continuity in India's Village* (New York: Columbia University Press).

Elder, H.J.S., 1970 'Rajpur: Change in the Jajmani System of an Uttar Pradesh Village' in K. Ishwaran (ed.), *Change and Continuity in India's Village* (New York: Columbia University Press).

Elwin, Verrier, 1943. *The Aboriginals* (Bombay: Oxford University Press).

Epstein, S., 1962. *Economic Development and Social Change in South India* (Manchester: Manchester University Press).

Firth, R., 1964. 'Family and Kinship in Industrial Society', *Sociological Review Monograph,* Keele.

Fiske, M. Adele, 1977. 'Caste Among the Buddhists' in Harjinder Singh (ed.), *Caste Among Non-Hindus of India* (Delhi: National Publishing House).

Fox, R., 1971. *Kin, Clan, Raja and Rule,* Oxford.

Frank, A.G., 1970. 'The Wealth and Poverty of Nations', *Economic and Political Weekly*, 29-30.

Gadgil, D.R. (ed.), 1959. *Origins of the Modern Indian Business Class—An Interim Report* (New York: Institute of Pacific Relations).

———, 1969. 'Two Powerful Classes in Agrarian Areas' in A.P. Desai (ed.), *Rural Sociology in India* (Bombay, Popular Prakashan).

Galanter, Marc, 1961. 'Equality and Protective Discrimination in India', *Rutgers Law Review, 16*(1).

———, 1963. 'Law and Caste in Modern India', *Asian Survey, 3*(2).

———, 1968. 'Changing Legal Conception of Caste' in Milton Singer and B.S. Cohn (eds.), *Structure and Change in Indian Society* (Chicago: Aldine Publishing Company).

———, 1972. 'The Abolition of Disabilities—Untouchability and the Law', in J. Machael Mahared (ed.), *The Untouchables in Contemporary India* (The University of Arizona Press).

———, 1984. *Competing Inequalities: Law and the Backward Classes in India* (Delhi: Oxford University Press).

Gandhi, J.S., 1978. 'Lawyers at a District Court: A Study in the Sociology of Legal Profession', unpublished Ph.D. Thesis (Delhi: Jawaharlal Nehru University).

Ghosh, K., 1969. *Agricultural Labourers in India* (Calcutta, Indian Publications).

Ghurye, G.S., 1943. *The Aborigines—So-called and Their Future,* (Poona: Gokhale Institute of Politics and Economics).

———, 1945. *Caste and Race in India*, Oxford.

———, 1957. *Caste and Class in India* (Bombay, Popular Book Depot).

———, 1961. *Caste, Class and Occupation* (Bombay: Popular Book Depot).

Giri, V.V., 1958. *Labour Problems in Indian Industry* (Bombay: Asia Publishing House).

Gopal, S., 1965. *British Policy in India, 1858-1905* (Cambridge: Cambridge University Press).

Gore, M.S., 1994. *The Social Context of an Ideology: Ambedkar's Politics and Thoughts* (Delhi: Sage).

Gough, Kathleen, 1970. 'Palakkara: Social and Religious Changes in Central Kerala' in K. Ishwaran (ed.), *Change and Continuity in India's Village* (New York: Columbia University Press).

———, 1974. 'Indian Peasant Uprising', *Economic and Political Weekly* (Special Number), *9*(32-34), 1391-1412.

———, 1975. 'Changing Households in Kerala' in Dhirendra Narain (ed.), *Exploration in the Family* (Bombay: Thacker).

———, 1977. 'Colonial Economics in South East India', *Economic and Political Weekly, 12*(13), 541-54.

———, 1979. 'Dravidian Kinship and Modes of Production', *Contributions to Indian Sociology* (N.S.), *13*(12), 265-91.

————, 1980. 'Modes of Production in Southern India', *Economic and Political Weekly* (Annual Number), *15*(5-7), 337-64.

Gould, H., 1961, 'Sanskritization and Westernization: A Dynamic View', *Economic Weekly*, 13.

Gould, Harold A., 1968. 'Time Dimension and Structural Change in an Indian Kinship System: A Problem of Conceptual Refinement'; in Milton Singer and Bernard Cohn (eds.), *Structure and Change in Indian Society* (Chicago: Aldine Publishing Co.).

Gouldner, A., 1970. *Coming Crisis in Western Sociology* (New York: Free Press).

Guha, A., 1970. 'The Comprador Role of Parsi Seths, 1950-1850', *Economic and Political Weekly*, 5 (48), 1933-6.

Guha, B.S., 1937. 'An Outline of the Racial Ethnology of India', in *An Outline of the Field Sciences of India*, Calcutta.

Gune, T.V., 1953. 'The Judicial System of the Marathas', *Deccan College Dissertation Series*, 12, Poona.

Gupta, Dipankar, 1977. 'The Shiva Sena Movement 1966-74: A Sociological Analysis', unpublished Ph.D. Thesis (Delhi: Jawaharlal Nehru University).

Gupta, S.C., 1969. 'Some Aspects of the Indian Agriculture' in A.R. Desai (ed.), *Rural Sociology in India* (Bombay: Popular Prakashan).

Habib, Irfan, 1963. 'An Examination of Wittfogal's Theory of Oriental Despotism', *Enquiry*, *6*, 54-78.

————, 1963. *The Agrarian System in Mughal India* (Bombay: Asia Publishing House).

Hagen, E.E., 1962. *On the Theory of Social Change* (Illinois: The Dorsey Press).

Hall, Stuart, 1977. 'The Hinterland of Science: Ideology and the Sociology of Knowledge' in *On Ideology* (Birmingham: University of Birmingham).

Hampel, C.G., 1959. *Aspects of Scientific Explanation and Other Essays in the Philosophy of Science* (New York, Free Press).

Hardgrave (Jr.), R.L., 1968. 'Caste Fission and Fusion', *Economic and Political Weekly* (Special Number), July.

Harper, Edward B., 1959. 'A Hindu Village Pantheon', *South Western Journal of Anthropology*, 227-34.

————, 1968. 'Social Consequences of an "Unsuccessful" Low Caste Movement' in James Silverberg (ed.), *Social Mobility in the Caste System in India* (The Hague: Mouton).

Harrington, M., 1963. *The Other America*, London.

Hazari, R.K., 1966. *The Corporate Private Concentration Ownership and Control* (Bombay: Asia Publishing House).

Hazelhurst, P., 1966. *Merchant Entrepreneurship and Caste in a Punjabi City*, Duke University Press.

Hazlehurst, L.W., 1966. *Entrepreneurship and Merchant Caste in a Punjab City*, (Durham: Duke University).

———, 1968. 'Caste and Merchant Communities' in Milton Singer and Bernard Cohn (eds.), *Structure and Change in Indian Society* (Chicago: Aldine Publishing Co.).

Holmstrom, Mark, 1972, 'Caste and Status in an Indian City', *Economic and Political Weekly*, 7(15), 769-74.

Homans, G.C., 1964. 'Bringing Man Back In', *American Sociological Review*, 29.

Hopkins, E. Washburn, 1901. 'Ancient and Modern Hindu Guilds', *India: Old and New* (New York).

Hutton, J.H., 1955. *Caste in India: Its Nature, Function and Origin*, Cambridge University Press.

Ibbetson, D.C.J., 1916. *Panjab Castes* (Lahore: Government Publication).

Inden, Ronald, 1990. *Imagining India* (Cambridge, Basil Blackwell Ltd).

Irschick, E.F., 1969. *Political and Social Conflict in South India: the Non-Brahmin Movement and Tamil Separatism (1916-1929)* (Berkeley: University of California).

Isaacs, H., 1964. 'A Reporter at Large—The Ex-Untouchables', *The New Yorker*, December.

Iswaran, K., 1970. 'Introduction' in K. Iswaran (ed.), *Change and Continuity in India's Village* (New York: Columbia University Press).

Ito, Shoji, 1966. 'A Note on the "Business Cambine" in India', *The Developing Economies*, September 4(3).

Jackson, J.A., 1968. *Social Stratification* (Cambridge: Cambridge University Press).

Jain, R.K., 1977. 'Classes and Classification Among the Peasantry of Central India: Relations of Production in Village Parsania, Madhya Pradesh', *Sociological Bulletin*, 26(1), 91-115.

Jain, R.K. (ed.), 1977. *Text and Context: The Social Anthropology of Tradition* (Philadelphia: Institute for the Study of Human Issues).

Jha, S.N., 1970. 'Caste in Bihar Politics', *Economic and Political Weekly*, 5(7), 341-4.

John, P.V., 1968. *Some Aspects of the Structure of Indian Economy, 1947-48 to 1961-62* (Bombay: Asia Publishing House).

Joshi, P.C., 1969. 'Land Reform in India' in A.R. Desai (ed.), *Rural Sociology in India* (Bombay: Popular Prakashan).

———, 1971. *Land Reform and Agrarian Change in India and Pakistan* (Report).

———, 1978. 'Agrarian Structure and Employment: Some Aspects of Historical Experience', *Economic and Political Weekly* (Annual Number), 13(6-7), 315-31.

Kalia, S.L., 1959. 'Sanskritization and Tribalization', *Bulletin of the Tribal Research Institute,* Chindwara.

Kamat, A.R., 1979. 'The Emerging Situation: A Socio-Structural Analysis', *Economic and Political Weekly, 14*(7-8), 349-54.

Kapadia, K.M., 1958. *Marriage and Family in India* (Madras: Oxford University Press).

———, 1959. 'The Family in Transition', *Sociological Bulletin, 8*(2).

Karve, Irawati, 1961. *Hindu Society: An Interpretation* (Poona: Deccan College).

Khare, R.S., 1970. *The Changing Brahmans* (Chicago: The University of Chicago Press).

———, 1978. 'Structuralism in India: Some Issues and Observations', *Contributions to Indian Sociology* (N.S.), *12*(2), 253-78.

Khusro, A.M., 1958. *Economic and Social Effects of Jagirdari Abolition and Land Reform in Hyderabad.*

King, A.D., 1970. 'The IIT Graduates: 1970—Aspirations, Expectations and Ambitions', *Economic and Political Weekly, 5*(35), 1497-1510.

Klass, Morton, 1980. *Caste: The Emergence of the South Asian Social System* (Philadelphia: Institute for the Study of Human Issues).

Kochanek, S.A., 1968. *The Congress Party of India* (Princeton: Princeton University Press).

Kolenda, Pauline M., 1968. 'Region, Caste and Family Structure: A Comparative Study of the Indian "Joint" Family' in Milton Singer and Bernard Cohn (eds.), *Structure and Change in Indian Society* (Chicago: Aldine).

———, 1978. *Caste in Contemporary India: Beyond Organic Solidarity* (California: Benjamin Cummings).

Kosambi, D.D., 1956. *An Introduction to the Study of Indian History* (Bombay, Popular Book Depot).

———, 1956. *Indian History* (Bombay: Popular Book Depot).

———, 1969. 'Indian Feudalism', in A.R. Desai (ed.), *Rural Sociology in India* (Bombay: Popular Prakashan).

Kothari, Rajni (ed), 1970. *Caste in Indian Politics* (Delhi: Orient Longman).

———, 1970a. *Politics in India* (Delhi: Orient Longman).

———, 1970b. *Caste in Indian Politics* (Delhi: Orient Longman).

Kotovsky, Grigory, 1964. *Agrarian Reforms in India* (Bombay: Peoples' Publishing House).

Kovalevsky, M.M., 'Communal Landholdings: The Causes, Character and Outcome of its Disintegration', Thorner's *Contributions to Indian Sociology,* No. IX, Old Series.

Kroeber, A.L., 1930. 'Caste', *Encyclopaedia of the Social Sciences,* vol. III.

Kuppuswamy, B., 1962. *Socio-Economic Status Scale (Urban)* (Delhi: Mansayan).

Kuppuswamy, B. and B. Singh, 1967, 'Socio-Economic Status Stratification in Western Uttar Pradesh', *Sociological Bulletin,* March, *16*(1).

Kurup, A.M., 1971. 'Status of Kerala Scheduled Tribes: A Study Based on Ethno-Demographic Data', *Economic and Political Weekly,* 6(34), 1815-20.

Ladejinsky, Wolf, 1964. 'Agrarian Reform in Asia', *Foreign Affairs,* April.

Lamb, Helen B., 1959. 'The Indian Merchant' in Milton Singer (ed.), *Traditional India: Structure and Change,* (Philadelphia: The American Folklore Society).

Lambert, C.L. and D. Richard, 1963. *Workers, Factories and Social Change in India* (Princeton: Princeton University Press).

Lambert, R.D., 1963. *Workers, Factories and Social Change in India* (Princeton: Princeton University Press).

Lasswell, H.D., D. Lerner and C.E. Rothwell, 1952. *The Comparative Study of Elites: An Introduction and Bibliography,* (Stanford: Stanford University Press).

Leach, Edmund R., 1960. 'What Should We Mean by Caste' in E.R. Leach (ed.), *Aspects of Castes in South India, Ceylone and North West Pakistan,* Cambridge University Press.

Leach, Edmund R. (ed.), 1960. *Aspects of Caste in South India, Ceylon and North West Pakistan* (Cambridge: Cambridge University Press).

———, 1967. 'Caste, Class and Slavery: The Taxonomic Problem' in Anthony de Reuck and Julie Knight (eds.), *Caste and Race,* London.

Leach, E.R. and Mukherjee, 1970. *Elites in South Asia* (Cambridge University Press).

———, 1972. in M.N. Srinivas, *Social Change in Modern India* (Berkeley: California University Press, reprinted (Delhi: Orient Longman).

———, 1971. 'Eprit in Homo Hierarchicus', *Contributions to Indian Sociology* (N.S.), 5, 1-81.

Lenski, G.E., 1966. *Power and Privilege: A New Theory of Stratification,* McGraw Hill.

Levy, M.J. (Jr.), 1949. *The Family Revolution in Modern China* (Cambridge: Harvard University Press).

———, 1966. *Modernization and the Structure of Societies* (Princeton: Princeton University Press).

Levy, M.J. and L. Fallers, 1959. 'The Family: Some Comparative Considerations', *American Anthropologist,* 61.

Lieten, G.K., 1979. 'Caste in Class Politics', *Economic and Political Weekly* (Annual Number), *14* (7-8), 313-28.

Lipset, S.M., 1960. *The Political Man*, New York.

Lockwood, D., 1958. *The Black-Coated Workers*, London.

————, 1960. 'The New Working Class', *European Journal of Sociology*.

Lokur, B.N., 1965. *The Report of the Advisory Committee on the Revision of Lists of Scheduled Caste and Scheduled Tribes* (Delhi: Manager of Publications).

Lynch, Owen M., 1968. 'The Politics of Untouchability—A Case from Agra, India' in Milton Singer and B.S. Cohn (eds.), *Structure and Change in Indian Society* (Chicago: Aldine Publishing Co.).

Madan, T.N., 1962a. 'The Hindu Joint Family', *Man*, 62.

————, 1962b. 'The Joint Family: A Terminological Clarification', *International Journal of Camparative Sociology*, 3.

————, 1971. 'On Understanding Caste', *Economic and Political Weekly*, 6(34), 1805-8.

————, 1972. 'Religious Ideology in a Plural Society: The Muslims and Hindus of Kashmir', *Contributions to Indian Sociology* (N.S.), 6, 106-41.

Madan, T.N. and P.C. Varma, 1971. *Development and Professions in India* (Delhi, Institute of Economic Growth).

Madan, T.N. *et al.*, 1971. 'On the Nature of Caste in India: A Review Symposium on Louis Dumont's *Homo Hierarchicus*', *Contributions to Indian Sociology* (N.S.), 5, 1-81.

Maine, Sir H., 1890. *Village Communities in the East and West*, London.

Malaviya, H.D., 1955. *Land Reform in India*.

————, 1969. Agrarian Unrest after Indepencence' in A.R. Desai (ed.), *Rural Sociology in India* (Bombay: Popular Prakashan).

Mankidy, A., 1976. 'Scheduled Caste Entrants into Banking Industry', *Economic and Political Weekly* (Supplement), *11*(19), M11-M16.

Mann, H.H., 1921. *Land and Labour in a Deccan Village* (Bombay: Oxford University Press).

Marglin, F.A., 1977. 'Power, Purity and Pollution: Aspects of the Caste System Reconsidered', *Contributions to Indian Sociology* (N.S.) *11*(2), 245-70.

Marriott, McKim, 1955. 'Little Community in an Indigenous Civilization' in McKim Marriott (ed.), *Village India: Studies in the Little Community* (Chicago: Chicago University Press).

————, 1965. *Caste Ranking and Community Structure in Five Regions of India and Pakistan*, Poona.

————, 1968. 'Caste Ranking and Food Transactions: A Matrix Analysis' in Milton Singer and B.S. Cohn (eds.), *Structure and Change in Indian Society* (Chicago: Aldine Publishing Co.).

————, 1968. 'Multiple Reference in Indian Caste System' in Jame Silverbert (ed.), *Social Mobility in the Caste System in India* (The Hague: Mouton).

Marx, Karl, 1853a. in *New York, Daily Tribune*, 25 June.

————, 1853b. in *New York, Daily Tribune*, 8 August. These despatches of Marx have also been published by People's Publishing House of Bombay in 1945 under the title, 'Articles on India', by Karl Marx.

————, 1904. *Critique of Political Economy* (Chicago: Charles H. Ker. & Co.).

Mayer, A.C., 1965. 'The Significance of Quasi-Groups in the Study of Complex Societies' in H. Banton (ed.), *The Social Anthropology of Complex Societies* (London: Tavistock).

Mayer, Adrian C., 1960. *Caste and Kinship in Central India*, London.

Mayer, K.B., 1964, 'Social Stratification in two Equalitarian Societies: Australia and United States', *Social Research*, Winter, *31*(4).

McCormack, W., 1959. 'Factionalism in a Mysore Village' in Park and Tinker (eds.), *Leadership and Political Institutions in India*, Princeton University Press.

Mehta, Udai, 1969. 'The Problems of the Marginal Farmers in Indian Agriculture' in A.R. Desai (ed.), *Rural Sociology in India* (Bombay: Popular Prakashan).

Meillassoux, C., 1973. 'Are There Castes in India?', *Economic and Society*, February, 89-111.

Mencher, J.P., 1970. 'Change Agents and Villages: Their Relationships and Role of Class Values', *Economic and Political Weekly* (Special Number), *5*(29-31), 1189-97.

————, 1974. 'Conflicts and Contradictions in the Green Revolution: The Case of Tamil Nadu', *Economic and Political Weekly* (Annual Number), *9*(6-8), 309-23.

————, 1978. Agrarian Relations in Two Rice Regions of Kerala', *Economic and Political Weekly* (Annual Number), *13*(6-7), 349-66.

Meszaros, I. (ed.), 1971. *Aspects of History and Class Consciousness* (London: Routledge and Kegan Paul).

Mhatre, S., 1970. 'Caste and Prejudice', *Economic and Political Weekly*, *5*(35), 1461-2.

Mines, Mattison, 1977. 'Social Stratification Among Muslim Tamils in Tamilnadu, South India' in Harjinder Singh (ed.), *Caste Among Non-Hindus of India* (Delhi: National Publishing House).

Misra, B.B., 1961. *The Indian Middle Classes*, London.

Moffatt, Michael, 1975. 'Untouchables and the Caste System: A Tamil Case Study', *Contributions to Indian Sociology* (N.S.), *9*(1), 111-22.

Moore, W.E., 1953. 'But Some Are More Equal Than Others', *American Sociological Review*, 28 February.

Mukerji, D.P., 1942. *Modern Indian Culture*, People's Publishing House.

————, 1958. *Diversities*, (Delhi: People's Publishing House).

Mukherjee, Radha Kamal and B. Singh, 1961. *Social Profile of a Metropolis* (London: Asia Publishig House).

————, in Barnes and Backer (eds.), *Social Thought from Lore to Science,* Vol. III.

Mukherjee, Radha Kamal and S.D. Misra, 1955. 'Inter-Caste Tensions in India' (mimeo).

Mukherjee, Ramakrishna, 1957. *The Dynamics of a Rural Society,* Berlin.

————, 1958. *The Rise and Fall of the East India Company,* Berlin.

————, 1965. *The Sociologist and Social Change in India Today* (Delhi: Prentice Hall).

————, 1969. 'Empirical Social Research on Contemporary India', *Social Science Information,* Paris.

————, 1970. 'Study of Social Change and Social Development in the Developing Societies', *Economic and Political Weekly (Special Number),* 5(29-31), 1159-70.

————, 1973. *The Rise and Fall of the East India Company* (Bombay: Popular Prakashan).

————, 1976. *Social Indicators* (Delhi: Macmillan).

Mukherjee, S.N., 1970. 'Caste, Class and Politics in Calcutta, 1815-38' in E.R. Leach and S.N. Mukherjee (eds.), *Elites in South Asia.*

Mukherji, P.N., 1977. 'Social Movement and Social Change: Towards a Conceptual Clarification and Theoretic Frame-work', *Sociological Bulletin,* 26(1)' 38-59.

Mundle, Sudipto, 1976. 'The Bonded of Palamau', *Economic and Political Weekly,* II(18), 653-6.

Murdia, Ratna, 1975. 'Land Allotment and Land Alienation: Policies and Programmes for Scheduled Castes and Tribes', *Economic and Political Weekly,* 10(32), 1204-14.

Murdock, G.P., 1949. *Social Structure* (New York: Macmillan).

Myrdal, Gunnar, 1944. *An American Dilemma: The Negro Problem and Modern Democracy* (New York: Harper).

————, 1968. *Asian Drama: An Inquiry into the Poverty of Nations* (Harmodsworth: Penguin Books), vol. I.

Nadel, S.F., 1957. *The Theory of Social Structure,* Cohn and West, 154.

Nadkarni, M.V., 1976. 'Tenants from the Dominant Class: A Developing Contradiction in Land Reforms', *Economic and Political Weekly* (Supplement), 11(52), A137-A146.

Namboodiripad, E.M.S., 1979. 'Caste Conflicts vs. Growing Unity of Popular Democratic Forces', *Economic and Political Weekly* (Annual Number), 14(7-8), 329-36.

Nandy, Ashis, 1973. 'Entrepreneurial Cultures and Entrepreneurial Men', *Economic and Political Weekly* (Supplement), 8(47), M98-M106.

Narain, Iqbal, 1964. 'Democratic Decentralization and Rural

Leadership in India: the Rajasthan Experiment', *Asian Survery,* 4(8).

Navalakha, S., 1971. *Managers, Bureaucrats and Intellectuals: A Sudy of Elite Formation in India* (Delhi: Institute of Economic Growth).

Nesfield, John C., 1885. *Brief View of the Caste System of North Western Provinces and Oudh, Together with an Examination of the Names and Figures Shown in the Census Report,* Allahabad.

Nicholas, Ralph, 1961. 'Economy of Family Types in Two West Bengal Villages', *Economic Weekly,* 13.

———, 1963. 'Village Factions and Political Parties in Rural West Bengal', *Journal of Commonwealth Political Studies,* No. 2

———, 1965. 'Factions: A Comparative Analysis' in Michael Banton (eds.), *Political Systems and the Distribution of Power,* Association of Social Anthropologists, Monograph No. 4, (London: Tavistock).

———, 1968. 'Structure of politics in Village of Southern Asia' in Milton Singer and B.S. Cohn (eds.), *Structure and Change in Indian Society* (Chicago: Aldine Plublishing Company).

O'Malley, L.S.S., 1932. *Indian Caste Customs,* Cambridge University Press.

Omvedt, Gail, 1971. 'Jotirao Phule and the Ideology of Social Revolution in India', *Economic and Political Weekly,* 6(37), 1969-79.

———, 1976. *Cultural Revolt in a Colonial Society: The Non-Brahman Movement in Western India 1873-1930* (Bombay: Scientific Socialist Education Trust).

———, 1994. *Dalits and the Democratic Revolution, Dr. Ambedkar and Dalit Movement in Colonial India* (Delhi: Sage).

Oommen, T.K., 1970. 'The Concept of Dominant Caste: Some Queries', *Contributions to Indian Sociology* (N.S.), No. IV.

Orans, Martin, 1959. 'A Tribe in Search of a Great Tradition: The Emulation-Solidarity Conflict', *Man in India, 39.*

Orenstein, H., 1961. 'The Recent History of the Extended Family in India', *Social Problems,* 8.

———, 1965. *Gaon: Conflict and Cohesion in an Indian Village* (Princeton: Princeton University Press).

Ossowski, S., 1969. 'Old Notions and New Problems: Interpretation of Social Structure in Modern Society' in Andre Beteille (ed.), *Social Inequality* (Harmondsworth: Penguin Books).

Panikkar, K.M., 1955. *Hindu Society at the Cross Roads,* (Bombay: Asia Publishing House).

Panini, M.N., 1977. 'Networks and Styles: Industrial Entrepreneurs in Faridabad', *Contributions to Indian Sociology* (N.S.), *11*(I), 91-115.

Paranjpe, A.C., 1971. *Caste, Prejudice and Individual* (Bombay: Lalvani).

Park, R.L. and I. Tinker (eds.), 1959. *Leadership and Political Institutions in India* (Princeton: Princeton University Press).

Parsons, Talcott, 1940. 'An Analytical Approach to the Theory of Social Stratification', *American Journal of Sociology*, November, *14*.

———, 1953. 'A Revised Analytical Approach to the Theory of Social Stratification' in R. Bendix and S.M. Lipset (eds.), *Class, Status and Power, A Reader in Social Stratification*, Glencoe, Ill.

———, 1964. 'Evolutionary Universals in Society, *American Sociological Reveiw*, No. 3.

Parvathamma, C., 1978. 'The Remembered Village: A Brahmanical Odyssey', *Contributions to Indian Sociology* (N.S.), *12*(1), 91-6.

Patankar, Bharat and Gail Omvedt, 1979. 'Dalit Liberation Movement in Colonial Period', *Economic and Political Weekly* (Annual Number), *14*(7-8), 409-24.

Patil, Sharad, 1979. 'Dialectics of Caste and Class Conflict', *Economic and Political Weekly* (Annual Number), *14*(7-8), 287-96.

Patnaik, Utsa, 1972. 'On the Mode of Production in the Indian Agriculture: A Reply', *Economic and Political Weekly* (Supplement), *7*(40), A145-A151.

———, 1976. 'Class Differentiation within the Peasantry: An Approach to Analysis of Indian Agriculture', *Economic and Political Weekly* (Supplement), *11*(39), A82-A101.

Patwardhan. S., 1968. 'Social Mobility and Conversion of Mahars', *Sociological Bulletin*, September, *17*(2).

Pavlov, V.I., 1964. *The Indian Capitalist Class: A Historical Study*, (Delhi: People's Publishing House).

Phule, J., 1991. *Collected Works of Mahatma Jotirao Phule, Volume II, Selections*, trns. P.G. Patil (Bombay: Government of Maharashtra).

Pocock, David, 1957. 'Inclusion and Exclusion: A Process in Caste System of Gujarat', *South-Western Journal of Anthropology*, *13*(1).

Pocock, D.F., 1974. *Mind, Body and Wealth: A Study of Belief and Practice in an Indian Village* (London: Blackwell).

Pouchepadas, J., 1980. 'Peasant Classes in Twentieth Century Agrarian Movements in India' in E.J. Hobsbawn *et al.* (eds.), *Peasants in History* (Delhi: Oxford University Press).

Prasad, Narmadeshwara, 1970. *Changing Strategy in a Developing Society: India* (Meerut: Meenakshi Prakashan).

Prasad, Pradhan H., 1974. 'Employment and Income in Rural India', *Economic and Political Weekly* (Special Number), *9*(32-34), 1305-8.

———, 1975. 'Agrarian Unrest and Economic Change in Rural Bihar: Three Case Studies', *Economic and Political Weekly*, *10*(24), 931-7.

———, 1976, 'Poverty and Bondage', *Economic and Political Weekly* (Special Number), *11*(31-33), 1269-72.

Premi, Kusum K., 1974. 'Educational Opportunities for the Scheduled Castes: Role of Protective Discrimination in Equalization', *Economic and Political Weekly*, *9*(45-46), 1903-10.

Raghavan, V., 1959. 'Methods of Popular Religious Instructions in Southern India', in Milton Singer (ed.), *Traditional India: Structure and Change*, Philadelphia.

Ram, Nandu (ed.), 1993. 'Social Composition and Role of Limited Elite (Creamy Layers) among Minorities, Deprived Communities and other Marginal Groups', Report of the National Seminar, May 10-11 (mimeo).

Ramaswamy, Uma, 1974. 'Scheduled Castes in Andhra: Some Aspects of Social Change', *Economic and Political Weekly*, 9(29), 1153-8.

Ranadive, B.T., 1979. 'Caste, Class and Property Relations', *Economic and Political Weekly* (Annual Number), 14(7-8), 337-48.

Rao, Hanumantha, 1986. 'Changes in Rural Poverty in India', *Mainstream*, January, 11.

Rao, M.S.A., 1964. 'Social Stratification and Social Change in South-East Asia', *Sociological Bulletin*, March, 13(1).

———, 1970. *Urbanisation and Social Change* (New Delhi: Orient Longman).

———, 1979. *Social Movement and Social Transformation* (Delhi: Macmillan).

Rao, R.S., 1970. 'Search of the Capitalist Farmer: A Comment', *Economic and Political Weekly*, 5(51), 2055-6.

Reddy, N.S., 1973. 'Caste in a Tribal Society: The Formative Process', *Contributions to Indian Sociology* (N.S.), 7, 159-67.

Redfield, R., 1955-6, 'The Social Organisation of Tradition', *Far Eastern Quarterly*, 15, 13-21.

Reissman, Leonard, 1967. 'Social Stratification in Neil J. Smelser (ed.), *Sociology: An Introduction* (New York: John Wiley and Sons).

Rhys Davids, C.A.F., 1923. 'Economic Conditions According to Early Buddhist Literature' in. E.J. Rapson (ed.), *Cambridge Ancient History of India* (New York: Cambridge University Press).

Rocher, Ludo, 1975. 'Caste and Occupation in Classical India: The Normative Texts', *Contributions to Indian Sociology* (N.S.), 9(1), 139-57.

Rosen, George, 1966. *Democracy and Economic Change in India*, (Berkeley: University of California Press).

Rosenthal, Donald B., 1970. *The Limited Elite: Politics and Government in Two Indian Cities* (Chicago: University of Chicago Press).

Rowe, William K., 1963. 'Changing Rural Class Structure and the Jajmani System', *Human Organisation*, 22(1).

———, 1968. 'Mobility in the Nineteenth Century Caste System' in Milton Singer and B.S. Cohn (eds.), *Structure and Change in Indian Society* (Chicago: Aldine Publishing Co.).

Rudolph, L. 1965. 'The Modernity of Tradition: The Democratic Incarnation of Caste in India', *American Political Science Review*, LIX, (4), December.

Rudolph, L. and S.H. Rudolph, 1967. 'The Political Role of India's Caste Associations' in C.E. Welch, Jr. (ed.), *Political Modernization* (Belmont, Cal.: Wadsworth Publishing Company).

————, 1969. *The Modernity of Tradition* (Delhi: Orient Longman).

Rudra, Ashok, 1970. 'In Search of the Capitalist Farmer', *Economic and Political Weekly* (Supplement), *5*(26), A35-A87.

————, 1975a. 'Loans as a Part of Agrarian Relations', *Economic and Political Weekly*, *10*(28), 1049-53.

————, 1975b, 'Indian and the Colonial Mode of Production—Comments', *Economic and Political Weekly*, *10*(42), 1668-70.

————, 1978. 'Class Relations in Indian Agriculture', *Economic and Political Weekly*, *13*(22), 916-23.

Ruhudkar, W.B., 1960. 'A Scale of Measuring Socio-Economic Status Scale in Indian Farm Families', *Nagpur Agricultural College Magazine, 34.*

Runciman, W.G., 1968. 'Class Status and Power' in J.A. Jackson (ed.), *Social Stratification* (Cambridge, Cambridge University Press).

————, 1969. 'The Three Dimensions of Social Inequality' in Andre Beteille (ed.), *Social Inequality*, (Harmondsworth: Penguin Books).

Saberwal, Satish, 1976. *Mobile Men: Limits to Social Change in Punjab* (Simla: Indian Institute of Advanced Study).

————, 1977. 'Indian Urbanism: Socio-Historical Perspective', *Contributions to Indian Sociology* (N.S.), *II*(1), 1-17.

————, 1979a. 'Inequality in Colonial India', *Contributions to Indian Sociology* (N.S.), *13*(2), 241-64.

————, 1979b. 'Sociologists and Inequality in India: The Historical Context', *Economic and Political Weekly* (Annual Number), *14*(7-8), 243-54.

Saini, G.R., 1976a. 'Green Revolution and the Distribution of Farm Incomes', *Economic and Political Weekly* (Supplement), *11*(13), A17-A22.

————, 1976b. 'Green Revolution and Disparities in Farm Incomes: A Comment', *Economic and Political Weekly*, *11*(46), 1804-6.

Sartk, W., 1958. *Social Theory and Christian Thought* (London: Routledge and Kegan Paul).

Sengupta, N., 1977. 'Further on the Mode of Production in Agriculture', *Economic and Political Weekly* (Supplement), *12*(26) A55-A63.

Shah, A.M., 1964. 'Basic Terms and Concepts in the Study of Family in India', *Economic and Social History Review*, vol. I.

Shah, A.M. and R.G. Shroff, 1959. 'The Vahivanca Barots of Gujarat: A Caste of Genealogists and Mythographers' in Milton Singer (ed.), *Traditional India: Structure and Change* (Philadelphia: American Folklore Society).

Shah, G., 1977. *Caste Associations and the Political Processes* (Bombay: Popular Prakashan).

Shah, S.M., 1969. 'Rural Class Structure in Gujarat' in A.R. Desai (ed.), *Rural Sociology in India* (Bombay, Popular Prakashan).

Shanin, Theodor, 1977. 'Measuring Peasant Capitalism: Russia's 1920s and India's 1970s', *Economic and Political Weekly*, *12*(47), 1939-48.

———, 1980. 'Measuring Peasant Capitalism' in E.J. Hobsbawn *et al.* (eds.), *Peasants in History* (Delhi: Oxford University Press).

Sharma, Baldev R., 1970. 'The Industrial Worker: Some Myths and Realities', *Economic and Political Weekly*, 5(22), 875-8.

———, 1976. 'Professionals in the Making: Their Social Origin', *Economic and Political Weekly* (Supplement), *11*(19), M5-M10.

Sharma, K.L., 1970. 'Modernization and Rural Stratification: An Application at the Micro-Level', *Economic and Political Weekly*, 5(37), 1537-43.

———, 1974. *Changing Rural Stratification System: A Compara-tive Study of Six Villages in Rajasthan* (Delhi: Orient Longman).

———, 1976. 'Jharkhand Movement in Bihar', *Economic and Political Weekly*, *11*(1-2), 37-43.

———, 1980. *Essays on Social Stratification* (Jaipur: Rawat).

Shekhar, M.C., 1968. *Social Change in India* (Poona: Deccan College), 339, 342, 347.

Shils, Edward A., 1961. *The Intellecyual between Tradition and Modernity: The Indian Situation* (The Hague: Mouton).

Siddiqui, M.K.A., 1973. 'Caste Among the Muslims of Calcutta' in Imitiaz Ahmad (ed.), *Caste and Social Stratification Among the Muslims* (Delhi: Manohar).

Silverberg, James, 1968. 'Colloquium and Interpretative Conclusions' in James Silverberg (ed.), *Social Mobility in the Caste System in India*, (The Hague: Mouton).

———, 1959 'Caste-Ascribed "Statis" Versus Caste Irrelevant Roles', *Man in India, 39*.

Singer, Milton, 1955-6. 'Cultural Patterns of Indian Civilization: A Preliminary Report of a Methodological Field Study', *Far Eastern Quarterly, 15*.

Singer, Milton (ed.), 1959. *Traditional India: Structure and Change*, (Philadelphia: American Folklore Society).

———, 1968, 'The Indian Joint Family in Modern Industry' in Milton Singer and Bernard Cohn (eds.), *Structure and Change in Indian Society* (Chicago: Aldine Publishing Company), 423.

Singh, Harjinder (ed.), 1977. *Caste Among Non-Hindus of India* (Delhi: National Publishing House).

Singh, Hira, 1979. 'Kin, Caste and Kisan Movement: Some Questions to the Conventional Sociology of Kin and Caste', *The Journal of Peasant Studies*, 7(1).

Singh, Inder Paul, 1977. 'Caste in a Sikh Village' in Harjinder Singh (ed.), *Caste Among Non-Hindus of India* (Delhi: National Publishing House).

Singh, K.S., 1978. 'Colonial Transformation of Tribal Society in Middle India', *Economic and Political Weekly*, 13(30), 1221-32.

———, 1992. *People of India: An Introduction* (Calcutta: Anthropological Survey of India).

———, 1994. *The Scheduled Tribes* (Delhi: Oxford University Press).

Singh, Nirmal, 1979. *Politics, Society and Education: A Political Sociology of Private Colleges* (Delhi: Ajanta Book International).

Singh, R.S., 1979. 'Rural Leadership, Entrepreneurship and Social Change: A Sociological Study of Bilariganj Block in Azamgarh District', unpublished Ph.D. Thesis (Delhi: Jawaharlal Nehru University).

Singh, Rajendra, 1974. 'Agrarian Social Structure and Peasant Unrest: A Study of Land Grab Movement in District Basti, East U.P.', *Sociological Bulletin*, 23(1), 44-70.

———, 1978. 'Peasant Movement in Uttar Pradesh: A Study in the Politics of Land and Land Control in Basti District, 1801-1970' in M.S.A. Rao (ed.), *Social Movement in India, Vol. I: Peasant and Backward Classes Movements*, (Delhi: Manohar), 91-148.

Singh, Yogendra, 'Historicity of Modernization', *Professor Kapadia Commemoration Volume* (Bombay: University of Bombay).

———, 1961. 'Caste and Emotional Integration in India', *National Integration in India* (Agra: Institute of Social Sciences).

———, 1967. 'Sociology for India: The Emerging Perspective' in T.K.N. Unnithan *et al.* (eds.), *Towards a Sociology for India* (Delhi: Prentice Hall).

———, 1967. 'The Scope and Method of Sociology in India and Sociology for India: the Emerging Perspective' in T.K.N. Unnithan *et al.* (eds.), *Sociology for India* (Delhi: Prentice Hall).

———, 1968 'Caste and Class: Some Aspects of Continuity and Change', *Sociological Bulletin*, September 17(2).

———, 'Village Community' in A.R. Desai (ed.), *Rural Sociology in India* (Bombay: Popular Prakashan).

———, 1969a. 'The Changing Power Structure of Village Community' in A.R. Desai (ed.), *Rural Sociology in India* (Bombay: Popular Prakashan).

———, 1969b. 'Social Structure and Village Panchayats' in ibid.

———, 1970. 'Chanukhera: Cultural Change in Eastern Uttar Pradesh' in K. Ishwaran (ed.), *Change and Continuity in India's Villages* (New York: Columbia University Press), 269-70.

————, 1971. 'Political Modernization in India: Concepts and Processes' in A.R. Desai (ed.), *Essays on Modernization of Underdeveloped Societies,* vol. II (Bombay: Thacker & Company).

————, 1973. *Modernization of Indian Traditions: A Systematic Study of Social Change* (Delhi: Thomson Press).

————, 1976. 'Role of Social Sciences in India: A Sociology of Knowledge', in S.C. Dube (ed.), *Social Sciences and Social Realities: Role of the Social Science in Contemporary India* (Simla: Indian Institute of Advanced Study).

————, 1977. *Social Stratification and Change in India* (Delhi: Manohar).

————, 1979a, 'Constraint, Contradictions and Inter-disciplinary Orientations: The Indian Context', *International Social Science Journal, 31*(1), 114-22.

————, 1979b. 'Ideology, Theory, and Methods in Indian Sociology' in Stein Rokkan (ed.), *Quarter Century of International Social Science: Papers and Reports on Development 1952-1977,* (Delhi: Concept Publishing Co.).

————, 1986. *Indian Sociology: Social Conditioning and Emerging Trends* (Delhi: Vistar).

————, 1993. *Social Change in India: Crisis and Resilience* (Delhi, Har Anand).

Sinha, Surajit, 1957. 'Tribal Cultures of Peninsular India as a Discussion of Little Tradition in the Study of Indian Civilization,' *Man In India,* 27.

Sirsikar, V.M., 1970. *The Rural Elite in a Developing Society* (Delhi: Orient Longman).

Sivakumar, S.S., 1978. 'Aspects of Agrarian Economy in Tamil Nadu: A Study of Two Villages (II)', *Economic and Political Weekly, 13*(19), 812-21.

Sivakumar S.S. and Chitra Sivakumar, 1979. 'Class and Jati at Asthapuran and Kanthapuran', *Economic and Political Weekly,* February.

Smelser, Neil J., 1968. *Essay in Sociological Explanation* (Engewood Cliffs, N.J.: Prentice Hall).

Sorokin, Pitrim A., 1965. 'Sociology of Yesterday, Today and Tomorrow', *American Sociological Review,* 833.

Spear, Percival, 1970. 'The Mughal Mansabdari System' in E.R. Leach and S.N. Mukherjee (eds.), *Elites in South Asia,* Cambridge.

Spodek, Howard, 1969. 'Traditional Culture and Entrepreneurship: A Case Study of Ahmedabad', *Economic and Political Weekly* (Supplement), *4*(8), M27-M31.

Srinivas, M.N., 1952. *Religion and Society Among the Coorgs of South India* (Bombay: Oxford University Press).

————, 1955. 'The Social System of a Mysore Village' in McKim

Marriott (ed.), *Village India* (Chicago: University of Chicago Press).

——, 1959. 'The Dominant Castes in Rampura', *American Anthropologists*, LXI.

——, 1962. *Caste in Modern India* (Bombay, Asia Publishing House).

——, 1966. *Social Change in Modern India* (Berkeley: California University Press).

——, 1968. Mobility in the Caste System' in Milton Singer and Bernard Cohn (eds.), *Structure and Change in Indian Society*, (Chicago: Aldine Publishing Co.).

——, 1976. *The Remembered Village* (Delhi: Oxford University Press).

——, 1979. 'Future of Indian Caste', *Economic and Political Weekly* (Annual Number), *14*(7-8), 237-42.

Srinivas, M.N. and Andre Beteille, 1969. 'Harijans of India' in Beteille (ed.), *Caste Old and New* (Bombay: Asia Publishing House).

Staal, J.F., 1955-6. 'Cultural Patterns of Indian Civilization: A Preliminary Report of Methodological Field Study', *Far Eastern Quarterly*, 15, 23-36.

Stark, W., 1958. *Social Theory and Christian Thought* (London: Routledge and Kegan Paul).

Stein, Burton, 1968. 'Social Mobility and Medieval South Indian Hindu Sects' in James Silverberg (ed.), *Social Mobility in the Caste System in India* (The Hague: Mouton).

Stern, Henri, 1979. 'Power in Modern India: Caste or Class? An Approach and Case Study', *Contributions to Indian Sociology* (N.S.), *13*(1), 61-84.

Steward, J.H., 1955. *Theory of Culture Change* (Urbana: University of Illinois Press).

Stinchcombe, A.L., 1963, 'Some Empirical Consequences of the Davis-Moore Theory of Stratification', *American Sociological Review*, October, *28*.

Stokes, Eric, 1970. 'Traditional Elites in the Great Rebellion of 1857: Some Aspects of Rural Revolt in the Upper and Central Doab in South Asia' in E.R. Lelach and S.N. Mukherjee (eds.), *Elites in South Asia*, Cambridge.

——, 1978. *Peasant and the Raj* (Delhi: Vikas).

Swamy, Dalip S., 1976. 'Differentiation of Peasantry in India', *Economic and Political Weekly*, *11*(50), 1933-9.

Thapar, Romila, 1972 'Past and Prejudice', Patel Memorial Lectures (mimeo).

Thorner, Daniel, 1956. *The Agrarian Prospect in India*,

——, 1966. 'Marx on India and the Asiatic Mode of Production'.

——, 1969. 'Capitalist Farming in India', *Economic and Political Weekly* (Supplement), *4*(52), A211-A212.

——, 1969. 'Land Reforms' in A.R. Deasi (ed.), *Rural Sociology in India* (Bombay, Popular Prakashan).

Tinker, H., 1966. in Ralph J. Brabanti (ed.), *Asain Bureaucratic Systems Emergent from the British Imperial Traditions, (S. No. 28), (Duke: Commonwealth Studies Centre).

Titmus, R.M., 1962. *Income Distribution and Social Change*, London.

Townsend, Peter, 1965. 'The Meaning of Poverty', *British Journal of Sociology, 13*(3).

Tumin, Melvin, M., 1953. 'Some Principles of Stratification: A Critical Analysis', *American Sociological Review, 18*(4).

————, 1963. 'On Inequality', *American Sociological Review*, February, *28*(1).

————, 1965. 'Reward and Task Orientations', *American Sociological Review*, August, *20*(4).

————, 1967. *Social Stratification: The Forms and Functions of Inequality* (New Jersey: Englewood Cliff).

Uberoi, J.P.S., 1974. 'For a Sociology of India: New Outlines of Structural Sociology, 1945-1970', *Contributions to Indian Sociology* (N.S.), *8*, 135-52.

Unnithan, T.K.N., Indra Deva, and Yogendra Singh (eds.), 1965. *Towards a Sociology of Culture in India* (Delhi: Prentice Hall).

Van Der Veen, J.H., 1976. 'Commercial Orientations of Industrial Entrepreneurs in India', *Economic and Political Weekly* (Supplement), *11*(35), M91-M94.

Verma, K.K., 1979. *Changing Role of Caste Associations* (Delhi: National Publishing House).

Vyas, V.S. and George Mathai, 1978 'Farm and Non-Farm Employment in Rural Areas: A Perspective for Planning', *Economic and Political Weekly* (Annual Number), *13*(6-7), 333-47.

Warner, W.L., 1960. *Social Class in America* (New York: Harper).

Warriner, Dorren, 1969. *Land Reform in Principle and Practice*, Oxford.

Weber, Max, 1952. *Essays in Sociology* (London: Routledge & Kegan Paul).

Weiner, Myron, 1963. *The Politics of Scarcity* (Bombay, Asia Publishing House).

Weiner, Myron and Rajni Kothari, 1965. *Indian Voting Behaviour* (Calcutta: K.L.M. Mukhopadhyaya).

Wesolowski, W., 1966. 'Some Notes on the Functional Theory of Stratification' in R. Bendix and S.M. Lipset (eds.), *Class Status and Power*, New York.

————, 1969. 'The Notion of Status and Class in Socialist Society' in Andre Beteille (ed.), *Social Inequality*, (Harmondsworth: Penguin Books).

Wiebe, Paul D. and G.N. Ramu, 1975. 'Caste and Religion in Urban India: A Case Study', *Contributions to Indian Sociology* (N.S.), *9*(1), 1-18.

Wiebe, Paul D. and S. John Peter, 1977. 'The Catholic Church and

Caste in Rural Tamilnadu in Harijinder Singh (ed.), *Caste Among Non-Hindus of India* (Delhi: National Publishing House).

Wilke, Arthur S. and Raj P. Mohan, 1978. 'Caste, Caste Ass.)-ciations, Caste Traditions and Inequality as Vocabularies, *Contributions to Indian Sociology* (N. S.), 213-37.

Wiser, W.H., 1936. *The Hindu Jajmani System* (Lucknow: Lucknow Publishing House).

Wolf, Eric, 1966. *Peasant* (New York: McGraw Hill).

Wright Mills, C. 1959. *The Sociological Imagination* (New York).

Wright, P. Theodore, Jr., 1965. 'Muslim Legislators in India: Profile of a Minority Elite', *Journal of Asian Studies*, February, *24*.

Wrong, Dennis H., 1959. 'The Functional Theory of Stratification: Some Neglected Considerations', *American Sociological Review*, December, *24*.

————, 1973. *Modernization of Indian Tradition: A Systematic Study of Social Change* (Delhi: Thomson Press)

Young, Michael, 1961. *The Rise of the Meritocracy*, London.

Zagoria, Donald S., 1969. 'The Social Bases of Indian Communism' in Richard Lowenthal (ed.), *Issues in the Future of Asia* (New York: Frederick A. Praeger).

Zetterberg, Hans, 1965. *On Theory and Verification in Sociology*, The Bedmister Press.

Zweig, F., 1961. *The Worker in an Affluent Society*, London.

REPORTS

Backward Commission Report (Government of India), 1981.

Census of India, 1931, vol. I, pt.-I, p. 472.

National Sample Survey No, 30, 122, 146.

National Sample Survey-Round 37, 1982.

Report of Agricultural Labour Enquiry, Rural Manpower and Occupational Structure, 1954.

Report of the Backward Classes Commission (Government of India), 1956.

Report of the Commissioner for the Scheduled Castes and Scheduled Tribes, 1964.

Report of the Commissioner of Scheduled Caste and Scheduled Tribes, (Government of India) 1987.

Report of the Committee on Distribution of Income and Levels of Living, pt.-I, p. 53, February 1964.

Report on the Industrial Licensing Policy Inquiry Committee, Main Report, 1969.

U.P. Zamindari Abolition Committee Report, 1948.

Index